SOLDIER'S HEART

SOLDIER'S HEART

Reading Literature Through Peace

and War at West Point

◆

Elizabeth D. Samet

Farrar, Straus and Giroux

New York

Farrar, Straus and Giroux
19 Union Square West, New York 10003

Portions of this book originally appeared, in different form, in *The American Scholar*, vol. 74, no. 3 (Summer 2005); and in *Armed Forces & Society*, vol. 31, no. 4 (Summer 2005), and vol. 29, no. 1 (Fall 2002). Copyright © 2005 by Elizabeth Samet.

Grateful acknowledgment is made for permission to reprint the following material:

Brigit Pegeen Kelly, "Wild Turkeys: The Dignity of the Damned," from *Song*. Copyright © 1995 by Brigit Pegeen Kelly. Reprinted with permission of BOA Editions, Ltd., www.boaeditions.org.

"The Snow Man," copyright © 1923 and renewed 1951 by Wallace Stevens, from *The Collected Poems of Wallace Stevens* by Wallace Stevens. Used by permission of Alfred A. Knopf, a division of Random House, Inc.

Quotes from "The Road Not Taken" from *The Poetry of Robert Frost*, edited by Edward Connery Lathem. Copyright © 1916, 1969 by Henry Holt and Company. Copyright © 1944 by Robert Frost. Reprinted by permission of Henry Holt and Company, LLC.

Five lines from "P.O.E." reprinted with the permission of Scribner, an imprint of Simon and Schuster Adult Publishing Group, from *The Poems of Lincoln Kirstein* by Lincoln Kirstein. Copyright © 1987 by Lincoln Kirstein. All rights reserved.

"The Death of the Ball Turret Gunner" from *The Complete Poems* by Randall Jarrell. Copyright © 1969, renewed 1997 by Mary von S. Jarrell. Reprinted by permission of Farrar, Straus and Giroux, LLC.

ISBN-13: 978-0-7394-9376-2

Designed by Jonathan D. Lippincott

Happy are these who lose imagination:
They have enough to carry with ammunition.
Their spirit drags no pack.
Their old wounds, save with cold, can not more ache.
Having seen all things red,
Their eyes are rid
Of the hurt of the colour of blood for ever.
And terror's first constriction over,
Their hearts remain small drawn.
Their senses in some scorching cautery of battle
Now long since ironed,
Can laugh among the dying, unconcerned.
                    —Wilfred Owen, "Insensibility" (1920)

In every campaign there are large numbers of soldiers invalided home with the affection of the circulation commonly called "soldier's heart" . . . The treatment is not that of ordinary heart disease, but should be directed to in every way increasing the general tone, including the mental tone, of the sufferers . . . The patients should not be told, or allowed by our bearing towards them to think, that they have "heart disease," as such is not strictly the case.
          —Robert Dawson Rudolf, "The Irritable Heart of Soldiers (Soldier's Heart)," *The Canadian Medical Association Journal* (1916)

Contents

Author's Note

———◆———

The people in this book are real, the events true to my memory. In early drafts of the manuscript I had changed all of the names, but when I asked several of those about whom I had written what they thought of certain passages, the usual reply was something along these lines: "Everything looks fine except for that silly fake name. I wish you would use my real name." I have preserved a silly pseudonym, however, in a few cases.

I thank David Kuhn for his confidence in me and his sure guidance. I am also grateful to Billy Kingsland at Kuhn Projects for his enthusiasm and graceful efficiency. My editor, Eric Chinski, provided constant encouragement while also listening carefully and challenging me at every stage to think more deeply and precisely. Everyone at Farrar, Straus and Giroux has been a pleasure to work with; Gena Hamshaw especially helped the publication process to move swiftly and smoothly.

Charles Freund and Jeffrey Frank first nourished the idea for this book; I'm more appreciative than they can know for their generosity and counsel. Anne Taranto, Frank Rotondo, Daisy Miller, Seth Armus, and my parents have been especially good sports throughout. My mother, in particular, is possessed of patience beyond measure.

Rick Kerin, my faculty sponsor at West Point when I first arrived in 1997, and now head of its Department of English, has seen fit to arm me against confusion over the years with some essential weapons, including *Army Officer's Guide* and *The 1865 Customs of Service for Officers of the Army*. The latter's description of a nineteenth-century commander also suits Rick: "He, of course, is presumed to be a man of greater experience, education, and information, and his aid and counsel, conscientiously given, will always be appreciated." Finally, I am fortunate to have encountered students and colleagues who can look with such honesty at the costs and rewards of the profession they have chosen.

The views expressed in this book are my own and do not necessarily reflect those of the United States Military Academy, the Department of the Army, or the Department of Defense.

SOLDIER'S HEART

Year of the Plague

———◆———

SHAKESPEARE 3, THIS IS SHAKESPEARE 6—OVER

I had forgotten all about the radio in my hand. I was so startled when it crackled to life I nearly dropped it:

> *SHAKESPEARE 3, THIS IS SHAKESPEARE 6—OVER*
> *SHAKESPEARE 6, THIS IS SHAKESPEARE 3—OVER*
> *SHAKESPEARE 3, GIVE ME A SITREP WHEN YOU HAVE*
> *THE ENEMY IN SIGHT—OVER*
> *WILCO—OUT*

I have said "out" when I should have said "over." I have taken far too long to figure out that "SITREP" means situation report. Somewhere this might be fatal. Here the amused voice on the other end, that of my colleague Dan, grumbles that I'm not allowed to end a transmission I didn't start:

> *YOU CAN'T SAY OUT, SHAKESPEARE 3, ONLY I CAN*
> *SAY OUT*
> *OOPS*

I had volunteered for this mission: standing guard at the doors of the United States Military Academy's Department of English, during the school's annual Plebe Parent Weekend, which is immediately abbreviated—as all things military must be—PPW. This event is designed to gratify the curiosity of parents who have only recently surrendered their children to the United States Corps of Cadets, West Point's student body. In their first semester, plebes take English 101, an introductory composition course that is part of the Academy's thirty-course core curriculum, which includes everything from engineering to philosophy, military history to information technology, economics to psychology. The plebes dwell at the bottom of a four-class hierarchy in which sophomores, juniors, and seniors go by the names yearlings, cows, and firsties respectively. All of this terminology takes some getting used to. Even when you think you know what things are, you can't be sure you know what to call them.

It had been decided that every department needed a presence at the door of its open house. To lend myself the aura of officialdom, I retrieved from the bottom of my desk drawer a name tag I hadn't worn since new faculty orientation several years before. Identifying me as PROF SAMET, DEPT OF ENGLISH, it was emblazoned with the belligerent Academy crest of Pallas Athena and the microscopic words CIVILIAN SERVICE, a designation that turns out to be a statement of the obvious: if you aren't in uniform—even in civilian clothes most cadets and officers give themselves away by their bearing, their haircuts, and their fashion choices—it is pretty clear what you are. And while a few tourists have mistaken me for a cadet over the years, the cadets themselves have never been confused.

There are civilian professors at all of the service academies (Army, Navy, Air Force, Coast Guard), as well as on the faculties of the military's various staff and senior service colleges. At the Military Academy, civilian professors are considered emergency personnel; we acquire the magnificently redundant epithet "key and essential." In weather-related emergencies, when West Point, which like other Army installations is referred to as a "post," goes to a condition called "Code Red," some civilian employees can stay home, but as the memo issued at the start of each academic year explains, I need to make arrangements for an emergency billet with someone on post in the event that nature threatens to derail my commute. The strategic advantages of the terrain that made this location attractive in the eighteenth century, when Fort Putnam was built high up on the west bank of the Hudson River, make the approach on winter days rather daunting. Civilians who live "off post," and most do, must venture over one of the surrounding mountains. Should a dangling modifier need reattaching, a sentence fragment suturing, or a metaphor anatomizing in a storm, however, I will be first on the scene. That's a set of priorities an English professor can embrace.

The mothers and fathers I greeted at the door during that Plebe Parent Weekend knew none of this trivia. To them, I was simply a nuisance; a guard at a border checkpoint who stood between them and news of their children. Briefed on my duties, I took up my post armed with half of a two-way radio set issued to me with mock solemnity by the head of the department, a position always occupied by a colonel, who had borrowed it from his grandchildren for the occasion. There I waited for the mothers and fathers of the plebes to invade our open house in search of their sons' or daughters' professors. I had orders to bar the suspicious, to interrogate all those unaccompanied by a cadet, and to send the rest upstairs.

Why all the fuss? Because it was October 2001, and everything, as it quickly became fashionable to say, had changed. Once an open post with a friendly MP who waved visitors through the gates, West Point, like military installations everywhere, had responded to the events of September 11 by instituting a variety of force-protection measures. Unsettled as I initially was by the idea of being greeted each morning by a soldier with an M-16, I knew I would get used

even to that. Before September 11, life at West Point had been—
there's no other word for it—peaceful. When I arrived, in the summer of 1997, the Army to which the school contributes about a
thousand second lieutenants each spring wasn't at war with anyone.
Firsties knew that they could look forward to a series of stateside assignments and a tour in Germany or Korea, but they couldn't really
count on combat unless perhaps they joined the Special Forces,
and then they wouldn't be able to tell anyone about it anyway. In
1999, I attended a belated but symbolically significant ceremony at
which officers were awarded Recognition Certificates for their
faithful service during "the Cold War era" (September 2, 1945–
December 26, 1991). Even the Russians weren't there to kick
around anymore. The most heated debates of the day centered on
whether it was appropriate for the Army, and for the country, to engage in peacekeeping and humanitarian-aid missions. These debates haven't been resolved, only eclipsed.

As I processed the parents, one of my colleagues—usually Dan,
who was rather amused by all of this—would check in periodically.
Dan had served for several years with the Army's prestigious 82nd
Airborne Division before earning his Ph.D. in philosophy. There
are three main constituencies on the West Point faculty: civilian
Ph.D.s (20 percent); a rotating military component of captains
and majors who earn a master's degree, serve for three years, and
then return to the field Army (60 percent); and a senior military
contingent of lieutenant colonels and colonels who have gone back
to graduate school for the Ph.D. (20 percent). Dan had done a
three-year tour at West Point earlier in his career, but I met him
when he returned as a member of the senior military faculty. He
is from Montana, and its wide-open spaces have shaped his attitudes toward people and society. He is a man of the west who has
spirit, rough humor, and generosity; a cowboy who happens also to
have read an enormous amount of Kant. Dan's speech is a wonderfully improbable amalgamation of the scatological and the ac-

ademic. He wrestles with philosophical theories as if they are calves to be roped or deer to be butchered.

After he took me deer hunting one winter morning, I took to calling Dan "Elmer Fudd." We had gone out to the woods with the aim of "knocking something over," but our crunching footsteps in the overnight snowfall made us about as stealthy as cartoon killers: "Be vewy quiet. I'm hunting wabbits." I felt slightly ridiculous (and very cold) tromping around in the snow with my bright orange safety vest and hat. Dan, by contrast, is utterly at home in the woods stalking his prey, alert and light on his feet. Of only medium height, he's got the athletic build and movements of a former wrestler and the soldier's no-nonsense, close-cropped haircut. Put all that together with a knowledge of his physical competitiveness and incredible capacity for pain—something I learned when he almost sliced his thumb off but refused at first to go to the hospital—and you behold a fairly intimidating figure in camouflage. At the end of the day, I fired a few rounds from Dan's .270 rifle, which has a kick so strong that it almost knocked me over. I also had a ringing in my ears for a day, and I suddenly understood why so many of my military friends have suffered serious hearing loss. Like many officers, Dan has especial patience when it comes to training novices, and even the most incurable city mouse can emerge from a day in the woods under his tutelage with a richer understanding of nature, wildlife, and firearms.

On the day of the open house, Shakespeare call signs seemed appropriate:

SHAKESPEARE 3, THIS IS SHAKESPEARE 6, HAVE YOU SECURED THE PERIMETER?—OVER
SHAKESPEARE 3, THIS IS SHAKESPEARE 6, DO YOU NEED RELIEF AT YOUR POST?—OVER
NEGATIVE—OVER
ROGER—OUT

Relief? No way. Refusing to surrender my post, I processed legions of parents with dispatch. In they pressed, fathers carrying video cameras, mothers wearing black parkas with gold letters indicating their children's class, USMA 05. These parkas are standard issue for cadets, who often buy extra ones for their mothers, girlfriends, and, occasionally, fathers.

In the "gray days" of winter, when the castellated stone buildings blend with the sky and the wind rips off the Hudson, these parkas and the winter caps that go with them are the emblems of shared misery. There is a profound sense in which an eighteen-year-old plebe needs to feel that he has suffered, and suffered cruelly. Reporting to West Point sometimes only days after high school graduation, the "new cadet" spends the summer trudging through the humid woods of the Hudson Valley in face paint and camouflage imagining her friends sleeping late or going to the beach. In the fall, when he has exchanged his Army combat uniform (ACU) for a more businesslike as-for-class uniform and plunged into a heavy load of required courses, the shorn plebe's friends instant-message him with tales of growing beards, rushing fraternities, and signing up for (but not necessarily attending) whatever classes strike their fancy. Surrendering a great deal, plebes cultivate a compensatory aura of martyrdom.

On their parents, the parkas seemed a strange show of solidarity. For identification purposes, the mothers and fathers had been issued personalized pins in the shapes of their home states. It was almost impossible to decipher the surnames, but I thought that if I could identify the states, I would be able to gain the upper hand with my dazzlingly thorough knowledge of capitals. Texas was easy, so was California, but the nondescript square states proved a challenge, and I found myself staring a bit too long and hard at the chests of parents from Wyoming and Colorado. Who but a native can tell the difference between the isolated silhouettes of North and South Dakota?

As the day wore on, an entire nation assembled before me. They say every fourth cadet is from Texas, but in fact all fifty states are represented. A West Point class is not the gung-ho, red-state monolith an outsider might expect. I've known of cadets who grew up on Manhattan's Upper East Side and cadets who spent part of their childhood on the streets; cadets who were Eagle Scouts and cadets who played in garage bands; cadets whose fathers are ministers and cadets whose fathers have long ago disappeared; cadets from families with a tradition of military service dating back to the nineteenth century and cadets whose parents protested the Vietnam War. Ironically, for a young man or woman in this last category, joining the military proved to be the ultimate act of defiance.

One officer told me he went to West Point in the late 1960s, perversely, to avoid being sent to Vietnam (but ended up being sent after graduation anyway), and more than one has made a career out of the Army largely because their fathers were convinced that they weren't quite "man enough" to do it. Some of my colleagues are zealots; others have come back from Iraq in profound distress. A few haven't come back at all. What everyone who graduates from West Point shares, no matter the personal history, is a willingness to devote their twenties to military service—a minimum of five years on active duty and three more in the Reserves—in exchange for a free undergraduate education.

Like the identical gray uniforms worn by the cadets, the black parkas tended to mask the abundant parental variety. Their individuality was eclipsed as well by a sense of communal predicament. They were all eager mothers and fathers whose concern about their children's progress in composition hid a deeper anxiety about what distant corner of the world they might be deployed to in a few years. Some of them must have wondered what all of their ambitions had wrought, to what violent end their enthusiasm had potentially consigned those beings whose safety had been for eighteen years their chief object.

Organized parental visitations have always struck me as somewhat infantilizing. I remember my mother and father going to elementary school, even high school, open houses, but they never met any of my college professors, nor did they know the names of the courses they were paying for. Mine are not parents anyone would call uninterested, but there was a stage after which it became unseemly to manifest their interest on site. Yet my parents didn't drop me off in Harvard Yard for freshman orientation with the fear that I might one day be returned to them in a flag-draped coffin. One of my former students, Joey, while serving with the Old Guard in Washington, D.C., routinely escorted such coffins from Dover Air Force Base, and he has told me it is the most difficult assignment he's had, more brutal in its way than was his tour in Iraq. The administration of the Academy recognizes the deep-seated need of the parents whose children it admits to see firsthand something of day-to-day operations. The opportunity to visit with an English professor for a few minutes and to get a report on their children's progress in class is therefore something, if not always enough, for parents wrapped in apprehensions as tightly as they are in those black parkas. Some trepidation must always accompany pride for the families of soldiers, but the imaginings of those parents in October 2001 were far more desperate in view of the fact that the stakes of American soldiering had suddenly been raised.

The stakes of *teaching* at West Point have also been raised by the events that followed September 11. The institution always felt different from a civilian college, but it used to be much easier for me as well as for the cadets to confuse their chosen profession with just another career. The Army itself had encouraged this kind of thinking in the 1980s with its "Be All You Can Be" slogan and its emphasis on adventure and technical training over the deadlier aspects of the military profession. The September 11 attacks, the War on Terror, Operation Enduring Freedom in Afghanistan, and, most important, Operation Iraqi Freedom and the ongoing occupation have altered the perspectives of cadets and forced them to consider more closely what it is they have signed up for. The nebulous struggle against terror that we have now learned to call the Long War has likewise forced me to reexamine what it means to teach literature to these particular young women and men.

My association with the Army has persuaded some people that I am invested with particular affinities, arcane knowledge, or special powers. When I give a lecture or present a paper at a conference, strangers materialize to tell me of past associations with anyone or anything military. They seek to forge a bond, however tenuous. The most bizarre such encounter occurred at a convention in New Orleans. After giving a paper about poetry and soldiers, I was approached by a spectral figure, turned out in beret and cape, and carrying a silver-headed cane. Following me through the French Quarter, he confided that Robert Graves, the author and World War I veteran, had been his dear friend. Before "Robert" died, he said, visibly moved, "he asked me to forgive him. You see, he had done some unspeakable things in the war. But who was I," demanded my ghostly confidant before wandering off down Royal Street, "who was I to absolve him?"

Others assume I have an intimate knowledge of long-range military strategy or of the inner workings of the secretary of defense's mind. I am routinely asked what "the Army" thinks about x or y. My ignorance about these matters no doubt disappoints the curious. Also chagrined are those who assume that I've met everyone in the Army, as if the entire organization were confined to one tiny post. Most are keenly interested in the generals: "What do you know about Wesley Clark?" topped the list of questions in 2004. Now it is General David Petraeus about whom everyone is curious. Most common, however, are inquiries about cadets or officers who have been assigned to West Point at some stage of their careers:

"You teach at West Point? I know someone who went to West Point! Maybe you taught him. Honey, what was Margie's son's name? William, Willard, Wilbur? Don't you remember?"

"I don't know. I thought it was Mark."

"Well, anyway, his last name is Johnson, and he graduated about two years ago."

"Seems to me it was longer than that. More like five, I'd say."

"Oh, maybe five then. Did you know him?"

Friends and relatives imagine that, by working in a military environment, I have become a master logistician. On trips people throw road maps at me and tell me to find the best route to our destination. Whenever I visit my parents, my mother confronts me with large pieces of furniture that must be moved through very small doors: "We've been saving this for you," she'll say. "I've decided that it really belongs in the other room." I'm routinely given missions involving reservations, tickets, optimal modes of transport, alternative routes, itineraries for places I've never even visited, questions of procedure or of rules and regulations: "You're good at that." "You ought to be able to figure that out."

One morning not long after I had come to work at West Point, a friendly groundskeeper I routinely passed on my way to the gym shouted, "Miss, what's your function?" over the roar of his power mower. "Excuse me?" "What's your function?" he repeated, cutting the engine. "What do you do around here?" "Oh," I shouted back, "I teach English." And that, essentially, was what I did. Sure my students wore uniforms and called me "ma'am"; sure a brigadier general showed up in my class one day, but such oddities didn't change what I was doing in any fundamental sense. Increasingly, however, as more of the junior officers to whom I once taught English have made their way to, and not always home from, Iraq, it has become more difficult to describe my "function" even to myself. I believe as much as ever in the importance of teaching literature to future Army officers; moreover, the cultural awareness fostered by such study is vital to the Army's current missions. At the same time I feel that I have become ineluctably involved in something much larger than an academic discussion or a particular discipline.

My ongoing conversations with students, some of which began when men and women who are now lieutenants and captains were plebes, reveal the ways in which literature helps them to understand their own increasingly complicated lives. Having chosen a profession that cannot often afford to indulge their desire for reflection, they make courageous attempts to bridge active and contemplative selves. This is a story about my intellectual and emotional connections to military culture and to certain people in it, but the real drama lies in the way the cadets I teach and the officers with whom I work negotiate the multiple contradictions of their private and professional worlds. Because they serve at the bottom of a hierarchy not especially interested in their opinions, cadets, especially plebes, at once crave and fear the freedom to wonder. Few people really know this part of their story: the courage with which they challenge accepted truths; the nuanced way they read literature and culture; and the ingenious methods they have for resisting conformity in lives largely given over to rules and regulations. Our national fondness for celebrating the physical heroism of soldiers—the apparent readiness with which they sacrifice their lives to larger causes—eclipses the far less romantic displays of moral and intellectual fortitude that also distinguish so many of them. In turning them all into heroes, we have lost a sense of the individuality they also fight to preserve.

I imagine it would be difficult to know that your students are going to war under any circumstances. As it happens, I remain unconvinced by any of the stated reasons given for the invasion of Iraq and dismayed by its civilian architects' apparently cavalier lack of foresight, and because many of my former students, in whom I very much believe, participated in the invasion and continue to serve in the occupying force, it is an adventure that has provoked in me deep sorrow and anger. As I look back on the last few years, I realize how frustrated I've become about not only the prosecution of the war in Iraq but also the ways in which our own country, even as it celebrates the abstraction of the military's sacrifice, has become disconnected in the absence of a draft from the individuals who fight.

In the years after Vietnam, renewed attention to war's psychological costs and a proliferation of studies on post-traumatic stress disorder (PTSD) helped to teach Americans to distinguish the soldier from the war. No matter what they think about this war, the public and the media celebrate soldiers returning from it as heroes or pity them as victims rather than vilifying them as baby killers. Absence of malice notwithstanding, such sentimentality has a dehumanizing effect: it is not the same thing as a true sympathetic accord. Soldiers have become assuaging symbols of sacrifice; they allow us at once to feel and not to feel that we are at war: to go shopping, as we have been encouraged to do, in cars adorned with flags, bumper stickers, and comparable emblems of a sacrifice by proxy.

The condition we now call PTSD was first diagnosed as a malady of the heart, that figurative seat of our emotional life, by physicians treating otherwise healthy Civil War soldiers presenting symptoms that mimicked cardiovascular disease. Because medical practitioners had yet to identify the psychosomatic cause of this illness, the soldiers were often said to be suffering from "disorderly action of the heart," "irritable heart," or, by World War I, "soldier's heart." Armies themselves tend at once to the clinical and the mawkish; their necessary embrace of hard facts drives them periodically to compensatory excesses of sentiment. They must be "all heart" yet have no hearts at all: "steel my soldiers' hearts," Shakespeare's Henry V prays to the God of battles on the eve of Agincourt. "Possess them not with fear! Take from them now / The sense of reck'ning, if th' opposed numbers / Pluck their hearts from them." Exhorted as they are to be lionhearted but also to remain impervious to the organ's stirrings, is it any wonder that soldiers find themselves with disordered hearts?

Is it any wonder that my own confidence in literature's potential to enlarge intellectual and emotional capacities battles on occasion with a suspicion that at least sometimes my students might find more effective protection in what Wilfred Owen, a poet who knew firsthand the terrors of the World War I trench, described in "Insensibility" as "hearts . . . small drawn"? "Happy" are the soldiers "whom no compassion fleers," writes Owen, who "cease feeling / Even themselves or for themselves. / Dullness best solves / The tease and doubt of shelling." But Owen doesn't end his poem there, for he recognizes that such insensibility is a dangerous seduction. It is the necessary precondition of brutality on the part of soldier and witness. He ends by cursing those who remain "as stones" in the face of battle's horrors: "Wretched . . . and mean / With paucity that never was simplicity" are those who have willingly "made themselves immune" to "whatever shares / The eternal reciprocity of tears."

Different as their war may be, soldiers today still face the shelling's "tease and doubt," and the ones I know fight against insensibility with everything they've got. I've discovered this through my correspondence with young officers deployed to Iraq. We exchange thoughts about books, baseball, movies. They ask me what I'm teaching or writing. Lieutenants are often extremely interested in what's happening in the classrooms from which they have so recently graduated; they are concerned that cadets' minds be exercised with sufficient vigor. Their own minds, they complain, are not.

When these young officers come home from Iraq or Afghanistan, they often use part of their leave to visit West Point. Returning to the Academy when it no longer has them in its clutches seems a necessary ritual for many. I have no doubt that I am as likely as anyone to romanticize these encounters, yet when a lieutenant calls or drops by the office, I sense an ineffable change. He or she often seems more serious, more adult, more circumspect. I often get the feeling that these officers have something they want to say but can't. Perhaps they simply want to acknowledge the change, to resume a normal acquaintance, or to tell me about something

that happened in the desert. Whatever they know can't be pried
loose by a lot of questions. It has to come voluntarily and perhaps
only much later, when distance permits reflection. More often than
not we end up talking about where they read a particular book and
what they found in it that helped them better understand what they
have been asked to do. Thus when people ask me today about my
"function," I can't answer so glibly because when I look out at those
newly shorn plebes who appear so eager to please on the first day of
the semester, full of good faith and idealism, I see not simply students of literature or numbed soldiers but citizens who are willing
to make a very real sacrifice.

Major William F. Hecker, III, who graduated from West Point in
1991, the same year that I graduated from Harvard, was killed in
January 2006, when the HMMWV in which he was riding rolled
over an improvised explosive device (IED) in Iraq. Bill was the
second of my colleagues to die in Operation Iraqi Freedom. The
first was Colonel Theodore S. Westhusing, who died in June 2005,
when he committed suicide in his trailer in Baghdad. Ted, who was
serving at the time with the Multi-National Security Transition
Command—Iraq, responsible for training Iraqi security forces,
couldn't seem to reconcile his own conceptions of honorable service with what he was witnessing: the large amounts of money
changing hands, the role of private contractors, the nature of the
mission itself. Watching the Tour de France each summer since his
death, I've thought a lot about Ted, who never betrayed his impatience while waiting for me to pedal uphill after him on one of our
rides and whose shouts of *"Allez! Allez!"* always got me through,
even when one of the hills above the Hudson Valley began to feel
like L'Alpe d'Huez to me. Because it occurred in the summer, Ted's
funeral seemed somehow disconnected from the world of cadets
and the classroom, but Bill's funeral took place at West Point on a

stormy day at the beginning of the semester in January 2006. I remember because that was the day the roof blew right off the place.

I was working at my desk when a colleague poked his head into the office. "Did you hear that? There was a horrible noise, and I think I saw a piece of the roof pass by my window." "It was just the wind, Chicken Little. Relax." "No, really, I think the roof blew off." "Uh-huh." I tried to get back to work, but all my attempts at concentration were thwarted by the growing hum in the halls, by shouts and scurrying feet. The windows always rattle on a windy day in our building, and there are often strange noises coming from somewhere inside its walls. A few shingles blew off, big deal, I thought (conveniently forgetting that the building doesn't have a shingled roof). Whatever had happened certainly didn't warrant the watercooler melodrama ensuing out there in the hall. Exasperated, I was just about to get up to close the door when the fire alarm went off. The roof *had* blown off—right off the department. Warped pieces of metal lay all around: debris on the grass, in the middle of the road, even in the parking lot across the street. A length of gutter had sheared away from the building, and an enormous piece of copper sheeting hanging over the walls yawned menacingly in the wind. I heard the heavy footsteps of firemen's boots, and the serious men inside them told us to evacuate immediately. You don't argue with a man brandishing an ax.

It was a fitting—and to an English professor a somehow satisfyingly poetic—punctuation mark to what I had already come to think of as the Year of the Plague. The news from Iraq; Guantánamo, which Amnesty International had judged "the gulag of our times"; the bracing catalog of natural disasters (tsunami, earthquake, hurricane); the grave warnings about a flu pandemic worse than that of 1918; the rhetoric about America's imperial legions . . . 2005 had been tuned to apocalyptic strains. War and sickness, each a metaphor for the other, seemed once again to be marauding together through the land, just as they do in the *Iliad*. I remembered teaching that poem to a class of plebes in the spring of 2001. How different our experience would have been, especially perhaps our reading of Homer's opening description of the corpses of all those killed by the plague, only months later.

I wasn't the only one thinking about the Greeks, of course. Like Homer, the Athenian historian Thucydides had enjoyed a revival since September 11. Everyone from journalists to retired generals and pundit-academicians found in him what they needed either to celebrate the responsibilities of democracy or to lament the perils of empire. Preparing to teach a senior seminar on London and its twin seventeenth-century calamities—the plague epidemic of 1665 and the Great Fire of 1666—I had dusted *History of the Peloponnesian War* off to revisit its account of the fifth-century B.C. Athenian epidemic, which forensic scientists now think was typhoid: "Nor was any other human art or science of any help at all," writes Thucydides, who survived his own bout with the disease. "Equally useless were prayers made in the temples, consultation of oracles, and so forth." The desperation was compounded by the migration of people from the countryside to Athens: "The bodies of the dying were heaped one on top of the other, and half-dead creatures could be seen staggering about in the streets or flocking around the fountains in their desire for water." One of the things that Thucydides found peculiar about this plague was that birds and dogs instinctively refused to feed on the corpses. This time, I thought, images of Hitchcock fusing with Thucydides in my all-too-susceptible brain, the birds will bring it.

The cadets whom I bombarded with tales of plague and fire—with the diaries of Samuel Pepys and John Aubrey, and with Daniel Defoe's *A Journal of the Plague Year* (1722)—in the fall of 2005 confronted me in turn with a new sadness and a sober, quiet skepticism. They voiced it in a refrain uttered in response to any unwelcome news or setback, from a bad grade to a draconian regulation: "What's the difference, ma'am? I'll be in Iraq within a year anyway." "We are more cynical than your average college student," one senior informed me after an especially grim conversation in a poetry elective that same semester. "You are cynical," I replied, "about different things." As I reflect on the seniors in those courses, they remind me of Jaques, the melancholy poet of Shakespeare's *As You Like It*, who tries throughout the play to find words adequate to his feelings in "a miserable world."

When I later mentioned the cadets' new refrain to a retired colonel who had taught at West Point after serving in Vietnam, he told me they used to say the same thing back then. By contrast, a friend who was a cadet during Desert Storm recalled that watching that war on television had boosted morale and convinced cadets of their invincibility; he has difficulty imagining what is going through their heads as they watch our current operations. In the minds of today's cadets, Desert Storm, to say nothing of Vietnam, seems part of a distant past. In the old days, cadets, who were not permitted radios or televisions, had access to few media sources beyond the newspaper. Now, with computers and Internet connections, they can get their war in real time just like the rest of us. In addition to the news, they get more personal updates from deployed friends via e-mail and Instant Messenger. Thus war is never very far from our minds even as we immerse ourselves in the work of writers as diverse as Edith Wharton and the T'ang Dynasty poet Li Po.

Our department assembly point for fire alarms, and now for flying roofs, is Cullum Hall, a stately McKim, Mead, and White building that overlooks the Hudson River. It soon became clear that we weren't going to get back into our building anytime soon, and a command post was set up. As the firemen assessed the damage, our executive officer, working her way down an emergency telephone tree, made alternate arrangements for classes and meetings. Something was happening. Cell phones came out of every pocket. Plans were made. Someone had unearthed an ancient easel with a big pad of butcher paper where announcements were posted for cadets and faculty. Instead of feeling frustrated and helpless, as soldiers who are not fighting when there is a war on often do, my colleagues felt useful. All around me they were going into what one major laughingly called "action mode." She gave me a demonstration complete with running commentary of the various poses an officer might adopt in such a situation: "Hands on the hips, that's the most common one, of course, but you can also fold your arms in front of you and gravely survey the scene. My favorite is this one: arms folded, with chin resting in one hand. It looks like you are thinking—hard—about something."

Soldiers rise to emergencies. I don't mean that they like them or even secretly hope for them, but crises are what they train for; presented with one, they immediately feel more at ease, more comfortable in their roles. They can do something, even if it is only surveying the wreckage. At other times they are like policemen in a city without crime or physicians in a kingdom of androids. And perhaps soldiers, like statesmen, believe more passionately than most of the rest of us what Abigail Adams once told her son John Quincy, whom she feared insufficiently ambitious: "It is not in the still calm of life, or in the repose of a pacific station, that great characters are formed . . . Great necessities call out great virtues." To *act* was what so many of them had needed after September 11. That need expressed itself much less often as a simple desire for vengeance or payback than as sadness, even guilt, at having somehow failed to defend what they had sworn to defend.

When Joey reported from Washington that he felt guilty for not being in Iraq, I told him that guilt seems to be yet another hazard of his profession. Andy, another former student, reported the emptiness he felt at having to leave Iraq in the middle of his second tour in order to begin law school. Andy decided to become an Army lawyer because he has come to believe that the laws of land warfare have been outpaced by our present conflicts; he wants to help resolve the ambiguity that seems to have facilitated detainee abuse and other war crimes. But this long-term vision did little to alleviate the immediate regret he felt for leaving his soldiers behind. I can still remember one agonized e-mail soon after September 11, from my friend Scott, an officer who had just entered a Ph.D. program in preparation for returning to the permanent faculty at West Point. His last assignment had been at the Pentagon, and he knew some of the people who had been killed in the attack. While he understood that his "duty" was to go to graduate school—that was, after all, the job the Army had assigned him—he was embarrassed by the timing and felt that his immediate moral obligation lay elsewhere. The wise colonel who headed our department at the time of the attacks called a faculty meeting on September 12 in which he urged the officers in the room to recall that their mission—to teach cadets—was no less important than it had been before. If the Army needed them to do something else, it would call them. It has called many of them in the years since.

Bill Hecker's death, rolling over an IED in his HMMWV, has become an emblem of the current war. I have discovered that this particular end has assumed in the minds of many soldiers the importance that the fate of the gunners, exposed in a bomber's tail or ball turret, occupied for the airmen of World War II. That fate is encapsulated in Randall Jarrell's 1945 poem "The Death of the Ball Turret Gunner":

From my mother's sleep I fell into the State,
And I hunched in its belly till my wet fur froze.
Six miles from earth, loosed from its dream of life,
I woke to black flak and the nightmare fighters.
When I died they washed me out of the turret with a hose.

Like Jarrell, my father served in the Army Air Corps during World War II. My idea of an army grew out of his stories of serving as an air traffic controller. It was also shaped by the movies we sometimes watched together. A movie junkie since childhood, I grew up with *To Hell and Back*; *Guadalcanal Diary*; *Wake Island*;

Five Graves to Cairo; *Desperate Journey*; *Sergeant York*; *They Were Expendable*; *Run Silent, Run Deep*; and *Patton*. These films were my link to my father and to a world completely unlike the one I knew. This was back in the dark, pre-cable age when a show called *The Movie Loft* ran on a local Boston UHF station. It showed movies so old that our antiquated black-and-white television deprived me of nothing. It was a black-and-white universe that connected me to my parents' and my country's pasts. It was a world away from days at an all-girls private school, filled with Latin declensions and field hockey tournaments. My father, a CPA and an attorney, was rarely home before I went to sleep during tax season, and he is still the hardest worker I know. But he made a point of driving me to school in the mornings, and on the weekends, if I could find a World War II movie on TV, I could sometimes tempt him to set aside (or at least to look up from) whatever project he had brought home.

One of the most appealing ideas those films emphasized was that of the citizen-soldier. Even the apparent naturals—the born soldiers, the heroes—wanted nothing more than to return home, like the ancient Roman Cincinnatus, once their duty was done. In *Sergeant York*, Alvin York, World War I's most highly decorated soldier, rejects his newfound celebrity to go back home to farm in Tennessee. The fame he acquires through his battlefield heroism is simply a means to that end. Today, in the era of the all-volunteer military, the rhetoric of citizenship, of resuming one's place in civil society, has been eclipsed by one of professionalism, but even in a force structured by a professional military ethic (PME), the principle of citizen-soldiering still animates the exchange of military service for an undergraduate education at West Point and in the nation's ROTC programs.

Like their teacher, most of my students first encountered war and military life through the stories of their fathers and from the movies. For cadets, it might have been *Braveheart*, *Black Hawk*

Down, or *Jarhead*. In this sense, and perhaps in this sense alone, our situations are analogous. The signal difference is that they have actually agreed to turn make-believe into real life. All cadets graduate from West Point with a bachelor of science degree, but they can major in anything from mechanical engineering to Arabic. Those who elect to study in our department's art, philosophy, and literature program are the ones I know best, but in the core courses I also get the opportunity to see a cross section of cadets at work. Recent cataclysms have made me far more self-conscious about the romantic assumptions we all bring to the table and about what the institution asks cadets to do during what is referred to as their "forty-seven-month experience" at West Point.

The national crisis has accentuated a tension between training and education present at the Military Academy since its founding. I hear the word *relevance* much more often than I used to. What does it mean for a student to spend the morning reading Milton's *Paradise Lost* and the afternoon jumping out of an airplane? To spend a summer in the field learning how to defuse an IED and a winter writing about the poetry of Anne Sexton? To read T. E. Lawrence's account of his operations in Mesopotamia in *Seven Pillars of Wisdom* as a firstie in a British literature elective and to be deployed to Iraq the following year? Sometimes the sheer variety of their experiences causes cadets to become confused about what it is they are supposed to be. One asked me whether West Point wanted him to be a soldier or a scholar. If it wanted him to be both, he added, the days needed to be much longer.

Bill Hecker took the notion of being a soldier-scholar very seriously. In the hours before his funeral, I sat in Cullum Hall grading papers. The early commotion had subsided, and I found myself almost alone in a building that has become one of my favorite places at West Point. Its walls are lined with plaques and a huge portrait of General Pershing and his horse. Upstairs there is a still-beautiful if somewhat neglected ballroom with the names of battles carved into the molding along the tops of the walls. Cullum reminds me of a college rather than a military school, despite the fact that its story is so unambiguously one of war.

Sitting before Pershing's portrait, I thought of Bill's fanatical devotion to the poetry of Edgar Allan Poe. Poe was (briefly) a cadet; within a year of his arrival at West Point, he was court-martialed for gross neglect of duty and disobedience of orders. The apocryphal story that he got himself kicked out for showing up naked at formation one day is still popular with cadets, as of course it would be. Poe's 1831 *Poems*—Bill edited and introduced a facsimile edition before he died—was financed by the scofflaw's classmates and dedicated to the Corps. Bill's affinity for Poe stemmed in large measure from the fact that the latter had served as an enlisted soldier in the artillery before coming to West Point. Bill was also an artilleryman, and he delighted in discovering technical terminology and artillery allusions in the poems. The opening stanza of Poe's "The City in the Sea," first published as "The Doomed City" in 1831, seemed apt on that day:

Lo! Death has reared himself a throne
In a strange city lying alone
Far down within the dim West,
Where the good and the bad and the worst and the best
Have gone to their eternal rest.
There shrines and palaces and towers
(Time-eaten towers that tremble not!)
Resemble nothing that is ours.
Around, by lifting winds forgot,
Resignedly beneath the sky
The melancholy waters lie.

The services for my two colleagues constituted my first experience of military funerals, which have a kind of earnestness for which I was not entirely prepared. On unusually intimate terms with violence throughout their professional lives, soldiers know things that many of the rest of us do not. The most elemental thing they know, or are at least prepared to know, is death. Another is what the twentieth-century French aviation pioneer and author of *Le Petit Prince* Antoine de Saint-Exupéry called "craft." For Saint-Exupéry it was the craft of flying: "We understand . . . that what constitutes the dignity of a craft is that it creates a fellowship, that it binds men together and fashions for them a common language." Soldiers, too, are bound and dignified by craft, and they speak a language that announces their membership in it. Yet there are times, and this is one, when what soldiers end up with is less a common craft than, to borrow a phrase from Shakespeare, a royal fellowship of death.

Uncomfortable with peace, armies are precisely calibrated to manage death and dying. The machine of military culture works to turn each death, no matter the cause or circumstance, into an occasion for celebrating the warrior spirit. In the most thoughtful warriors, such deaths also occasion reflection about the nature of military service and the relationship between soldiers and the society they serve. When I read ancient epics with cadets or talk them over with my colleagues, we often find less truth and power in the rousing battle cries of Agamemnon and his fellow bloody-minded enthusiasts than in the disillusion of Achilles, the humanity of Hector, or the ambivalence of Aeneas.

At a military funeral, however, you forget any ambivalence in a wash of heroic sentiment and patriotic feeling. No matter how gruesome the details—no matter how unrecognizable the remains lying in that flag-draped coffin—ceremony turns death into something beautiful and fine. For me, it is chiefly the sounds: the snap of the flag in the wind, the rifle volleys fired in valediction, and the throb of "Taps" from a muted bugle. Ceremony provokes what Shakespeare calls the "awe and fear" that vanquish reason. And this is what I felt at Bill's funeral. The tearful eulogies of his friends and classmates were tinged as well with envy: Bill had died a soldier's death, and they must all secretly have hoped their own ends would be as honorable. After Bill's funeral I could understand the pride and pleasure of Tolstoy's Prince Andrey—disillusioned as he has become with the pursuit of glory—when General Kutuzov recalls the courageous charge in which Andrey had been given up for dead. "I remember you at Austerlitz," the old general tells him. "I remember, I remember you with the flag!" Attend a military funeral, where all is plaintive beauty, and you cannot quarrel with this moment in *War and Peace* or with the otherwise reasonable people who confess to you that the best death is a death in battle.

Whereas civilian funerals seem to cling to the idea that a unique individual has died, military funerals turn everyone into a symbol of epic sacrifice. I felt this strongly at Bill's funeral, as I do whenever I visit the West Point cemetery. Most of the headstones there are standard issue, although there are some outrageously ornate exceptions from earlier times: atop Daniel Butterfield, a Civil War general, stand sixteen gaudy columns commemorating his forty-three battles; the gravestone of Major General George W. Goethals is made of stone taken from the Panama Canal, which he built; George Armstrong Custer's grave still attracts attention despite the fact that his wife had the original bronze figural statue replaced with an obelisk and because of the rumor that the remains buried there are not even his. The freshest graves in this cemetery that is almost filled to capacity lie at the north end under a hedge. These are the graves dug since the start of the current war. Memorial eccentricity now a thing of the past, all of these graves are uniformly marked by the official military headstone.

At the beginning of Charles Dickens's *Great Expectations* the orphan narrator, Pip, having never seen father, mother, or any of his siblings, draws his impression of their likenesses from the shapes of their tombstones. The lettering on his father's grave gives him "the odd idea that he was a square, stout, dark man, with curly black hair," the inscription on his mother's that she "was freckled and sickly." Of the identical stones marking the graves of his five brothers Pip notes:

> To five little stone lozenges, each about a foot and a half long, which were arranged in a neat row beside their grave, and were sacred to the memory of five little brothers of mine,—who gave up trying to get a living, exceedingly early in that universal struggle,—I am indebted for a belief I religiously entertained that they had all been born on their backs with their hands in their trousers-pockets, and had never taken them out in this state of existence.

My problem is the reverse of Pip's: when I wander through the cemetery, my impressions of the stones are drawn from the lives. Instead of seeing uniform symbols of sacrifice in those military headstones, I think of the unique and unfinished individuals concealed beneath. And the longer I stare at the stones, the more "key and essential" and the more confusing my function comes to seem.

1

Not Your Father's Army

In 2006, on the fifth anniversary of 9/11, those great twin beams of light again reached up into the Manhattan sky. Their glow was visible miles away—even to a traveler on the Palisades Parkway, which connects West Point to New York City—yet they illuminated nothing. At West Point we had by this time been trained to expect the news of daily sniper attacks and bombings from Iraq and of the quieter but no less significant deterioration of Afghanistan. In September, I was reading Montaigne with nine cadets in a senior seminar on literary representations of the self, a course that also featured Plutarch, Horace, Shakespeare, Virginia Woolf, and Freud. The firsties were in a reflective mood; later that month, news of the death of a very popular recent graduate, Emily Perez, would carry them for a time into the doldrums. Ultimately, however, in contrast to their predecessors, with whom I had studied London the year before, these seniors remained strangely full of hope. Indeed, their attitude suggests to me that the romance of military life can withstand just about anything.

Perhaps the most resilient among this group was a trio of cadets I had first encountered a year earlier in the class of melancholy poets. I had come to call them the Three Musketeers. Thayer Hall, one of the Academy's main academic buildings, is a warren of corridors and multiple staircases. The Three Musketeers and I had to make our way out of Thayer and back to the English Department after poetry class, and they began to take playful delight in finding new places along the route to ambush me. Around whatever corner we met, we would immediately resume discussion about a point left unfinished in class, about the books they were reading, about the latest development in their summer plans: Grant was off to Kenya to work on his cousin's ranch, Renée to Vietnam, and Kevin home to Maryland before returning to West Point for his military duties in July.

Kevin switched his major early in his junior year to English from civil engineering. He is a young man of quiet intensity and wry humor who normally wears a very serious expression. When he does crack a joke, his deep brown eyes light up with mischief and the furrows in his brow relax. His grin is never too broad, his humor never cruel. Kevin speaks only after careful deliberation and then with a measured clarity that forces everyone to listen. He also has a disarming frankness characteristic of cadets. Unlike the jaded sophisticates with whom I went to college, Kevin will share with you his sense of wonder; he'll also tell you when he is fundamentally disappointed. Most important, he isn't afraid to admit there is something he doesn't know: "I feel inadequate having not been an 'English major' all my life," he told me one day during his junior year soon after making the change.

Kevin is a devoted reader—I guess he's making up for lost time—and he periodically sends me magazine articles of literary or historical interest. He wrestled for a long time with a thesis topic. At first, he had been interested in the Beats, but after reading too much of them, he grew weary and began to think on a larger scale about what it means to have a national literature: "The concept of America should be an important one to everyone who wears a uniform and faces the prospect of fighting for her," he wrote to me. "I've had that on my mind quite a bit over the past few months. It might be refreshing to pull something beautiful and unifying out from the shell of disappointing politics . . . I see . . . in my daily, CNN-consuming routine." What he pulled were the ideas of masculinity, honor, and patriotism, especially as they are negotiated by the stoic heroes of Ernest Hemingway.

Now that Kevin was a senior contemplating his impending graduation, the concept of honor began increasingly to consume his thoughts. He had been struck in our seminar by Montaigne's meditations on this virtue: "A man's worth and reputation lie in the mind and in the will," writes Montaigne in his essay "On Cannibals," "his true honour is found there." The idea of honor is inescapable at West Point: it lies at the heart of the motto "Duty, Honor, Country"; cadets live by the Honor Code; to be accused of violating that code is to be "brought up on Honor." This most romantic of virtues forms the core of the military ethos: "A man," declared Clark Gable, no doubt thinking about his service in the 8th Air Force as well as his approach to playing soldiers in the movies, "must be ready to choose death before dishonor without making too much song and dance about it." Kevin found himself writing about honor in all of his classes that semester: "I'm obsessed," he told me. As he continued to ponder what kind of officer he would become, he began to tease out honor's paradoxes, its fragility and elusiveness as well as its endurance: "Of the many romantic sensibilities the modern world has claimed as its casualties," he wrote, "I will not say that honor is one."

As is only appropriate, Renée, the second Musketeer, was a captain of the fencing team. Her weapon was the saber. She also had a hand in resurrecting Army Strings, a cadet string quartet that had fallen into abeyance for several years. It was her "dream" to reenergize the group, which under her stewardship began to get more gigs than it could manage. At the end of her e-mails, where other cadets might place a rousing "Beat Navy!" or a company motto like "Go Ducks!" or "Go Spartans!" Renée would append "Go Army

Strings!" Proof that another romantic notion, that of the Army as humanitarian instrument, has survived even the debacle of Iraq, Renée came to West Point because she believed that as an Army officer she could somehow help to alleviate the suffering of others.

Renée devoted much of her time during her senior year to a thesis on the iconography of Elizabeth I. The opportunity to write about one of history's most powerful women was certainly part of the attraction, but Renée seemed drawn as well to Elizabeth's intellectual agility and to her adroitness at managing her public image. Renée read everything, hunted down rare books and manuscripts, took research trips to Yale and to the Newberry Library in Chicago, and generally availed herself of every resource (material and human) she could find. Renée combines great energy with an aura of serene competence: there's never anything frenetic about her movements when it comes to either intellectual conversation or the armed "conversation," as the back-and-forth of blades is called, of fencing. There is a funny video of one of Renée's matches. She stands, saber in hand, awaiting her opponent's move with the aplomb of Douglas Fairbanks. As the other fencer lunges, Renée administers a touch with great finesse and watches her unbalanced opponent promptly fall over. Renée is wearing a face mask, but I suspect she permitted herself a gentle smile.

Military life is a family tradition for Grant, the third Musketeer: his grandfather and great-grandfather were in the Army, and his uncle was a Marine. "I've got very romantic ideas about the Army," he has told me on more than one occasion. When the time came for the seniors to select which military post they would attend after they finished the various schools new lieutenants must complete, Grant, who had already chosen the Infantry, based his decision on a calculation of which unit would be scheduled to deploy as soon as he arrived. He wanted to lead a platoon in combat. That was what West Point had prepared him to do, and now was the time, when he had no family, no distractions, no commitments beyond military service itself.

Grant is prey to nostalgia, if not quite its prisoner: "I want to be in my grandfather's army," he explained to me one afternoon as we walked across post. I think he imagines that army as having been imbued with lingering nineteenth-century ideas of honor and gallantry, to have been less corporate and bureaucratic, more maverick. When I suggested that his grandfather probably had the same complaint—that in imagining his grandfather's army Grant had almost surely conjured a utopia that lives only in oral family histories and literary accounts—he replied: "Yes, but isn't that the point?" At the time of this conversation, Grant had just finished interviewing for a cadet leadership position, and he had been grappling with matters of policy and styles of leadership. The Corps of Cadets is run by a Brigade Staff that consists of the first captain (Pershing and MacArthur both served as first captain) and several other cadet leaders. Grant was selected to be the operations officer, in charge of all the Corps's day-to-day activities. This is an extraordinarily time-consuming job, and Grant struggled to do it while writing a senior thesis on Milton's *Paradise Lost*. Whenever he came by my office to talk about his thesis, the discussion eventually turned to things military.

What Grant seemed to want most of all was greater autonomy. In Miltonic terms, he wanted the freedom to fall: "Many of my classmates and I, when we think of the Golden Age of the Corps, hearken back to the 40s . . . [when] our Lieutenants helped to win the war against the Axis powers. To us, those were the days when cadets were hard and gods roamed the Plain. Our perception of the Old Corps, or perhaps our myth, is that those cadets were granted command and exercised their authority with impunity." When Grant marches at the head of the Corps in parades, the pride and responsibility of ownership are almost palpable. He seems to be measuring himself against those hard gods who once stalked the Plain. Tall, lean, and ramrod straight, Grant "just looks like a soldier," as my neighbor in the stands declared one morning at a review. The degree to which Grant's romanticism is fueled by a rich literary sensibility can be seen in the following passage, which he wrote as a senior:

> As for me, I'll have the company of a thousand characters to walk with me into the future. When I am afraid, I can be a rough-skinned lion whose thirst for blood drives him into the middle of the slaughter. When I am overwhelmed, I can be the general [who] sits at the foot of the breach he means to take the next day and enjoys good conversation and fine foods with his friends; it is the paltry soul that when faced with many tasks cannot put them down and pick them up again. Should I fall into enemy hands, I will have the Greek tragedians to offer me perspective: Prometheus's fate will be forever worse.

In class the Three Musketeers fed off one another. Their intelligence and energy could carry the conversation. I loved to watch what happened whenever they grabbed hold of an idea, whether it was Wordsworth's contention in the preface to *Lyrical Ballads* that "all good poetry is the spontaneous overflow of powerful feelings" or Hamlet's recognition of the difficulty of distinguishing the performance of feeling from "that within which passeth show." They missed one another's company when they weren't all together in class, and in the spring of their senior year, they invited me to join them in an informal reading group on the *Iliad*. It is no hyperbole to say that the Three Musketeers gave me hope in a difficult time. Grant may worry that he isn't in his grandfather's army, but it strikes me that any army in which the Three Musketeers can flourish has some fine potential. One day, I found myself once again in step with the trio. "Ma'am," Renée announced, "we've got our own name for this group: the Fearsome Foursome." It's a quartet of which I'm proud to be a member, for it was this same sense of fellowship—the romance—that first drew me to the Military Academy as well, even if I couldn't have articulated it at the time.

My path to West Point was an unusual one that started with Ulysses S. Grant, USMA class of 1843. I first met Grant at the old Taft Hotel in New Haven, Connecticut. It was 1994 or 1995. The Taft had seen better days; so had Grant. It had long been fashionable to dismiss him as a hopeless drunk, a bumbler, or a callous brute. I don't remember who introduced us, but I can recall what an inspiring companion he proved to be after a few years on the obligatory graduate school diet. Relieved temporarily of the responsibility of teaching, I spent the majority of my Whiting Fellowship year at one of three activities: reading, writing, and working out. So here we were, a graduate student and the Butcher of Cold Harbor, an unlikely pair sitting on the sofa together for hours on end. I was supposed to be writing a dissertation on ideas of sympathy and political justice in eighteenth- and nineteenth-century literature. Only later did Grant become central to my investigation of American literature and to my understanding of a certain kind of democratic responsibility. What I later saw at West Point of a functioning military hierarchy prompted me to write a book about the ways in which Americans have imagined their obedience to the state or, as in the case of Grant, have gone about the project of commanding other Americans unused to subjection and taught to believe in their own liberty and autonomy.

But all of that was to come. For the moment, I found in Grant's *Personal Memoirs* a book that could keep one company—a book written by an adult, terminally ill with throat cancer, who confronted without flinching life's one grim certainty, its end. His words suggested to me across a temporal, professional, and personal divide that I was somehow not entirely alone in my various doubts and hopes. In the no-man's-land of graduate school, I was trying to prepare for a profession in a place where *profession* seemed to be a dirty word. We cultivated the sustaining fiction that it was a high-minded devotion to learning that had brought us to graduate school, while so many of our peers had sold out by studying law or business, but with high-mindedness came the pose of martyrdom. We surrendered rather easily to yet another romantic notion: that meaning is to be found only in misery.

Nor was Yale's sense of community especially strong. Departments felt like islands unto themselves. Seminars that drew students from different programs occasionally had the atmosphere of armed camps. I met wonderful teachers at Yale, mentors who went out of their way to help me and have been extremely generous in the years since. I also met professors from whom one learned a great deal despite the fact that they seemed a bit ambivalent about the whole enterprise. When the subject turned to Platonic ideals in one class, the professor sighed. "Well, in a Platonic universe I wouldn't have to teach this class." Another used to take a book from his office shelves but hold it just out of my reach so that I could scribble down the title without sullying the pages. "I'm sure the library has a copy," he would say, returning it to its place.

Grant's world was miles away from this one, and his *Memoirs* also introduced me to West Point, where its author spent four ambivalent years. The book widened my circle of acquaintance: Robert E. Lee, Winfield Scott, Zachary Taylor, Simon Bolivar Buckner, William Tecumseh Sherman. These were not people I normally thought a lot about. Grant was so different from many of the people I knew: he was entirely lacking in pretense—even as a general he still believed there were things others could teach him; he wasn't afraid to own up to a mistake; he didn't brag yet knew quite well his own mettle. Perhaps most important to me, eagerly participating as I was in a world of sometimes deliberate obfuscation, was the fact that Grant prized the ability to state his "meaning so plainly that there could be no mistaking it."

There was a lot to like about the General: the fact that he was shorter than almost everyone else; that he was the best horseman anyone had ever seen; that he didn't think all wars were equal or worth fighting and was candid enough to call the Mexican War "one of the most unjust ever waged by a stronger against a weaker nation." I even liked his idiosyncrasies: he hated the sight of blood; he never retraced his steps when lost but kept going if he overshot his destination until he found a road that turned in the right direction; at West Point, when he was supposed to be studying, he spent his time reading novels: "all of Bulwer's then published, Cooper's, Marryat's, Scott's, Washington Irving's works, Lever's, and many others I do not now remember." This admission created a kind of kinship between us, for campaigning with Grant was my escape.

Thus, when the Modern Language Association's Job Information List appeared in the fall of 1996, I read with otherwise unaccountable interest West Point's advertisement for an assistant professor of English. Military experience was not required, the job description said, but applicants should have "a genuine concern for the development of competent, committed military officers." I couldn't gainsay the value of educating military officers. In part because of my father, older than the baby-boomer parents of many of my peers, I didn't grow up imbibing an automatic mistrust of the military. West Point conjured up neither the vision of jackbooted government thugs nor the plot of *Seven Days in May*, in which a military cabal, sickened by the softness of civilian leadership, attempts a coup.

Nevertheless, curious as I was, I knew that West Point's priorities and protocols were not those to which I had grown accustomed. Would I be Rosalind in Arden or Marlow upriver at the Inner Station? It was, after all, a school that trained men and women in the use of the M-16 rifle, the M-203 grenade launcher, and the M-249 machine gun even as it educated them in foreign languages, mathematics, and literature. I am not, moreover, a joiner by nature, and the Army is the ultimate club, a paradoxically transparent but secretive society steeped in ritual and equipped with a private language. It is defiantly a men's club. Alien as West Point was to my own experiences, however, the prospect of teaching there also connected me in some way to my father's history.

Propagandists have long exploited the powerful influence exerted on daughters and sons by the legends of their fathers' armies: "Daddy," reads the caption of a well-known British World War I recruiting poster by Savile Lumley, "what did YOU do in the Great War?" Lumley's portrait of a pensive father and his inquisitive children, the son playing with tin soldiers and a toy cannon on the floor, was parodied by Donald McGill, whose cheap postcards George Orwell memorialized in "The Art of Donald McGill," an essay published in 1941. McGill's poster bore the same caption but depicted a soldier carrying two buckets of soup—or slop, it's hard to tell—from Field Kitchen No. 6. Despite their obvious stylistic differences, both images hint at the ever-present temptation for the soldier to tell another, perhaps more glamorous, war story than the one he may actually have lived. McGill's image in particular suggests that not all war experiences yield stories worth the telling to children hungry for the heroism of their parents.

"You don't tell stories in uniform!" Walter Pidgeon's General Kane reprimands a subordinate in MGM's 1948 *Command Decision*. This is not, of course, strictly true. The uniform may counsel prudence, but it does not mandate silence. War stories have always been the stock-in-trade of soldiers. Fame, the Greek *kleos*, is a most powerful motivator, and war stories, like fish stories, tend to get grander at each retelling. The desire for epic immortality led Alexander the Great to complain that he lacked a Homer to record his exploits. The figure of the storytelling soldier pervades the literature cadets and I read together. Perhaps its most evocative incarnation occurs in Shakespeare's *Henry V*. In the moments before Agincourt, the king eggs on his outnumbered, demoralized army with the promise that the soldier fortunate enough to survive the battle will one day be able to "strip his sleeve and show his scars, / And say, 'These wounds I had on Crispin's day.' / . . . This story shall the good man teach his son." Henry offers his men the opportunity not simply to display their wounds, those indelible badges of honor, but also to tell their sons the tales of how they got them.

Some soldiers, General Grant once noted, are "always aching for a fight." George S. Patton seems to have been one of them. The film *Patton* is a great favorite among cadets, some of whom have memorized the General's long opening speech in front of the giant flag. (I confess to knowing more of it by heart than is probably good for me.) In that speech Patton delivers his own version of Henry V's promise: "Thirty years from now when you're sitting around your fireside with your grandson on your knee and he asks you 'What did you do in the great World War II?' you won't have to say, 'Well, I shoveled shit in Louisiana.'"

Ironically, this film was made during the war that changed the prevailing assumption about what an American war story was supposed to sound like. Tim O'Brien strikes the keynote of the Vietnam war story in *The Things They Carried*:

> A true war story is never moral. It does not instruct, nor encourage virtue, nor suggest proper models of human behavior, nor restrain men from doing the things men have always done. If a story seems moral, do not believe it. If at the end of a war story you feel uplifted, or if you feel that some small bit of rectitude has been salvaged from the larger waste, then you have been made the victim of a very old and terrible lie.

In a style that blurs the line between fiction and fact, O'Brien insists on pursuing "truth" by means of narratives that resist satisfying moral or structural closure. Furthermore, by insisting on amorality, O'Brien forces his readers to think about what motivates soldiers to tell such stories in the first place and what compels the rest of us to listen. The tension between a contemporary urge to demythologize and a persistent desire to be seduced all over again by heroic tales animates the cadets' study of literature.

Perhaps nowhere is this dynamic clearer than in English 102, one of the courses plebes are required to take during the spring semester. This is the lone literature course of an entire undergraduate career for most cadets. After several years of teaching contemporary poetry and a smattering of older verse—Charles Wright, Alberto Ríos, Charles Simic, Deborah Digges, Jorie Graham, Robert Pinsky, and Marilyn Nelson were among the poets who came to read their work to cadets in the 1990s—the department shifted the focus of the course to war poetry during the spring of 2001. The presence of war literature persisted to greater or lesser degrees for the next several years; today the course has a broader range of both theme and genre.

I was not privy to all the reasons for the change, but I suspect that there was an underlying feeling that by setting the plebes to the study of war literature we would be seen to be making thoroughly businesslike use of their time. This is the kind of course many outsiders expect at West Point. They imagine that, if soldiers read anything all, it must be the vocationally relevant: a steady, manly diet of Kipling, perhaps. Kipling was not among the authors we read in 2001. Course texts included *Beowulf*, in Seamus Heaney's new translation; Robert Fagles's translation of the *Iliad*; *The Penguin Book of First World War Poetry*; and Shakespeare's *Troilus and Cressida*. For me the highlight of the semester was listening to Fagles reciting for a thousand plebes the first lines of the *Iliad* in Greek. For a moment the rhythm of Homer's hexameters transformed a vast and soulless auditorium usually devoted to Power-Point briefings into the plain before Troy.

As it turned out, the explicitly themed war literature course got mixed reviews from the plebes in my sections. Those who relished the opportunity to read something practical, pertinent, and martial grew impatient when various works proved short on belligerence and long on ambivalence. Others chafed at the subject matter: "Ma'am, English class is the only place where we don't have to read about war all the time. Can't we read something else?" This question brought home to me how difficult it is actually to avoid the theme of war in literature. You may not be interested in war, Trotsky warned, but war is certainly interested in you.

The entire second half of the course was devoted to the *Iliad*. I introduced Homer's poem to the plebes with the vignette that Alexander the Great kept Aristotle's annotated copy together with a dagger under his pillow while on campaign. After the defeat of the Persians, it was called the "casket copy" because Alexander put it, as his most valuable possession, in a jewel-encrusted casket taken from the vanquished Darius. According to Plutarch, Alexander regarded the poem as a "handbook of the art of war." "Now, ma'am," said one perplexed plebe—call him Paul—after we had read the first several books of the epic, "Alexander was a fool to carry this poem around with him." We had thus far been introduced to squabbling generals, sulking warriors, and prancing cowards, and Paul hadn't found one leader worthy of emulation in the bunch. What could Alexander possibly have drawn from that mess?

It wasn't until he reached the account of Agamemnon's *aristeia*, or day of glory, in book eleven that Paul changed his mind. At this point in the poem the Greek general finally gets his act together and transcends his habitual pettiness. The book opens with a marvelous description of him putting on his armor: greaves with silver clasps, a magnificent breastplate covered in gold and tin and adorned with twin serpents of blue enamel, a sword decorated with silver and gold, and a shield of blue steel crowned with a terrifying Gorgon's head—a warrior's haute-couture dream. Thus armed, Agamemnon rallies his badly demoralized army and leads the charge against the Trojans: spearing one in the chest, hacking another across the ear, dispatching twin brothers by spearing one and "slashing" the arms off the other before "lopping off his head" and sending his trunk "rolling through the carnage like a log." After reading this book, Paul declared: "Now I understand." There is a lot to sort out in this episode, for while it celebrates the embodiment of ancient battlefield prowess, it also exposes the extreme brutality that joining the army of our fathers might require. And I wasn't sure what, exactly, Paul understood.

As I read the *Iliad* with the plebes—this was about four months before September 11—the part I found most moving was Hector's departure from his wife and son at the end of book six. In the years since, its power has grown; I find myself returning often to the Trojan hero's valedictory to his family and his city. Hector is able to conjure with arresting clarity the vision of a postwar world in which he will have no part: he envisions with foreboding his fellow soldiers "tumble in the dust," his parents die, Troy itself "crushed by enemies." Heavier than all these griefs is the knowledge that his wife will become a Greek captive. To preserve her freedom in the face of all the prophecies that spell out Troy's doom, Hector leaves the city behind with the knowledge that he is behaving nobly, in the only way that "the one man strong enough / to fight off" his wife's "day of slavery" can. In saying goodbye to his son, Hector acknowledges simultaneously the full psychic cost of the warrior ethos and one of the driving forces behind it. Weary yet determined, he prays to Zeus that his son might one day carry home the bloody armor of a vanquished enemy—that he might, in other words, reprise, or even outdo, his father's battlefield heroics.

In Hector's wish for his son, I read the perdurability of war's romance, but I also like anachronistically to see a prototype of the citizen-soldier. Unlike Achilles, Hector isn't a killing machine, and his martial ambitions always seem to me bound up with the survival of the city and the culture he defends. The mythology of the citizen-soldier lies at the heart of the American military tradition. It was central to the political philosophy of West Point's civilian founders, John Adams and Thomas Jefferson, who were both deeply mistrustful of soldiers and standing armies, and it had its fullest flowering in the World War II G.I. At West Point, however, this archetype competes with a more old-world conception of the chivalric warrior (even if that figure goes by the modern name of *military professional*). It is this warrior who dominates the West Point romance.

Both Harvard and Yale are much older than the Military Academy, founded in 1802; both have robust institutional egos and strong traditions. Yet neither had seemed to me as preoccupied by its history or as insulated from the society of which it formed a part as West Point can sometimes feel. Or perhaps I was just too thoroughly acculturated to notice. West Point's mythology is nowhere more obvious than in the various monuments around post. A new one, Reconciliation Plaza, materialized several years ago, as the Academy prepared to celebrate its bicentennial by sprucing up the walkways between the barracks and the academic buildings. Given by the class of 1961 on the occasion of its fortieth reunion, the series of plaques commemorates one of the most important events in the nation's history, the Civil War, which divided the West Point class of 1861 just as it did the rest of the country.

West Point graduated two classes that year, one in May, whose motto was "Faithful to Death," the second in June: "Through Trials to Triumph." Both crops of new lieutenants diverged in their loyalties: some joined the Confederate States Army, while others remained loyal to the Union. The monument recasts the Civil War as a West Point story. It turns national history into an institutional narrative replete with aristocratic tableaux. Its panels rehearse the tales of various graduates who, finding themselves enemies on the field of battle, behave toward each other like knights of old despite the technical and ideological modernity of their war.

While most of the panels depict West Pointers, one recounts the story of a Harvard graduate, Oliver Wendell Holmes, at the battle of Antietam. Lying wounded in a farmhouse that temporarily falls into Confederate hands, Holmes is succored by a passing rebel who tosses him a canteen that is returned moments later when the Confederate soldier must himself retreat in the face of Yankee fire. A more typical tale involves George Custer, a member of the class of 1861, and a fellow Union officer, who watched through the night at the deathbed of a West Point friend mortally wounded while fighting for the South at Cedar Creek. Finally, Lee's surrender to Grant at Appomattox becomes a meeting between two great-souled West Pointers. Reconciliation Plaza's recasting of the Civil War as chivalric romance reveals a sympathy for aristocratic ideals—and for the Southern officers so preoccupied with them—that still attracts many who join today's democratic force.

The British military historian John Keegan once gave a lecture at West Point in which he noted that the gulf between officers and enlisted personnel has always been much wider in the American Army than in the British. American officers, lacking the inherited class authority of their British counterparts, he suggested, have had to manufacture their own. An identification with aristocratic ideals manifests itself among both officers and cadets in the veneration of figures such as Napoleon and Robert E. Lee. Growing up in Boston steeped in the lore of the Boston Massacre and Bunker Hill, I was largely ignorant of the rival mythography of the Lost Cause to which no few of my students and colleagues seem devoted. You can't escape the South at West Point; more specifically, you can't escape Lee, who graduated in 1829 and served as superintendent from 1852 to 1855. You jog or drive down his road, you live in or visit his housing area or his barracks, you see his portrait hanging opposite Grant's in the library's reference room, you read his quotations on various plaques and monuments, and you meet his adherents around every corner.

This is the fortress I proposed to invade back in November 1996, when I learned that I had been selected for an interview at West

Point. Most job searches in English involve a trip to the December MLA Convention, where interviews are usually held in hotel rooms. Sordid tales of candidates being forced to sit on beds in rooms that housekeeping has yet to visit are circulated in academic circles with the same zest with which cadets swap stories of the naked Poe or of the ghosts that haunt the barracks. While I was always given a chair at these interviews, I never got used to knocking on strange hotel room doors. The idea of interviewing by telephone created apprehension of a different kind. While setting up the interview, I was prepped by the very engaging and helpful department secretary: "The telephone interview is terrific," she insisted. "Get comfortable. You can wear pajamas and fuzzy slippers and drink hot chocolate, if you want. You'll be talking with four colonels. I'll be there, too, don't worry."

Preparing for such interviews, one anticipates all sorts of questions, ranging from the academic to the political (sometimes both at once): broad and seemingly innocuous questions full of traps; questions that are designed to be practical but which are necessarily hypothetical for a graduate student without extensive teaching experience; questions of fact that make you feel as if you are taking your Ph.D. qualifying exams all over again. On the phone with the colonels, there was at once less aggression and more mystery. Picture them naked, the old adage runs. I pictured them naked, all right, but with epaulets—outrageous, gaudy Napoleonic epaulets with looped gold braids and tassels. Such preparation turned out to be superfluous. The questions were eminently straightforward: What appeals to you about teaching in a military environment? How will you adjust to teaching in a curriculum that has less flexibility than you are used to? What are your long-term scholarly ambitions?

There was a slight pause after the technical questions were over, as if we had all crossed to safety and then, it happened: the question from left field. One of the colonels asked me what I did when I wasn't working. At first I didn't even know what he meant. Silence. He rephrased the question, slowly and deliberately for the obvious dolt on the other end of the line: "What do you do for fun? What do you like to do when you aren't working?" Fun? Had he actually asked me that? What could he possibly want with such information? Wasn't it illegal to ask such a question? I flashed to a recent conversation with a professor about which of two novels she preferred: "It is not," she had informed me, "a question of likes and dislikes." More silence before I ventured, "Um, well, I like to play squash." "Good," he replied, "you can come beat up on a bunch of old colonels on the squash court, and we'll even teach you how to play racquetball." Fair enough, I thought, but I also wondered, Who are these people?

The telephone interview had gone well, and a campus visit was scheduled for the week before the Army-Navy game. Never having made the trip and worried about the traffic I was likely to hit, I left New Haven in the early morning darkness. These were not people one kept waiting. I arrived ahead of schedule—way ahead of schedule. The itinerary, which I have saved all these years, said ARRIVAL: 1000. I arrived at 0730, and that only by driving well below the speed limit for the last several miles. The detailed instructions disseminated to all participants in a military operation indicate when various units should cross the Line of Departure (the LD). These times aren't approximate; if a unit arrives early or late, it can get other people killed. My gross miscalculation threw a wrench into the works: the major who was supposed to escort me was nowhere to be seen. But the secretary immediately (and characteristically) found a "work-around." One of the colonels stepped in to give me a tour of the post. I would later call him the "John Wayne Colonel" because of his imposing size and bearing (and to distinguish him in the stories I would later tell my friends from "Errol Flynn," the mustached colonel who joined us at lunch).

The atmosphere was full of spirit because of the upcoming football game. Some say that a coach at West Point can lose every game in a season as long as he beats Navy. As it happened, the 1996 season had been the most successful in years for the star quarterback Ron McAda and his team, and everyone was looking forward to Saturday's contest. It is traditional on Fridays and throughout the week before an important athletic event for cadets and officers alike to attest their support by wearing a field uniform—formerly the battle dress uniform (BDU) and now the ACU—in lieu of the more businesslike as-for-class and class B uniforms designated for cadets and officers respectively. The ACU is a practical uniform: digitized camouflage, cargo pockets, boots for rough terrain. Such sartorial expressions of military readiness are supposed to translate into victory on what Douglas MacArthur, a former superintendent who remains one of West Point's presiding geniuses, called "the fields of friendly strife."

The full dress uniform, with the "gilt bullet" buttons, worn with sash, saber, and shako for parades and ceremonies, is what most people think of when they imagine West Point, but it isn't what cadets wear every day to class. In fact the as-for-class uniform consists of a dark shirt and gray trousers. During Navy week, however, when everyone wears ACUs, West Point looks more like a regular Army post than it does at any other time of the year, and to a neophyte unfamiliar with military installations, this display of warrior spirit provided an especially dramatic introduction.

Camouflage is unambiguous: you know that you are dealing with a soldier. As a result, however, wearing it heightens the oddities of the cadet's quotidian experience. "Come on, ma'am," a cadet who knows me well will say on the term's first "casual Friday," as they call it, "tell everyone about your BDU theory." It would be more accurate to describe my theory as an opinion, but it is a mighty strong one. Dressed in their field uniforms, cadets are rowdier, louder, and less patient with the sedentary experience of the classroom than they otherwise are. The uniform seems to bring home to them the strangeness of their double lives. Sometimes I can channel the energy, but there are days when it is difficult to keep everyone focused. These are the days when, because they somehow feel most martial and because the activity of, say, reading sonnets seems most incongruous, we often end up talking about the larger issues of their existence at West Point and their future commitment. These are by no means wasted hours, and they are important conversations to have, but on Fridays I do think a lot about sumptuary laws.

The officer's green uniform was redesigned in the wake of Vietnam to look less martial and more corporate. A wool-polyester blend double-vent jacket is added to the class B to make what is called the class A, which is worn for ceremonies. It carries all of the awards, tabs, ribbons, and patches that reveal where an officer has been and what he or she has done. A few years ago, in a move that irked the beret-wearing Rangers, Airborne, and Special Forces, the beret became official headgear for all soldiers. My friend Al calls the beret a "hateful, two-handed hat" because of the maintenance it requires. There are occasional logjams at the mirrors mounted next to every outside door at West Point while officers adjust their berets. In one building the mirrors have the injunction "CHECK YOURSELF OUT. LOOK SHARP." taped below them.

The tour with John Wayne was my first exposure to an Army colonel and to West Point. Later I came to learn that he was a masculine icon for many junior officers: he could outrun and outdrink men twenty years his junior, and acolytes flocked to him. Not a West Point graduate, he had a warm affection for the institution. Some graduates, by contrast, seem simultaneously bewitched and repulsed by the place. "West Point," one of my colleagues proposed, "always looks better in the rearview mirror." In 1877, Grant told a correspondent that he liked visiting "the old academy now that the" authorities had "lost the power . . . of 'bulldozing'" him.

The Duke showed me the Cadet Library, which sits between the barracks and the academic buildings; it is in the process of being replaced by a new building across the street. The impressive collection of class rings encased in glass in the foyer becomes ghoulish once you realize that most of the jewelry has been donated by the families of graduates who have been killed. Our tour also included one of West Point's oldest buildings, Nininger Hall, which has a permanent exhibition of cadet rooms from different eras, such as Sheridan's and Pershing's. My guide showed me his favorite view of the Hudson River from the balcony of Cullum Hall. Gazing up at the names on the ballroom walls, I recognized a few of Grant's battles. When I mentioned my newfound interest, my guide talked about what the Mexican War had taught Grant and how it had shaped him as an officer. "The key to Grant's whole career," he insisted, "is Mexico."

It was on this visit that I first saw the Pershing portrait and another painting that would become important to me later on, that of Colonel Lucius H. Holt, Professor of English and History (1910–1920), and Professor of Economics, Government, and History (1920–1930). Holt came to West Point from Yale when MacArthur was superintendent and great curricular revisions were afoot. Receiving a direct commission as a lieutenant colonel, Holt devoted two decades to the evolving humanities and social sciences programs. In the portrait, he wears the World War I–era tunic with its Sam Browne belt. That was a fine uniform—damned decent and military—but he looks like a bespectacled English professor all dressed up (and rather pleased with himself) for a scene in *The Big Parade*. During his tenure, Holt introduced the study of poetry and literary prose into the curriculum. In 1908 *Palgrave's Golden Treasury of English Verse* was added, and the years that followed also saw Joseph Addison; Thomas Carlyle; Alfred, Lord Tennyson; Shakespeare; Richard Brinsley Sheridan; and Robert Louis Stevenson. Colonel Holt doesn't loom large in official histories of West Point, but I like to imagine him as the department's resident spirit.

There were other memorable encounters on that first day. I was introduced to one officer (who later became a good friend), as a man who had "ruined his life in the Gulf War." He had been in a Gulf War syndrome screening program because he suffered for a time from a cluster of symptoms. When he learned that, as part of my visit, I would be teaching a group of students who were preparing to retake a writing examination they had failed a few weeks before, he exclaimed: "Those sorry-ass bastards! Good luck with them." It was a strange way to talk about students, I thought, but I have since learned how typically military is that toughness that conceals a genuine devotion to soldiers' well-being. This was an officer who in fact spent inordinate amounts of time and energy on his students: years after taking his class, they lined up outside his office door to ask for help.

Most of the people I met were officers, but I do recall one encounter with a civilian faculty member in the library. John Wayne introduced us. Giving me a tentative handshake, he asked: "Are you terrified? I was terrified." I looked at him and at the colonel, who was really a most affable escort, and said, "No, I'm not terrified at all. Should I be?" In fact, it is almost impossible to feel truly afraid at West Point. I'm not talking about a sense of physical security, although, compared with New Haven, West Point feels safe in that way as well. Unless you are a plebe, hounded from reveille to retreat by all manner of villains, you feel a certain sense of belonging. People care what happens to you. And even a plebe knows that his classmates have got his back.

Before I left West Point that day, I had a long interview with the head of the department, a man who looked like an emissary from the nineteenth-century British Army, an impression that only grew over the years. It was easy to picture him with Wellington at Waterloo, or with Gordon at Khartoum. A swagger stick and khakis would have suited him far better than green poly-blend. With wit like a stiletto but a countenance of stone, he would signal emotion only by the widening of his eyes. One of the things that set him apart was his refusal to wear any medals or ribbons except for his parachutist badge, referred to as "jump wings," and the Combat Infantryman Badge (CIB), a rifle overlaying a wreath.

The CIB is a coveted mark of distinction: created during World War II, it is awarded for participation in ground infantry combat. Evidence of the impact of Iraq and Afghanistan on the Corps is the presence today of not a few cadets who earned CIBs as enlisted soldiers before enrolling at West Point. Evidence of the absence of a front line in these conflicts is the new Combat Action Badge (CAB), awarded to soldiers from branches other than Infantry or Special Forces "who personally engage the enemy." People had invented all sorts of stories to account for the Colonel's refusal to wear any ribbons. One apochryphal story had it that he had been a sniper in Vietnam. "Is it true," an eager cadet whispered to me one day, "that Colonel ———— has the highest number of kills of any sniper in the history of the U.S. Army?" I suspect this rumor secretly delighted the Colonel even if his impassive face would never betray it. As I have suggested, this officer and his wife were vestiges of another army—an army of the imagination that perhaps never existed at all. Their peculiarities and priorities were only partially understood. As one of their fiercest admirers put it, "We are well yet oddly led."

One summer I traveled with them in Italy. When I got off the plane in Rome, they were waiting for me in a red Alfa, in which we climbed to what must have been every hill town in Umbria and Tuscany. Sitting in the "death seat" next to the Colonel, who drives at suicidal speeds with an eerie calm, huge hands draped over the steering wheel, I read the map and listened to tales about the Pentagon and Vietnam. In Washington, the Colonel and his wife had met many of the people who later populated what amounted to a kind of salon in their lovely quarters at West Point. They had stables of exotic guests: photographers, journalists, poets, members of the Foreign Service. In fact, they knew so many interesting people that they were relieved of the obligation to be interesting themselves, but they delivered nonetheless, exerting a relentless fascination on those who knew them.

One night at dinner I found myself at the right hand of the late Smith Hempstone, the journalist and former ambassador to Kenya. He had a voice like a newspaper's nestle and snap. He began the conversation by telling me he had recently lost a tooth and so could no longer be an Aztec sacrifice, one of the sleek boys sent to glut a feeding sun. I learned that he had first found his way to Africa, where he eventually made his career, because Hemingway had told him the hunting was good in between drinks in a Venice hotel. But my favorite memory of time spent at their quarters was a commissioning ceremony the Colonel and his wife hosted for John, a diminutive, brilliant, mercurial young man in our program who wrote his thesis on *Hamlet's* skepticism. We were all wearing leis— John is from Hawaii—and with his new lieutenant's bars pinned to his shoulders, he sat down at the piano to accompany his father, who sang arias for us in a room filled with dark oil paintings and antique furniture, while the afternoon sun shimmered on the Hudson below.

By the time the Colonel retired, my enthusiasm for Lucius Holt was well known. At special departmental occasions I had taken to delivering verses I claimed had been dictated by the old man's ghost. Holt was a Macaulay specialist, and his edition, *Selections from the Prose of Macaulay*, was added to the cadets' reading list in 1916, the year of its publication. Before he left, the Colonel entrusted to me a copy of the first edition, originally the property of a former department head and inscribed on its flyleaf with the double-underlined words DO NOT REMOVE FROM MY DESK. Now it sits on my desk, not to be removed.

Back in 1996, as the Colonel and I talked in his office, which had a view of the Hudson, we could see a snowstorm moving in. The room's navy blue walls were decorated with African masks, a large screen depicting an elephant, and several pen-and-ink drawings.

On the floor was the foot of an elephant that had been turned into a planter. Perhaps it suggests something about the Colonel that he could delight in having the severed foot of his favorite animal close by. Years later I learned from a friend that no one could figure out why the interview took so long: What could we possibly have been talking about for hours? There was a different quality to this conversation than there had been to those earlier in the day. It had greater depth and broader range. The Colonel told me something of what it might be like to teach cadets. He also shared several hypotheses about how an institution might most effectively go about accomplishing the goal of preparing military officers: he presented arguments for an all-military faculty; more unexpectedly, for an all-civilian one; and, finally, for a postgraduate experience along the lines of the British Sandhurst. He asked about my work in a way that revealed wide reading and a fine ear. Finally, recalled by the darkening clouds sweeping over the river, he suggested that I should start my trip back. We would talk again, he said, and soon.

It certainly wasn't the kind of conversation I had expected. There was something unusual about his soft-spoken, looming presence. In a profession in which loud enthusiasm is common, he was remarkable for ironic understatement. As I drove home, I began to think about the week that lay ahead. I was preparing to teach *The Prince*, and as I thought about Machiavelli's book, it occurred to me that its scheme gave me a way to account for the Colonel. Finding himself among a pride of boisterous lions, he had chosen to play the fox. When I got back to New Haven, I opened Grant's *Memoirs* again and tried to learn more about the four ambivalent years he spent at West Point. In a letter to his cousin he wrote with the indifferent spelling and punctuation that charms when offered up by the famous:

> I have put asaid my Algebra and French and am going to tell you a long story about this prettiest of places West Point . . . From my window near I can see the Hudson; that far famed,

that beautiful river with its bosom studded with hundreds of snow sails. Again if I look another way I can see Fort Putnan [sic] frowning far above; a stern monument of a sterner age which seems placed there on purpose to tell us of the glorious deeds of our fathers and to bid us remember *their* sufferings—to follow their examples. In short this is the best of all places—the *place* of all places for an institution like this . . . Now all this sounds nice, very nice, "what a happy fellow you are" you will say, but I am not one to show fals colers the brightest side of the picture. So I will tell you about a few of the *drawbacks* . . .

Some of the drawbacks of military life were immediately apparent: severe discipline, restriction to post, taxing classes. Others would be revealed to Grant only in time—at Palo Alto, Shiloh, and Petersburg. But the fundamental "sternness" of both the place and the profession were clear to him from the start.

That Saturday I sat down to watch the Army-Navy game. I had seen it before without caring who won, but now I found myself cheering for Army, feeling some sort of allegiance, as if I already belonged. This is silly, I thought, they haven't even offered you the job. Army won. Then, early the following week, the Colonel called. Take a week, he said. I did, and then I accepted the position. When I told my friends and acquaintances at Yale that I was going to West Point, I got a range of responses. "You'll humanize them," said one well-meaning professor, leaving me puzzled. They had seemed pretty human to me. In fact, they may even have done a little in the years since to humanize me.

One of the oddest things about an army is that when it isn't getting you killed it works with enormous zeal to take care of you. At West Point, a tendency to cosset cadets coexists with the imperative to toughen them up. The cynical observer is likely to perceive hypocrisy in such contradictory impulses, but I am no cynic—well, at least not anymore. For if my undergraduate years launched me into skepticism and graduate school took me deeper still into waters of doubt and disenchantment, West Point won me back to a kind of idealism. Having been coached by professionals to cultivate ironic detachment, I allowed myself to be seduced by esprit de corps—by the worth of community and commitment, and by the prospect of surrendering myself to a shared mission. Yet, in the way of such stories, mine is punctuated by those moments of shuddering recognition and reversal that confront the objects of seduction as surely as novelty and shining armor captivate. The allure of military life and its heroic promise seem indestructible, but nothing threatens the romance of *war* more effectively than war itself. This is the treacherous terrain I have been learning how to navigate along with the cadets as we contemplate the various romances that have brought us together.

Grant the Musketeer is right, of course. The utopian lure of West Point makes any betrayal a cadet might suffer there potentially devastating. But despite the disillusionment that attends experience, a soldier must retain a small quotient of idealism in order to be willing to die for someone or something. That's why in Tolstoy's *War and Peace*, Prince Andrey, who comes back from the dead at Austerlitz with as clear a picture of glory's emptiness and war's futility as could be had, returns to fight at Borodino, not as a staff officer but at the head of a regiment for which he can feel responsible, leading men in whom he can believe. Hold both truths inside one's head at once, that's what officers like Grant, Renée, and Kevin try to do. In the words of the Academy's strategic vision, they "must be prepared for the uncertainty and ambiguity of military service." The cadet experience is divided into three programs: physical, military, and academic. There is a reassuring clarity and transparent relevance to the first two realms, but in the last, especially those disciplines in which results cannot be quantified, ambiguity holds dominion. In the classroom, cadets have their best chance to prepare themselves for uncertainty—to the extent that anyone can prepare for that.

When he returned to West Point as a lieutenant colonel after obtaining his Ph.D. at the University of Pennsylvania, my friend Scott took over direction of the plebe literature course. Like Prince Andrey, Scott has a stereoscopic vision of war. He had it when he wrote to me of his guilt and frustration at finding himself in graduate school on September 11, and he probably acquired it in the First Gulf War. Scott made it a priority to impart a complex understanding of the profession to cadets in English 102 and in the seminar he conducted as part of West Point's summer program for promising high school students. Among the poems he included in the latter was Wilfred Owen's "Dulce et Decorum Est." Its title alludes to an ode by the ancient Roman poet Horace, who wrote, *"Dulce et decorum est pro patria mori"* [it is sweet and fitting to die for one's country]. Owen, whose poem details the particular horrors of a poison gas attack, repudiates this sentiment as "the old Lie" in his condemnation of civilians who exhort "children ardent for some desperate glory" to go to war.

One of the students in the program wrote to Scott several months later to report that he had again read Owen's poem in his high school class. By that time the young man had decided to come to West Point, and his classmates took the opportunity presented by "Dulce et Decorum Est" to tell him that he had been duped. They assumed that West Point recruited candidates by perpetuating an unalloyed, uncomplicated romantic vision, which Owen attempts to debunk in his antiwar lyric. The young man knew better because of his experience in the summer seminar. Scott's response to his message reveals a serious officer at work as a teacher. Regarding the prospect of selling the old lie, he wrote:

Such an impression betrays common misperceptions about all the military academies and about military service in general. For soldiers and for the officers who lead them, the thought of sacrifice, of potentially losing what we hold most dear, is a constant fact of life . . . Officers in particular must be keenly aware of the sacrifices they might someday ask their soldiers to make—the price that might have to be paid. It is therefore vitally important that a cadet's education make him or her fully aware of all perspectives. To do otherwise would be to act dishonorably.

What Scott at once embodies and describes is a particular kind of sensibility that Aristotle associated with the virtuous man. Such self-awareness has a price; not all virtues, Aristotle suggests, are "pleasant" to exercise. The more a man "is possessed of virtue in its entirety and the happier he is," Aristotle insists, "the more he will be pained at the thought of death; for life is best worth living for such a man, and he is knowingly losing the greatest goods, and this is painful. But he is none the less brave, and perhaps all the more so, because he chooses noble deeds of war at that cost." To ask eighteen-year-old plebes to identify such distinctions and such costs is no small task; however, as Scott insists, it is the debt that anyone who teaches them owes.

2

"Books Are Weapons"

———◆———

In my first semester at West Point, I taught four sections of freshman composition. My only teaching experience thus far had been in graduate school at Yale, where students were never shy about telling me what they thought. One expectation I brought to West Point was that when I asked for a cadet's opinion, she would leap at the chance to provide it. With all the naïve earnestness of a new teacher, I sent carefully crafted questions out into the void and waited . . . and waited . . . and waited. "Silence is okay," a graduate school mentor used to reassure me. "Sometimes you need to wait them out." I have no problem waiting them out, and even in 1997, I had already learned to distinguish the I'm-thinking silence from the I-have-no-idea-what-she's-talking-about variety. But the plebes' silence was different again. Only later did I learn to think of it as the There's-no-way-in-hell-I'm-going-to-answer-that-question-because-we-all-know-it-isn't-really-a-question-at-all-but-a-trap-a-haze-a-claymore-mine-set-to-explode-if-I-can't-read-her-mind silence.

Plebes are people, too—at least nominally—but unlike their ancient Roman counterparts who gathered together to air their grievances in the Forum, they have no tribunes charged with their advocacy. Existing at the bottom of a chain of command that extends up through third-, second-, and first-class cadets to the officers who run the institution, they are unaccustomed to being asked for their opinions. While the administration endorses, indeed celebrates, intellectual inquiry and academic freedom, education necessarily coexists at West Point with the realms of training and indoctrination, and no one is more aware of this balancing act, or more baffled by it, than a plebe.

They may not have Michel Foucault's sophisticated theoretical vocabulary, but plebes understand more thoroughly than I ever did the dynamics of Jeremy Bentham's Panopticon, the 1787 prison blueprint—with its central observation tower designed to create the effect of constant surveillance even when there was no one in it—on which Foucault modeled his theory of social discipline. Bentham described his plan, which could serve the needs of various institutions from hospitals to schools, as "a new mode of obtaining power of mind over mind." "It is obvious," he wrote,

> the more constantly the persons to be inspected are under the eyes of the persons who should inspect them, the more perfectly will the purpose X of the establishment have been attained. Ideal perfection, if that were the object, would require that each person should actually be in that predicament, during every instant of time. This being impossible, the next thing to be wished for is, that, at every instant, seeing reason to believe as much, and not being able to satisfy himself to the contrary, he should *conceive* himself to be so.

Plebes "conceive" themselves to be under such scrutiny all the time. When I once showed a class of plebes the scene from the beginning of Fritz Lang's *Metropolis* in which files of robotic, shuffling, uniformed factory workers change shifts, they shouted out, "Look, ma'am, plebes!" Upperclassmen tend to lose the shock of recognition that the plebes manifest when confronted with *Metropolis* or another similarly dramatic model of disciplined lives.

Most of the time, no one gives a damn what a plebe thinks, only what she knows. Every year in late August, the plebes suddenly find themselves in the classroom after an entire summer of field training, during which they have operated almost exclusively in "receive mode." New cadets spend much of that first summer memorizing something called "knowledge." This process is designed to familiarize novices with military culture and custom. It is an exercise in habituation, and some of what they learn by rote has less immediate practical than ritual value. Gradually, some of the more esoteric facts—the number of gallons in the reservoir, the number of lights in Cullum Hall, the number of names on a particular monument—are being replaced by the names of weapons systems and other military terminology. But in those early years, the plebes and upperclassmen participated in mystifying catechisms. If asked, "How's the cow?" a plebe would reply, "She walks, she talks, she's full of chalk, the lacteal fluid extracted from the female of the bovine species is highly prolific to the nth degree." When asked for "the definition of leather," any plebe (and several forty-year-olds of my acquaintance) could automatically reply: "If the fresh skin of an animal, cleaned and divested of all hair, fat and other extraneous matter, be immersed in a dilute solution of tannic acid, a chemical combination ensues; the gelatinous tissue of the skin is converted into a nonputresible substance, impervious to and insoluble in water; this is leather."

Plebes are still frequently called upon by upperclassmen to recite such pieces of knowledge in addition to current events, the Mess Hall meals for the week, and the number of days left until important events such as the Army-Navy game or graduation. Physical hazing has been prohibited, but even in its absence, this is still a lot to process; indeed, another motive for this routine is to accustom cadets to being bombarded by more tasks than they think they can handle. To survive, they consult a publication called *Bugle Notes*, known informally as "The Plebe Bible," which contains all of the items for which they are responsible.

It is no surprise that the mind-set of summer bleeds into the academic semester. Plebes want to please and tend to parrot. They derive great comfort from right answers. The hierarchical structure of West Point, moreover, abets a teacher's desire to be validated and vindicated, and an officer's to be obeyed. Military faculty face a special challenge, as a colonel once elucidated for me: "When most officers look at that classroom of cadets, they can't help but see future lieutenants rather than students, and no one really wants to know what a lieutenant thinks about anything." My military colleagues must juggle two identities, officer and teacher, while I have the luxury of working on just one.

During that first summer, cadets are authorized only four responses to most of the interrogators they encounter over the course of the day: "Yes, sir/ma'am," "No, sir/ma'am," "No excuse, sir/ma'am," and "Sir/Ma'am, I do not understand." The questions I was asking the plebes were of an altogether different kind. The answers couldn't be found through the process of memorization. The colonel who directed freshman composition that year had chosen a reader that provided ample fodder for discussion: everything from the feminist writings of Gloria Anzaldúa to the radical history of Howard Zinn. But it felt to me that the plebes and I spent a lot of time in a staring match, trying to figure one another out. It was a long first few months that revealed West Point at its most Dickensian. That classroom seemed like something straight out of *Hard Times*, only with the roles reversed. I was poor Sissy Jupe, Girl Number 20, a circus refugee who liked horses, wanted to learn more about them, and thought it was all right to paper the walls with their pictures. And there sat my students, as inflexible as Mr. Gradgrind, the patron of Dickens's school. They were all cannons loaded "to the muzzle with facts," shouting with Sissy's obedient classmate, the pale, almost translucent, boy Bitzer: "Quadruped. Graminivorous. Forty teeth, namely twenty-four grinders, four eye-teeth, and twelve incisive. Sheds coat in the spring; in marshy countries, sheds hoofs, too. Hoofs hard, but requiring to be shod with iron. Age known by marks in mouth," and wondering what more there was to say about the matter. I wanted them to indulge their "fancy," while they craved nothing more than to be "regulated and governed" like the pupils in *Hard Times*.

Eventually, I discovered that being more explicit about my expectations helped: I explained, for example, that I wasn't looking for the definition of leather. Now I know to make this clear at a first meeting with plebes. But it took me a semester—no, I'm revising history, much longer than a semester—to grasp the full extent of what I was asking them to do and the complexity of the adjustments they had to make in order to prepare for an hour of critical thought and reflection sandwiched between a session on tactics and another of parade-field drill. Cadets are tough, but they need a different kind of strength to figure things out for themselves.

Often in those early days I felt more than a little like a plebe myself. New faculty orientation was conducted in a patois in which even familiar words acquired strange meanings or appeared in new combinations: *Beast, Dirt, Juice, quills, squid, cow, gray hog, green girl*. Terms unintelligible even when spelled out had already been abbreviated or turned into acronyms before they made their way to me on PowerPoint slides. I was expected to know what it meant to finish CAS3 (Combined Arms and Services Staff School) and start CGSC (Command and General Staff College); to give AI (additional instruction) and to get an MOI (memorandum of instruction); to look for someone at his TOC (tactical operations center); to be listed on someone's TDA (Table of Distribution and Allowances) and to know that a TDA was different from a TOE (Table of Organization and Equipment); and—this one I learned quickly—to be OBE (overcome by events).

The Army is a giant found poem, its newness intriguing and exciting, but it also seemed immune to my interpretative powers. I couldn't even read the ranks on people's uniforms, especially field uniforms, on which subdued insignia blend in with the camouflage pattern. A general can sneak up on you before you know it. Cadet rank proved even more confusing: members of each class sport a shield of a particular color on their collars, but they wear other badges of achievement and indications of status that take more time to decipher. The only saving grace for the newcomer is that plebes wear no insignia at all.

During those first few weeks, messages filled with hieroglyphs instructed me to be somewhere at a particular time, dressed a certain way. My faculty sponsor took pity on me, and in the years since, he has continued patiently to answer questions asked initially out of an instinct for self-preservation but, as day-to-day operations gradually became more transparent, out of a desire to satisfy a growing preoccupation with military culture and traditions. Over the years he has presented me copies of not only *Bugle Notes* but also the invaluable *Army Officer's Guide* and, for historical comparison, *The 1865 Customs of Service for Officers of the Army*. Armed with these tomes, I could at least begin to penetrate military mysteries.

One of the mysteries to which I was introduced is something called the Thayer Method. Sylvanus Thayer, often called the Father of the Military Academy, served as superintendent from 1817 to 1833. He made many changes to both the military and academic programs, and it is in the latter context that the term *Thayer Method* is invoked. Thayer's innovations included aspects of what educators today call *active learning*: small classes in which the professors did no lecturing; daily cadet participation in activities such as solving problems, answering questions, or reciting material they had prepared beforehand. Integral to the method was something referred to as taking boards, or writing solutions on the chalkboard. If an instructor gives the command "Take boards!" today, cadets will still leap from their seats, grab a piece of chalk, and start writing.

Classes at West Point remain small, officially capped at eighteen, and they are conducted as seminars for which cadets are expected to be prepared every day. This does indeed encourage active learning. However, the Thayer Method has been variously interpreted by instructors since the early nineteenth century, and it has always been better suited to some disciplines than others: taking boards isn't always the best way to analyze a sestina or a tragedy. As my former colleague Robert Gibson has written, however, "the term 'Thayer Method'" has become "entrenched in Academy lore." For cadets in particular, Thayer himself has become a byword for education by sinking or swimming. Some have described the process as being thrown into the deep end on the first day: a cadet struggles to understand new concepts before coming to class for the express purpose of having all of his muddled notions corrected in front of his peers. A misunderstanding of the legacy and the passage of time itself has had the unfortunate effect of permanently linking poor Sylvanus to the worst of times. When a cadet first announced to me that she was having "a Thayer week" I had no idea that she had to complete an English paper, a history paper, a math project, and a psychology test. By now, however, I have grown accustomed to hearing about the miseries of Thayer days, Thayer weeks, and, from one especially oppressed cadet, a Thayer year.

Another of the initially confusing things I encountered in those early years was the intensity with which plebes attempt to compensate for their relative powerlessness by insisting that they have access to knowledge their civilian counterparts do not. I started to teach Jarrell's "Death of the Ball Turret Gunner" long before our current engagements in Afghanistan and Iraq had made us too familiar with the phenomenon of death by IED. I learned from experience to withhold until the end of our discussion the information that Jarrell served as a celestial navigation instructor rather than on the crew of a bomber. The cadets seemed manifestly untroubled by some of the poem's more vexing elements: by the fact, for example, that the speaker is describing his own death apparently from beyond the grave, or even by the brutality of his end, washed out of the turret with a hose. Whenever I asked them if it mattered whether the poet had actually served as a ball turret gunner, however, they would become passionately insistent: "Yes, ma'am, of course it matters. If he didn't, it ruins the poem." "But he couldn't

experience his own death and then write about it, could he?" I
would venture. "No," came the reluctant response, "but it still matters. Somehow, it still matters." Because it matters so very much,
many of the plebes did not at first see the incongruity of demanding
more of Randall Jarrell than they did of themselves.

Cadets tend jealously to guard territory about which they do
not, at least in a majority of cases, have any actual knowledge. When
they get to know you a bit better, they will admit that they wonder
sometimes if they have what it takes, but they are trained to be sure,
to bluff it out—impulses inimical to the intellectual inquiry that
erodes certainty—and owning war is one of the things for which
they will fight hardest. How much their solidarity with soldier-poets
in particular can mean was revealed to me through long conversations with Adam, a 2005 graduate who addressed the poetry of war
from the twinned perspective of soldier and critic in a senior thesis
on Wilfred Owen. Adam felt very much the way Owen did: all that
mattered was the knowledge born of experience. Think of George
Orwell reminding literary adversaries such as W. H. Auden and
Stephen Spender about his "bullet hole" in an argument over the
Spanish Civil War. Adam has a wonderfully supple mind, but he was
inflexible when it came to the issue of who had the authority to
write about war. After graduation, he e-mailed me from flight
school, where he was learning how to fly Kiowa helicopters, with a
change of heart about the exclusivity of military experience: "You'll
be happy to know that my views on the . . . debate have softened
dramatically. I think that, like many cadets, I held idealistic and ro-
manticized notions about war. My training thus far has certainly
driven home some realities that seemed very far away when I was a
cadet."

I *am* happy, not merely because I seem to have won the battle
but because denying this one crucial arena of human experience to
the poetic imagination doesn't help us better to understand war and
the people who fight it. As Adam's own example reveals, the warn-

ings of Wilfred Owen—that the real poetry of war can be found only in the "pity" and not in the "heroes . . . deeds . . . honour . . . or power"—have not dissuaded thoughtful young men and women from joining armies or convinced them that there is no poetry in patriotism and valor. Owen's monitory poetry may have complicated heroic mythologies and helped to revolutionize writing about war, but the battlefield remains as seductive as ever.

Plebes confront Owen's challenge, as well as those of Homer, Virgil, and Hemingway, early in their cadet careers in English 102. The course was instituted in the 1980s, and the focus on contemporary poets came about a few years later. The then course director Colonel (Retired) Terry Freeman suggests that the attention to poetry afforded the necessary time and space "in a crowded core as heavy in mathematics and sciences as it is in the humanities" for cadets "to experience the mysteries available within the sanctum of language." By concentrating on poetry, with its economy and immediacy, cadets were able to confront language working at its hardest. When I arrived, we were studying four contemporary poets a year in addition to reading a Shakespeare play and a sampling of older poetry.

Imaginative literature also helps cadets to anticipate various eventualities. Aristotle suggests that "the poet's function is to describe, not the thing that has happened, but a kind of thing that might happen, i.e., what is possible as being probable or necessary . . . Hence poetry is something more philosophic and of graver import than history, since its statements are of the nature rather of universals, whereas those of history are singulars." Poetry offers a range of possibilities and probabilities, worlds full of contradictions. Some poems offer them in distinctly military terms. The speaker of Thomas Hardy's "The Man He Killed" muses that under different circumstances he might have treated the same "fellow" he has just shot to a drink at a bar. Isaac Rosenberg's "Returning, We Hear the Larks" proposes that death and birdsong "drop from the dark" with equal probability. Richard Wilbur's "First Snow in Alsace," offering a picture of nature momentarily blanketing the ugliness of war, closes with a soldier's "boyish boast" that "he was the first to see the snow."

The force of such poems strikes home for the cadets because it intimates something of the complexity of the profession to which they have dedicated themselves. It enables them to recognize in it a weld of prose and poetry. At a time when cadets are being required to imagine roles and missions for which history offers insufficient plots, the space between the fictive and the real often becomes a passage of illumination. Even, perhaps especially, those plebes who begin English 102 with a conviction that poetry can have nothing whatever to do with soldiering come away with a recognition of the long-standing connections between literature and war and of the role of poetry in shaping culture, attitudes, and values.

One of the hours in which English 102 is commonly taught immediately follows the period designated for military instruction, in which plebes learn, among other things, how to write operations orders. It was the facility for issuing transparent orders for which Ulysses S. Grant so admired his hero, Zachary Taylor: "Taylor was not a conversationalist," Grant wrote after having worked for him in the Mexican War. "But on paper he could put his meaning so plainly that there could be no mistaking it. He knew how to express what he wanted to say in the fewest well-chosen words, but would not sacrifice meaning to the construction of high-sounding sentences." The critical reading and writing that take place in English class reinforce the imperative for military officers to be able to use language with precision, but in literature, especially poetry, cadets encounter language that is far from transparent.

Poetry and military language share an impulse toward concision, but the brutal economy of military writing is a world away from the playful ellipses of poetry. In sharp contrast to the "bottom line upfront" (BLUF) mandate of operations orders, poetry is downright cryptic. From an hour of map reading or terrain analysis, plebes may be plunged into the chilling landscape of Wallace Stevens's "The Snow Man," a poem that opens with the proposition

"One must have a mind of winter / To regard the frost" and closes by asking us to behold the "Nothing that is not there and the nothing that is." By January the plebes have lost something of their initial numbness. They come back from holiday leave having been doted on by their parents and in some cases feted by their hometowns. They are refreshed, their confidence renewed, but "The Snow Man" seems initially beyond the pale.

The wonder of it is that plebes haven't forgotten how to play, and once they realize that language is one of the things over which they still retain command, they begin to want to exercise their power. They are game for anything, even if they think it's completely nutty: writing fables about Beast Barracks, engaging in collaborative poetry exercises such as a game of bout-rimes or a Japanese tanka-writing party, updating an Ovidian myth for the twenty-first century, racing across post in the rain to be the first to identify a literary allusion on a plaque or monument. To the victorious warriors of contests such as these I sometimes present a book or, with appropriate ceremony and gravity, a tin toy samurai or another similarly martial token. Just before he graduated in the spring of 2005, a firstie—a former Golden Gloves boxer who grew up over a gym in Pittsburgh—returned to me the samurai he had won as a plebe: "It served me well over the last four years," he said. "Now I hope you'll pass it along to another deserving plebe who might find himself in need of a talisman."

Some cadets doggedly but futilely search for the military lesson to be extracted from every piece of literature, no matter its ostensible subject, while others become passionately invested in separating the activities of the classroom from the business of soldiering. They take a more expansive view. When one plebe discovered that the statement "Hope springs eternal" comes from Pope's *Essay on Man*, he reported that he had initially looked it up only for the prize I had offered, "but after reading it," he continued, "I find it is actually very interesting. Perhaps hoping for the best even in the face of eternity is what sets humanity apart." Cadets sometimes resent it when I remind them of our immediate military context. One day I suggested to a class of plebes that the shape of a particular poem reminded me of the formations and cadences of military life: of marching and drilling on the parade field, for example. When I drew them out of the world of the poem and back into the martial rhythms of their own lives, the class decided that I had been rather too thoroughly acculturated, or "ruined," as they put it. "They've got you, ma'am," said one in mock horror.

In the literature they encounter, whether or not its subject is war, plebes must entertain what the poet Jane Hirshfield, who read her work to them in the 1990s, has called poetry's "non-dogmatic morality." In an environment in which the scope of physical movement and general conduct is so often delimited, cadets can find this indeterminate, open-ended mode of communication potentially unsettling. Jorie Graham, who gave a reading at West Point in 1996, was deeply moved by "the way [cadets] searched through the literature, from Shakespeare to contemporary poetry, in order to determine a right moral choice in a situation where, increasingly, that is impossible." Teaching in such a climate also sometimes entails explaining to cadets when you are asking them to understand rather than to endorse a particular attitude or point of view. When Hirshfield visited during the First Gulf War, in 1991, she understood her task as being to offer what she regards as poetry's "values": "a recognition of the interconnection and interdependence that exist between oneself and everything else; the openness to the unknown that is at the root of all imaginative thinking; a deep fidelity to individual perceptions, 'right speech,' in the Buddhist sense, and 'honest speech,' in the sense of being true to the wide view of things."

The charm of plebes owes largely to their frankness, to the ease with which they are disarmed, and to their wonderful willingness to encounter new ideas and new truths. For all of these reasons, English 102 has become one of the courses I most look forward to teaching. Even though the exclusive focus on poetry has been replaced by an examination of a wider variety of genres—short stories, novels, prose narratives, drama—in my own sections, lyric poetry, a genre of intimacy and introspection, still holds pride of place. I like to start plebes off with sonnets, each intricately arranged stanza a little space in which so much activity is compressed. The complexity of the form satisfies cadets' institutionally cultivated love of what's difficult even as it frustrates those who attempt to figure it out with the same tools they would apply to a problem of engineering. Poetry seems easy and arbitrary until a reader can discern its involuted structure, and perhaps no form shows its architecture off to better advantage than the sonnet. When the plebes write their own sonnets, poetry's rigors become even clearer: "That was hard, ma'am. I thought poets just sort of threw those things together."

Sonnets also help cadets accustomed to racing from one activity to another at warp speed to slow down and move, to borrow Napoleon's phrase, *avec ordre et méthode.* "Optempo," as the pace of military life is referred to, is high; in class they can afford to move slowly. At the end of one lesson in which we spent the entire hour on the first quatrain of an Elizabethan sonnet, one plebe, looking up in amazement at the clock, said with chagrin, "Ma'am, we must be really stupid. We just spent an hour on one sentence." It hadn't occurred to him that finding an hour's worth of things to say about four lines was in fact pretty smart. And once, when we finished Shakespeare's Sonnet 73, which discloses an accelerating series of metaphors like nested matryoshka dolls—the speaker compares his stage of life to autumn, twilight, and dying embers—one plebe blurted out, "That cat's a genius, ma'am."

A long-standing custom of memorizing and reciting poetry has survived the course's numerous transformations. Having grown so adept at memorizing "knowledge," plebes think that reciting a fourteen-line poem will be a cinch. Some go for the land speed record, while others take an agonizingly long time to negotiate a poem's tricky syntax. Recitations—sometimes referred to as "resuscitations" by a befuddled plebe—are a rite of passage, and for most, the shared challenge of performing in front of their peers proves a

sufficiently bonding experience. Furthermore, by the end of the semester, some are taking great delight in the sounds of poetry: in the
"luscious clusters" of Andrew Marvell's "The Garden"; in the "savage
servility" of Robert Lowell's "For the Union Dead"; in the "concupis-
cent curds" of Stevens's "The Emperor of Ice-Cream"—the more outrageous the better. Several have reported that particular poems stick,
reoccurring to them at opportune moments. Andy carried Stevens
with him in Iraq, while Joey had Marvell stuck in his head. David, a
captain who majored in engineering as a cadet but will return to
West Point to teach English, still signs off his e-mails with a line
from *Henry V*, long passages of which he memorized while a plebe.

Some plebes never get over their discomfort with recitations,
while others mask it by turning into outrageous hams. One plebe set
his selections to music and accompanied himself on the guitar like a
medieval minstrel; another insisted on declaiming all of Tennyson's
"Ulysses" from the top of my desk. A few reveal a marvelous affinity
for poetic language. Their readings make you hear something in a
poem that you had forgotten or didn't even know was there. A cadet
from South America—West Point has exchange programs with a
number of foreign countries—whose self-consciousness about his
accent initially made recitations painful events that I didn't intend
them to be, asked one day if he could choose a poet not in our anthology. He selected Pablo Neruda, who had particular significance
for him, and delivered a series of brilliant recitations. His rendering
of Love Sonnet 11 was so gorgeous it left the rest of us speechless.

Neruda was an unexpected choice; Robert Frost's "The Road
Not Taken" has been in the top ten for as long as I can remember.
The seeming transparency of Frost's poem, which many cadets first
encounter in high school, provides a reassuring link to their earlier
selves and a vindication of their decision to attend West Point,
where the Cadet Prayer enjoins them to "choose the harder right
instead of the easier wrong." They all see virtue in having taken a
less-traveled road, and they are right to see it. But they sometimes

shortchange the many other roads, some of them alternative roads of service, that beckon their peers.

Frost's poem is recited so often that I don't even bother to include it on the syllabus anymore. One day in the spring of 2006, the poet David Lehman visited with the class. David had come to talk to the upperclassmen in my film elective about Hitchcock; afterward he joined a seminar of sixteen plebes in the West Point Room on the top floor of the library. David had chosen several poems to discuss, and he happened serendipitously to begin with "The Road Not Taken." After reading it aloud, he asked the cadets about the speaker's choice. Conditioned from high school to imagine it a decisive one, they were surprised when David called their attention to those wonderfully ambiguous moments in the poem where Frost suggests that the two roads are more alike than different: both are worn "about the same," each has a largely undisturbed cover of leaves. The concluding stanza imagines the speaker's older self transforming what had been an arbitrary decision into a life-altering one: "I shall be telling this with a sigh / Somewhere ages and ages hence." The poem now had a new significance for them. People join the army for arbitrary reasons, too, but it is a choice that acquires momentousness as the years pass.

Adam, the aviator, tells me that what goes on in English class is the accelerated transformation of grade-three into grade-one thinkers. In flight school, Adam read William Golding's "Thinking as a Hobby," an essay that differentiates among three grades of thought: grade-three (less thinking than feeling); grade-two (ferreting out contradiction); and grade-one (attempting to find truth). "I haven't started *Bleak House* yet," Adam had written. "I plan to start it after this next checkride. I did read an interesting essay the other night. It's called 'Thinking as a Hobby' by William Golding . . . I really love that essay. I particularly enjoyed his discussion of the dangers posed by grade-three thinkers." Officers such as Adam find themselves living in two very different worlds, the private life of the mind and the public life of action—of rallying cries and derring-do. Adam wants both lives.

When I asked him what kind of helicopter he hoped to fly, he replied: "I think I'd like to fly the Apache or Kiowa. The attack/scout mission seems to fit my personality. It's a competitive community with just a bit more arrogance than the other aviation subcultures, and I kind of like that." No one would call Adam arrogant, but he has the intensity and grit that make him thrill to the idea of leading charges. Tolstoy's Nikolay Rostov thrills to the same things in *War and Peace*, yet he remains a "grade-three thinker" because reflection confuses him and destroys the comforts of his regimental routine: "If we were once to begin criticising and reasoning about everything," Rostov declares to his fellow officers after the czar's peace with Napoleon baffles them all, "nothing would be left holy to us." Adam is attempting to do something far more difficult.

All of this criticizing, reasoning, and grade-one thinking—to say nothing of the poetry—encouraged in the classroom is not without controversy for those who would prefer to imagine West Point as a kind of modern-day Sparta, where training and discipline trump creativity and independence of mind and spirit. In his biography of Lycurgus, the founder of the Spartan social system, Plutarch describes the Spartan way of life: "The boys learnt to read and write as much as they would need to get by, while all the rest of their education was geared towards inculcating ready obedience, the capacity to endure hard work, and the ability to win the battle." Disagreement over the role of academics in the cadet experience is as old as the institution itself. Little more than a decade after the Academy's founding as a school for engineering and artillery in 1802, Secretary of War John Armstrong supposedly reacted to the news that cadets were reading history by declaring: "Such books as Gibbon are luxuries of leisure, the mushrooms and truffles of literary sensualists." Armstrong's thoughts on poetry have not been recorded.

Historically, the academic program has been shaped at least in part by questions of professional application: in the nineteenth century, for example, French was considered essential because cadets had to be able to read Jomini and other military theorists then in vogue. Today the imperative to produce "culturally literate" soldiers has led to the addition of a third semester of foreign-language instruction. Along with modifications in military training made to keep pace with current operations—learning to defuse IEDs, for instance—there have been adjustments to the academic curriculum, such as the addition of minors in regional studies and in terrorism studies, in order to meet the urgent demands of the profession. Partial though I am, I am not surprised when some people want to know what the hell Sonnet 73 has to do with any of this.

Although literary models are so obviously central to military culture's idea of itself, there also exists a mistrust of literature (especially poetry) as an effete civilian pastime. This suspicion stems from a persistent anti-intellectual strain both within the Army and on the part of some of its analysts. The late David Hackworth, a highly decorated retired Army colonel and former battalion commander in Vietnam, who subsequently became a commentator on defense issues and a fierce critic of the military, used to like to insist that soldiers and books make bad bedfellows. He believed that the practice of "teaching poetry at West Point" succeeded only in producing more of what he called the "perfumed princes" who lost Vietnam. I enjoy the irony that the title of his last book, *Steel My Soldiers' Hearts*, is an allusion to the general in chief of poets: Shakespeare.

Champions of the liberal education cadets receive at West Point—and those champions include the general officers who lead the institution—are fond of the following quotation, sometimes attributed to Thucydides but in fact penned by the British general Sir William Francis Butler: "The nation that will insist upon drawing a broad line of demarcation between the fighting man and the thinking man is liable to find its fighting done by fools and its thinking by cowards." Those who reject the possibility of a synthesis of thought and action look instead to the Spartans. Borrowing the language of the political scientist Samuel Huntington, who once praised West Point as "a bit of Sparta in the midst of Babylon," James Miller proposed in a 2003 *National Review* article that the introduction of civilian faculty to the military academies had brought Babylon to Sparta. "One of the aims of a general education is to teach students how to think on their own," he wrote. Conjuring an officer corps of blindly obedient automatons, Miller continued, "A military education, on the other hand, requires officers-in-the-making to absorb the stern discipline of accepting orders without questioning them."

In Sparta, Plutarch tells us, "no one was allowed to live just as he pleased. Life in the city was like life in military camp: people lived in a prescribed way and spent their time on communal concerns, because it never occurred to them to regard themselves as autonomous rather than as subject to their country." It is difficult for many contemporary readers to encounter that passage without thinking of the literary dystopias of Huxley and Orwell and actual totalitarian nightmares of the twentieth century. Yet Huntington's allusion to Sparta comes from the peroration of *The Soldier and the State*, published in 1957. Much beloved by some soldiers, the book contains a description of West Point that suggests not only Sparta but also the privileged and similarly circumscribed warrior-guardians of Plato's *Republic*:

> The parts do not exist on their own, but accept their subordination . . . The post is suffused with the rhythm and harmony which comes when collective will supplants individual whim . . . Yet is it possible to deny that military values—loyalty, duty, restraint, dedication—are the ones America most needs today? That the disciplined order of West Point has more to offer than the garish individualism of Main Street?

All those who would celebrate the virtues of the Spartans seem to have forgotten that part of what destroyed the city in the end was that its inhabitants knew how to do little except make war. They also seem to forget that Spartan warriors had the luxury to devote themselves to training and to war because their economy was built on the backs of enslaved helots.

I sometimes call the English Department "The Last Outpost." It certainly must seem so to the plebes who find themselves assigned to a room in our basement rather than to one of the main classroom buildings. We sit on the edge of the Plain, the physical and psychological center of post, far from the barracks, and it is often something of an adventure for cadets to arrive within the time allotted for traveling between classes. "I had to get directions, ma'am," more than one has announced on the first day of term. "I didn't even know this building existed." Yet we are in our remoteness, on our best days, a place where curiosity and imagination can find refuge. Nick, who graduated in 1999, after completing a senior thesis on Yeats, is now a captain. Several years ago, while stationed in Korea, he wrote this note about the significance of his experience in the department:

> I found a group of cadets and professors with an insatiable appetite for knowledge . . . The atmosphere was [one of] wonder [and] of exploration. I could not have imagined a place where free thought and ideas were so well thought of . . .
> Someone once told me that "the most important book you will ever read is the first one after your graduation." I wish I could remember what it was—I have done more reading since graduation than I would have ever thought possible. When I was commissioned I thought I had a pretty good idea what I was getting involved with—I was wrong. I had not anticipated the sheer variety of tasks I would be given as a Lieu-

tenant. I was amazed at the lack of direction at times. Much of the early months at my first assignment [involved] simply teaching myself how to do the job I had been assigned. The more I learned, the more was pushed in front of me. My success in the jobs I have held stems from the formal training I received from the department as well as the . . . atmosphere that enveloped me while I was there.

In communicating what his academic work had meant to him and how it had also served as a professional foundation, Nick offered us one way to think about our function. Adam offered another, more succinct formulation: "The department doesn't teach us what to think; it teaches us how to think." Often, as Nick and Adam imply, imagination allows officers to meet everyday challenges. On occasion, I hope, perspective and independence might help them to solve extraordinary problems as well.

When teaching plebes in the basement of our building, I have the feeling of being in a kind of cocoon, not one that shields us from the profession to which they have committed themselves but one that fosters an unflinching look at both its romance and its reality: Jarrell's "Death of the Ball Turret Gunner" can coexist in our imagining with the chivalric knights of Malory's *Morte D'Arthur*. If, as C. S. Lewis proposed, "we read to know we are not alone," that roomful of plebes is the place I feel myself to be in the finest company. And one day, perhaps—in Baghdad, in a village of Afghanistan, in some remote outpost that none of us can anticipate—they, too, will read to know they are not alone.

Several years ago, in a British literature elective, I included a unit on the Victorian debate over education. Among the texts we read was Matthew Arnold's response to Thomas Huxley's insistence that scientific knowledge be taught in schools. In "Literature and Science" Arnold relates the story of a training-college student who tried to paraphrase Macbeth's appeal to the doctor to help the suffering Lady Macbeth. Shakespeare's "Can'st thou not minister to a mind diseased?" became in the student's mouth: "Can you not wait upon the lunatic?" "What a curious state of things it would be," Arnold concludes,

> if every pupil of our national schools knew, let us say, that the moon is two thousand one hundred and sixty miles in diameter, and thought at the same time that [this was] a good paraphrase . . . If one is driven to choose, I think I would rather have a young person ignorant about the moon's diameter, but aware that "Can you not wait upon the lunatic?" is bad, than a young person whose education had been such as to manage things the other way.

One of the cadets in the class proposed that this was the perfect argument for being an English major at West Point. I like to think that cadets, regardless of their major, can recognize the concomitant value of factual precision and imaginative rigor; know the diameter of the moon and a good paraphrase of Shakespeare; handle a grenade launcher and share an appreciation of Rumi with an Afghan colonel, as my friend Al did while deployed to Kabul in 2006. He had first read Rumi when teaching a class on Iran to the cows:

> [The Colonel] knew Rumi, was pleased to see that I knew Rumi, and [that] gave us a natural point of entry to substantial conversation. We referred to Rumi over and again. I don't know that I want to claim the liaison would have been a bust without Rumi, but it surely would not have been as good as it turned out to be without him. Rumi gave us a point of contact in our respective imaginations; he convinced each of us that we were more alike than unalike.

West Point isn't a Dickensian school where the literal alone holds sway, but it does prize a Gradgrindian triad of realities, facts, and calculations. Today its engineering programs are nationally ranked, and given that warfare is increasingly a technological affair, the military application of the sciences is clear, as is that of social sciences such as behavioral psychology or international relations and of a humanities discipline like military history. The "uses" of literature have always been more difficult to evaluate, the metrics for cultural awareness, empathy, or knowledge of the human condition being far less precise than the moon's diameter or the number of gallons of water in the reservoir. Nevertheless, it is almost sure to be the case that poetry is more important to the cultures with which U.S. troops will come in contact—to those of our allies and our enemies—than it is to our own. Rumi matters to Afghan colonels in a way that Whitman does not to us.

The two men who authorized the founding of the United States Military Academy were keen on instilling a sense of civic responsibility as well as technical precision in its graduates. Adams and Jefferson were deeply suspicious of the military's apparent affinity for kings. Jefferson saw an avenue to liberty and virtue through the study of science, while Adams tended to look to history: Plutarch, for example, provided models such as Epaminondas, the Theban general and statesman who resisted Spartan tyranny. When the Corps of Cadets marched to Massachusetts in the summer of 1821, Adams, by then an old man, addressed them at Quincy and enjoined cadets to comb accounts of history's "immortal Captains" to find models of excellence and to learn the difference between the Caesars and the Washingtons.

Some form of literature has been part of the West Point curriculum since the mid-nineteenth century, when it fell under the purview of a variety of departments—from the Department of Geography, History, and Ethics to that of Modern Languages. A provisional Department of English and History was formed in 1908 and made permanent in 1910. Congress at last authorized an independent English Department in 1926. Several years ago one of my students compiled a bibliography of texts read in West Point English classes from 1840 to 2002. The early days were marked by their attention to oratory, rhetoric, and literary history. Owing largely to the efforts of Colonel Holt, the study of poetry and literary prose was formally introduced into the curriculumin the twenties to complement the instruction in composition already being given.

College educators everywhere lament the decline of learning among high school students. A glance at entrance examinations from the early twentieth century reveals the kind of knowledge required to enter West Point. Applicants in 1927 had to identify in a "correctly constructed sentence" each of the following: Christopher Marlowe, Sir Roger de Coverley, Elia, Cordelia, Tom Jones, Anthony Trollope, *Modern Painters*, George Meredith, Henry Esmond, and John Silver. I wonder how many high school seniors could identify these names today; Sir Roger and several of his fellows would have stumped me. The most heavily weighted question on that examination invited candidates to help reformulate the literary canon: "Select and name one of the prose works, not fiction, regularly studied in class in the fourth (senior) year of your high school (or preparatory school) course. Submit an argument (about 300 words) either for or against the retention of this work in the course for future years. Include in your presentation of the case the value of the ideas in the book, the interest, the style, and something about the content." What intrigues me most about this question is its unexpected invitation: the prospective cadet's opinion is valued. It is precisely the kind of question I want cadets to be able to answer today. Current pedagogical theory likes to contrast the "active learning" of today with the "banker" model of decades ago. But in 1927, at least, West Point clearly wanted a self-aware learner able to devise his own reading list.

To teach at an institution that also has as its mission the cultivation of a specific set of values and virtues—duty, honor, country—and that prepares its graduates for military service is always to feel a palpable pressure to consider every moment's practical and moral weight. In order to impress upon new cadets the importance of attending to detail and being responsible for others, the upperclass-

men who train them like to call attention to each mistake by yelling
at the unfortunate tyro: "New Cadet, you just killed your platoon!"
The plebes have heard this exclamation so often by the end of summer training that they have turned it into a universally applicable
and invariably facetious response to any screwup. Everything from
a forgotten book to a misinterpreted assignment merits a "Yo, dude,
you just killed your platoon." It is sometimes difficult, however, *not*
to imagine a grim future for the perpetually absentminded cadet,
for the one with poor listening skills, or for the chronically clumsy.

Before September 11, decisions were always scrutinized against a
distant backdrop of war; today, the argument from relevance seems
even more compelling. It is no wonder that some officers recently returned from deployments believe that their primary mission —is to
teach cadets how not to get killed in Iraq. I understand this impulse,
but you can't protect cadets against death, no matter how thoroughly
you train them, especially when the weapons arrayed against them
owe so much of their success to the element of surprise.

Since the war began, I have often wondered exactly what cadets
most need, but the rejection of the value of a liberal education in a
time of war betrays the rich and vital connection between education and military service that has long distinguished the U.S. military. Perhaps there is no better example of this connection than
Al—"Old Redneck Al," as he styles himself. "The Army saved me,"
he has told me on a number of occasions, "the Army and my grandmother. I have got to be the luckiest redneck on the planet." There
is at once a practical and a more spiritual sense in which Al means
this. He initially enlisted because he and his wife were expecting a
baby and had no money to pay for it. "They'll pay for that baby," a
man he knew told him, and the man was right. The Army paid for
that baby and three more, for Al's undergraduate education at Mississippi State, and for his M.A. in philosophy at the University of
Virginia. In return, he served in the Infantry, first as an enlisted soldier and then, after college, as an officer, for close to thirty years.

His career included a variety of assignments: from commanding a company in the 101st Airborne Division at Fort Campbell to teaching philosophy at West Point. He also served two tours in Vicenza, Italy, the second as an inspector general. As brigade operations officer, he deployed to Rwanda in 1994, on a mission to secure Kigali's airfield for the Red Cross, which was attempting to save Hutu refugees dying of dehydration on the shore of a lake in Goma, Zaire. Al volunteered to go to Kabul just before he retired.

Al's grandmother was his first teacher; she had intelligence and a rare gentleness that survived a life of rural poverty, an astonishingly early marriage, and a rudimentary education. Through the Army, Al met with different kinds of teachers, other modes of inquiry, and new questions to ask. "The Army," he'll tell you, "did two things—life support and education . . . The Army kept me moving and kept giving me opportunities that would have otherwise been entirely unavailable—travel, other ways of seeing life, people from all over, and, of course, education. It was, all of it, an education that eventually helped me find the ground under my own legs and made my legs stronger at the same time." At college he encountered ideas so strange that he began to wonder what else they had been keeping from him all those years, and he also found a professor who told him something no one else had: "You have a good mind."

There's an irony to Al's use of the language of salvation to describe his experience in the Army. Once a staunch Baptist who went by the nickname "Preacher" because he always carried a Bible in his pocket, Al can still quote chapter and verse as effortlessly as anyone I know, but he is no longer, to use his word, a "thumper." Today he is more likely to cite Rumi, Aristotle, John Stuart Mill, or Joan Didion than he is scripture. In the Army, which is populated by a very vocal complement of fundamentalist Christians, Al lost one faith and gained another, a faith in education. To this second faith he brought all the zeal of the converted, and he was an extraordinary teacher who respected his students' right to sort things out for themselves. Al taught just as he gardens—by giving his charges the requisite light, space, and sustenance.

When I happened to mention to my father what Al said, he replied that the Army had, in a sense, saved him, too. Of course, my father wasn't a professional soldier. After a few years in the Army Air Corps, he was discharged at the end of the war. At the time he enlisted, he was eighteen, working days and going to night school, but he admitted that there was no guarantee he would have found a way to finish school without the G.I. Bill. I have the feeling that he would have figured something out, but I know only the successful professional. I never met the eighteen-year-old order picker at Decca Records who grew up in Depression-era bleakness. (I do, however, have a few souvenir 78s, including Jimmie Lunceford, "My Blue Heaven" / Coleman Hawkins, "Meditation," and Woody Herman, "Woodchopper's Ball" / "Big Wig in the Wigwam.") My father is less sanguine or more modest: "Who knows what would have happened?"

To me this is the Army at its best and most inspiring: in short, at its most American. Hearkening back to the founders' insistence on the new nation's need to educate its citizens to a sense of their social and political responsibilities, the Army is, both directly and indirectly, an extraordinary teacher. Today education remains perhaps the only just reward for those who volunteer to be coerced, but it was during my father's war that the Army began to educate as well as to wage war on a massive industrial scale. One of the great, if less heralded, achievements of World War II was the distribution of more than 100 million books. Generals have always brought books on campaign: Alexander the Great, as I noted earlier, kept the *Iliad* under his pillow. James Wolfe, commander of British troops in the French and Indian War, carried Thomas Gray's "Elegy Written in a Country Churchyard" with him to Quebec. The American Civil War was the first in which literacy was widespread throughout the force. During World War I, Everyman's Library and Oxford World's Classics made the short trip across the English

Channel to provide a steady diet for British readers of all ranks in the trenches, but by World War II easily portable paperbacks were supplied to soldiers and sailors around the globe.

Hurry up and wait, the old expression goes. My father used to spend a lot of time waiting for planes to land. Having trained as an air traffic controller at a series of stateside bases, he made sergeant, and in 1944, he shipped out to India, where he spent the rest of the war monitoring radio-range beacons. Over the years he occasionally rewarded my requests for wartime stories: the time in Muskogee, Oklahoma, when he told an impatient general screaming into his radio for taxiing instructions to cut his engine and "stand by" while he cleared the field for an emergency. The morning in Agra when a Gurkha presented on a bayonet the rat that had earlier awakened my father by nibbling on his hand. Or one of his first training missions as a radio operator on a B-17, when the pilot coolly mentioned that the landing gear didn't seem to want to come down. I never imagined that these adventures were not equally thrilling to him—that he might in fact have craved distraction from that very life while living it.

Thus, in spite of the fact that I talk about literature with soldiers every day, it never occurred to me until the current war began to ask my father what he read during his war. He immediately recalled a long list of books read off-duty in India, while overhead the Skytrains ferried the wounded to Karachi; brought in tungsten, green tea, and tin from China; or took spare parts to Chittagong. There was a lot of Somerset Maugham and C. S. Forester. There were also *The Postman Always Rings Twice*, *Lord Jim*, *The Grapes of Wrath*, and Ben Ames Williams's best-selling *Leave Her to Heaven*, which I know only in the deliciously lurid film version with the deadly Gene Tierney.

Many of the books my father remembers, potboilers and classics alike, found their way to G.I.s throughout Europe and the Pacific in the form of Armed Services Editions (ASEs): oblong, cargo-pocket-size paperbacks printed in pairs on rotary presses normally used for producing magazines. My father's reading was shaped by the

Council on Books in Wartime, which was made up of publishers, librarians, and booksellers working together with the Army and Navy. There was little censorship. Disagreements, explains John Y. Cole in *Books in Action: The Armed Services Editions*, usually occurred over "matters of taste," or over the feasibility of abridging long works. The Westerns of Zane Grey made the cut, as did Laurence Sterne's *Tristram Shandy*, T. E. Lawrence's translation of the *Odyssey*, and the poems of Edna St. Vincent Millay—more than thirteen hundred titles in all. Making a case for the real as well as symbolic importance of books and reading in wartime, Christopher Loss maintains that the Council's promotion of "the free production, dissemination, and reading of books" was "a vital source of democratic rejuvenation in the face of Nazi fascism abroad and memories of World War I propagandizing at home."

Books came from private donors as well, and paperbacks produced for sale in the United States often carried instructions for delivery to the USO or for mailing overseas. Dell War paperbacks, for example, carried the following message: "BOOKS ARE WEAPONS—in a free democracy everyone may read what he likes. Books educate, inform, inspire; they also provide entertainment, bolster morale. This book has been manufactured in conformity with wartime restrictions—read it and pass it on. Our armed forces especially need books." Modern technology accelerated slaughter on the twentieth-century battlefield, but it also enabled the mass production and circulation of approximately 123 million ASEs made exclusively for overseas distribution to military personnel. Soldiers read them even in the landing crafts on their way to Normandy. In an account of the D-Day landings published in *The New Yorker* on July 15, 1944, the war correspondent A. J. Liebling reported a miraculous meeting on the beach in Normandy with several sailors he had last seen in port in Britain. The meeting put Liebling in mind of an earlier exchange with an infantryman who had been reading *Candide* in an Armed Services Edition: "Voltaire used the same gag too often," the soldier had complained.

"The characters are always getting killed and then turning out not to have been killed at all, and they tell their friends what happened to them in the meantime."

As the online catalog to the University of Virginia's 1996 exhibition on ASEs reveals, these books helped to fashion a reading identity for the many American soldiers and sailors who were their primary consumers. Michael Hackenberg records, for example, that Katherine Anne Porter, whose *Selected Short Stories* appeared as an ASE, received hundreds of letters from soldiers, many of whom aspired to become writers. Similarly, Wallace Stegner taught students on the G.I. Bill who had read his novel *The Big Rock Candy Mountain* as an ASE: "The book," Stegner wrote, "gave us a bond." The Armed Services Editions ended in 1947, but the Army Library Program has continued in every conflict since to supply soldiers on deployment with paperbacks and other reading material. Librarian of the Army M. Ann Parham reports that paperback book kits are today supplemented with temporary libraries and e-library kiosks in Iraq, Afghanistan, Bosnia, Kosovo, and elsewhere. Army librarians maintain a network of more than 125 libraries: they can be found on every post in the United States and throughout the world from Ansbach, Germany, to Camp Zama, Japan.

Today the phrase "books in wartime" again has currency. Even the ASEs have returned, this time sponsored by the Legacy Project, a nonprofit organization founded in 1998 by the historian Andrew Carroll to support military personnel. In the fall of 2002 several publishers agreed to contribute four titles: two classics, *Henry V* and Sun Tzu's *The Art of War*; and two new compilations, *Medal of Honor: Profiles of America's Military Heroes from the Civil War to the Present* and *War Letters: Extraordinary Correspondence from American Wars*. When the series was announced, Ben Macintyre noted in the London *Times* that it reflected none of the range and diversity of the original: "The choice is resoundingly patriotic, fairly unimaginative, and ramrod straight." A few more titles were subsequently added to the original list: Christopher Buckley's *Wry Mar-*

tinis; *The Man in the Arena*, selected essays, speeches, and letters of Theodore Roosevelt; and *One Thousand and One Arabian Nights*, translated by Geraldine McCaughrean. While the list is somewhat idiosyncratic, the impulse is beautiful. Yet these volumes, formatted to achieve "the same vintage appearance as the original ASEs from the second World War," nevertheless strike me as ersatz wartime books. There is something excessively self-conscious and perhaps dangerously nostalgic about all of this, almost as if retrofitted books can make us see today's ambiguous conflict with the same clarity with which we regard World War II.

The Long War demands a more expansive reading list. The new series produced in the vintage shape of the old ASEs misses the essential point of the originals. Those books were "weapons" because they embodied a transcendent idea, namely, as the Dell paperbacks put it, "in a free democracy everyone may read what he likes . . . Our armed forces especially need books." The notion that the U.S. Army delivers democracy, though not always in the form of books, is still very much alive. Indeed, it fires the imagination of many of the Iraq war's civilian architects, yet the freedom to read and to say what one likes always suffers during wartime, even in democracies. External threats tend to bring with them the impulse to restrict certain freedoms. From the Alien and Sedition laws of 1798 to the USA Patriot Act of 2001, American presidents have tended to meet crises with legislation designed to curtail and suspend rather than to enlarge freedoms, including intellectual freedom and freedom of expression. That's why I relish the idea that "books are weapons." It is terminology sufficiently combative for someone teaching students who may very well find themselves at the violent margins of experience, and over the past several years I've come to understand the many ways in which books can serve as weapons: against boredom and loneliness, obviously; against fear and sorrow; but also against the more elusive evils of certitude and dogmatism.

In the wake of September 11, everyone used to ask me how West Point had changed. After the initial shock, however, and beyond the heightened security, it seemed to me that we conducted business as usual. In 2006, I had the opportunity to revisit that cataclysmic moment five years earlier in the context of a department teaching practicum. We were reading a chapter about teaching in dark and difficult times from Elaine Showalter's *Teaching Literature*. One of the new faculty members at the session asked those of us who had been at West Point on September 11 what we had done after hearing the news. I told the group that I had carried on with my lessons as originally planned. To this day I don't know whether this was a responsible approach; I don't know whether my behavior came from weakness or strength. Perhaps I was influenced by the imperturbable calm I associated with the officers I most respected or by some more literary construction of stiff-upper-lip soldiering. Later, a cadet told one of my colleagues that I was the only one of her professors that day *not* to respond to what had happened. Perhaps I was a victim of my own emotional limitations.

Whatever the case, by the afternoon, when my class met, I was already frustrated by the blaring televisions, the wild speculations, and the cries for revenge (on whom?). The cadets looked somber but not frightened. No one asked for reassurance, so I didn't offer any. I don't pray; I'm no good at motherly consolation; I had nothing to tell them that they didn't already know. Later, once the event had a context, it sometimes resonated with something we were reading. I have discussed it and all that ensued in class many times since. At that moment, however, I had nothing to say, so I retreated to the syllabus. Showalter refers to this approach as the "Mr. Chips Model," in an allusion to the hero of James Hilton's novel *Goodbye, Mr. Chips*, about a classics master at a British public school who proceeds with his lesson on Caesar in the midst of an air raid. I remember being struck in the movie made of the novel by the fact that the unease and fear on the young boys' faces gradually dissipate, replaced as Chips carries on by engagement and even laughter. Perhaps that image counted for something with me as well.

On the afternoon of September 11, I went ahead with a screening of The Maltese Falcon in my American literature class. We attached no special significance to Sam Spade's ruminations on the inefficacy of torture or to his attempt to explain the nuances of his professional code of honor to an uncomprehending murderer whom he also happens to love. Instead of watching that seemingly endless loop of planes crashing into the Towers, we watched a bunch of eccentric crooks embarked on the fool's errand of searching for a jewel-encrusted bird. And on the morning of September 12, in a course on the Enlightenment, I turned, as the syllabus indicated I should, to Diderot's plan for the Encyclopédie, in which he admits to his own uncertainty and doubt even as he lays out his bold scheme for collecting and organizing all knowledge: "I am unable to believe that it is within the power of a single man to know all that can be known; to make use of all the knowledge that exists; to see all that is to be seen; to understand all that is comprehensible."

"I can't take that to Iraq," a plebe told me recently as I was writing some rhetorical terms and their Latin origins on the board. If the war charges every moment with unusual urgency, however, whatever professors owe to cadets is the same today as it has ever been. Taking the long view suggests two things: that war is always in the offing for a soldier, and that one day Iraq and Afghanistan will be replaced by other fields of battle. Yet it is decidedly the case that teaching certain texts now is a palpably different experience from teaching them before September 11, 2001.

In 2005, I read Macbeth with the class of melancholy poets. One of the companion texts we explored together was the actor Derek Jacobi's essay on playing the title role. When he discusses the "If it were done when 'tis done" soliloquy of Act 1, scene 7, in which Macbeth is trying to argue himself out of murdering Duncan, who is his king, kinsman, and guest, Jacobi claims to have discovered another side to the role:

The soliloquy is full of extraordinary images . . . all occurring
to him on the instant. He is a highly intelligent, imaginative
articulate man, quite unlike the brutal, nonthinking slasher
of the battlefield, the tried, and honed, killing machine.
Here we are in contact with that other side of him, the great
contrast with his life as a soldier . . . His head is full of the
mixture of good and evil. At this moment the evil side of
him, which we all possess, is getting the upper hand and in
order to balance it he brings up the best, the purest, the
most innocent of images, of angels, and newborn babies, and
the sky . . . And on the other side are the dark, blood-driven,
evil, dank thoughts.

This passage teaches differently at West Point now than it would
have once or than it would, say, at Yale. I started off class one day by
reading it aloud to the cadets: here we were presented with an actor's good-faith effort to understand his character, yet his conclu-
sions rested on certain presuppositions about what happens to
actors in the theater of war. The cadets took exception to Jacobi's
division of Macbeth into two distinct halves: the soldier and the
"imaginative articulate man." The actor's easy conflation of the soldier's participation in violence with the embrace of outright evil also
gave them pause.

The melancholy poets resented the wonder with which Jacobi
discovered Macbeth's rich imaginative life. Perhaps among no
group of cadets is the world of the imagination more highly prized
than it was among the fifteen men and women who had volunteered
for this poetry elective. Many of them wrote their own verse, contributed to the cadet literary magazine, or participated in poetry
readings held with students from Bard College. The cadet in charge
of the creative writing club was in the class. With their own participation in war on the near horizon, the seniors especially were un-
willing to accept Jacobi's characterization of war's effects on the
soldier: "I don't consider myself a 'nonthinking slasher,'" one said,

"and I don't think Iraq is going to turn me into one." None of them would accept that fighting in a war would brutalize or demonize them, yet as a colonel who served in Vietnam suggested to me recently, some of them it might. None of them wanted to believe that the surrender or partitioning of their private imaginative worlds is a condition of their service, but to a certain extent it is. Even knowing how to recognize a good paraphrase of *Macbeth* will not make every soldier invincible against war's corrosions.

3

Becoming Penelope,
the Only Woman in the Room

---◆---

For several years now, a male colleague and I have run an occasional evening film series for cadets in our program. After devouring a stack of mediocre pizzas, we make our way to an amphitheater classroom with a large screen to watch classics the cadets have somehow missed: *Casablanca*, *The Maltese Falcon*, *Yojimbo*. Recently, we featured *The Battle of Algiers*, a film that has enjoyed a resurgence of attention owing at least in part to a 2003 Pentagon screening organized by the Directorate for Special Operations and Low-Intensity Conflict. The Pentagon flyer announcing the film billed it as a depiction of "how to win a battle against terrorism and lose the war of ideas." Our film nights were originally inspired not by politics but by a group of movie-crazy cadets who already knew something about film history and technique and wanted to learn more. Even in the early days of the film series, however, many of those who attended were just looking for diversion. The cadets' running commentary made me feel as if I had landed in a lost episode of *Mystery Science Theater 3000*.

One day I had the bright idea to show *Sunset Boulevard*. I have watched this movie countless times: I love it for its acid take on Hollywood; for the ways in which the autobiographies of Gloria Swanson and Erich von Stroheim intertwine with their performances as the silent star Norma Desmond and Max von Mayerling, the director turned butler; and for the arresting prealcoholic beauty of William Holden. The film historian David Thomson gets it right when he says that Holden would later look like "the most 'used' man in Hollywood," but in 1950 he looked terrific. Obviously, I had always seen this movie from a particular point of view. On this night, however, I watched it for the first time with a bunch of straight nineteen- and twenty-year-old men. Glimpsed through their eyes, it turned out to be a different film entirely.

At first things seemed to be going well. Several cadets were pleased to catch the allusion to Dickens's Miss Havisham, the old woman in *Great Expectations* who was long ago left at the altar but refuses to remove her wedding dress, in the opening description of Norma's neglected-looking Sunset Boulevard mansion. The evening began to get a bit more interesting during the New Year's Eve party scene in which Norma reveals her love for Holden's down-and-out writer Joe Gillis. As the pair dance together across the newly waxed floor—"Valentino said there's nothing like tile for a tango," Norma tells Joe—the cadets began to get as uncomfortable as Joe looks in his white tie and tails. When he complains, "I felt caught like the cigarette in that contraption on her finger," I heard a murmured "Yeah, buddy." And at the moment when Joe, overwhelmed with the desire "to be with people my own age," momentarily escapes to a friend's raucous party, a universal sigh of relief rose from the audience.

As I alone knew, Joe Gillis was destined to return to that old house on Sunset Boulevard, drawn back by his guilt over Norma's suicide attempt. And the closer Joe got to Norma's boudoir, the more insistent the cadets' panic became: "No, no," they intoned with the foreboding of a Greek chorus, and then one of them shouted: "Get out of there, Joe!" At the stroke of midnight, to the tune of "Auld Lang Syne" drifting in as the orchestra plays downstairs to an empty room, Joe walks up to that bed that looks like a

Spanish galleon, sits down, and pulls Norma's bandaged wrists from her face with the words, "Happy New Year, Norma." Triumphant, she responds by clutching him by the lapels of that ritzy vicuña coat she has paid for, dragging him toward her, and saying "Happy New Year, darling." It was a good thing I had already memorized these lines, for they were inaudible under the crescendo of groans and screams. As the scene faded to black on the couple's embrace, there were a few last shudders and spasms of physical revulsion from the cadets (and from my colleague), who watched the rest of the movie in a kind of exhausted stupor.

It was clear to me by now that they were watching a horror film. In Norma Desmond they must all have seen their mothers. Gloria Swanson looks pretty good in that movie, even with "the half-a-pound of makeup" she is accused of wearing. She doesn't much resemble any cadet mother I've ever seen—whenever I encounter them, they are clad cap-a-pie in black, gray, and gold West Point sportswear—but there was undeniably something primal going on in that room. I have never again been able to watch the scene without hearing the cadets' cries of terror as they all pictured themselves in Joe Gillis's shoes, as it were, hooked but good by Norma Desmond's neurotic claws. It was the kind of revelation you get when you are the only woman in the room.

Over the past decade, I have grown so accustomed to being the only woman in the room that I need occasionally to be reminded that I used to be in rooms full of women all the time. I spent six formative years (seventh through twelfth grade) at an all-girls private school in Boston called the Winsor School. In the spring of 2006, I was reminded of how much my life had changed when I attended a reception organized to introduce the school's new director to graduates living in the New York area. I haven't been to my reunions, and my contact with classmates has been sporadic over the years. When I got this invitation, however, it awakened a surprising desire to reconnect with the place and its people. The party was held at an East Side town house garrisoned by white-gloved waiters. When the hostess responded to a guest's inquiry about the extraordinary size of the house with the words "Yes, it's a double-width," I flashed immediately to a colleague's recent musings that if his post-Army law school plans didn't work out, he would be able at least to purchase a "double-wide" trailer with his retirement pay: "somewhere for the wife and kids," he said with a wink. My galaxy seemed pretty wide that day, too.

When I looked around the room to see alumnae of various generations, I realized how strange it was to be among such women once again and to take my place in their continuum. The new director fielded questions about curricular minutiae. The continued teaching of Latin was celebrated; the addition of Chinese was received with enthusiasm; the disappearance of Greek went unremarked. The most controversial topic of the evening was the movement of an expository writing class, long an eleventh-grade rite of passage, to the ninth. Older alumnae, already persuaded that the world was ending, shook their heads and threw up their hands at this news, but my nearer contemporaries articulated patiently and carefully their doubts about the wisdom of shifting a class that had done them so much good where it was. Every one of us seemed burdened with her own educational idée fixe, determined in part by age, in part by experience. No doubt some of us were guilty of simple nostalgia, but there seemed as well to be a genuine interest in trying to measure the good our education had done us out in the world and how it might have done even more.

Unhappy alumni are a fact of institutional life, but every institution, as an anthropologist friend likes to tell me, has its own particular pathology. When West Point graduates (or cadets) are displeased by some change, they will often say "Corps has," as in "the Corps of Cadets has gone to hell." "Back in the day . . . ," they'll sigh before launching into a catalog of the now-obsolete hardships that forged them into tempered steel. On the part of many, this grousing is playful and self-aware. Think of a military version of Monty Python's Four Yorkshiremen, whose increasingly competitive tales of privation embrace the fantastic horrors of living in a septic tank, licking a gravel road clean, being thrashed to death every night by bread-knife-wielding parents, and getting up four hours before they go to bed to work twenty-seven hours a day at the mill. "But then again," one of the Yorkshiremen says, "we had it tough."

I-had-it-tough stories are the currency of military culture, and part of what plebes figure out is how and when to tell them. You can see the learning process at work among them: one plebe will go too far—his voice might lose the requisite edge of self-mockery—and the rest of the class will swarm like a school of piranhas. If, for example, a plebe starts to complain or make excuses on his own behalf rather than on that of the group, his peers will castigate him for weakness and shut him up. You've got to be working for the team. Dissatisfied graduates tend to voice their complaints to the superintendent, the three-star general who is West Point's equivalent of a college president. The most excited inquiries—those that become public knowledge through grapevines such as alumni online chat rooms, parents' clubs, and cadet e-mail chains—often concern some long-standing tradition that has been done away with or the fortunes of the football team. Sometimes alumni issue declarations instead of questions.

Soon after my arrival in the late 1990s, I was made aware of a white paper, submitted by a class from the 1950s, lamenting several changes they believed had degraded the West Point experience. There was the requisite allusion to Sparta and the suggestion that the Academy was becoming just another college campus and, what I think amounted in their minds to the same thing, feminized. The arrival of women, the paper baldly stated, had been accompanied by a not-coincidental relaxation of standards. These proponents of Sparta had nothing to say of the homoeroticism that fueled the Greek city-state's culture, and they would almost certainly have rejected as unendurably feminizing Herodotus's portrait of the naked Spartans combing their trademark long hair in preparation for the battle of Thermopylae. Nevertheless, graduates who deplore the arrival of women at West Point as the beginning of the end are emphatically Spartan in their belief that military discipline can be achieved only in an exclusively male environment.

In the spring of 2006, as I reconnected with Winsor, the thirtieth anniversary of women at West Point was being celebrated. In October 1975, President Ford signed the bill mandating the admission of women into the service academies, and the first coed class arrived at West Point in the summer of 1976. It was the nation's bicentennial year, and I was walking Boston's Freedom Trail for the first time, a seven-year-old being steeped by my parents in the city's revolutionary history. The 1960s and 1970s were turbulent times at the Military Academy. President Johnson expanded the Corps from approximately 2,500 to more than 4,400 cadets in 1964; Samuel W. Koster, superintendent from 1968 to 1970, prohibited much of the physical hazing to which plebes had been subjected for decades; and a cheating scandal in 1975, the year before women were admitted, led the secretary of the Army to commission an external investigative panel chaired by Eastern Airlines president Frank Borman.

According to *Time*, 1,519 new cadets reported for summer training in 1976; 119 of them were women. By November 1979, 57 had dropped out, leaving a total of 334 women in a corps of 4,338. *Time* also reported that Superintendent Andrew Goodpaster—the general had been called out of retirement to replace Koster, who had resigned amid charges that he had failed, while in command of the 23rd Infantry Division (Americal), to investigate reports of a massacre at My Lai—had been summoned to Washington to answer questions about persistent hazing. That summer, according to the magazine, male cadets had forced a female cadet "to bite off the head of a live chicken" as punishment for dating a man in her company (the primary unit of organization in the Corps) and thus violating an unwritten cadet rule. A number of the women who endured those early days have written about their experiences. Carol Barkalow, whose memoir *In the Men's House* was published in 1990, dramatically described the abuse she encountered: "Hazing was constant, emotional, mental. It was like a form of terrorism, because we never knew when it was coming and where it was coming from." Abuse ranged from the symbolic, a ketchup-coated saber plunged into a woman's pillow, to the dangerously real: sexual assault.

Colonel (Retired) Pat Hoy, who taught for many years in the English Department, has written eloquently about the Academy's culture. Of the violence with which those early women met, he asserts:

West Point breeds restraint deep into a man's soul . . . But when the female cadets came in 1976, restraint within the male world gave way to occasional violence. Neither alcohol nor academic pressure had anything to do with the change. The violence was deliberate—a group of misogynous young men trying to preserve the sanctity of an all-male world that was disappearing. Instead of adjusting to a new idea about West Point, the men were holding on.

Some men tutored under the old system still cling to history even as they acknowledge that the process of gender integration in the Army and other services is irreversible. Misogyny percolates beneath the surface of discussions about the "civilianizing" or weakening of military culture. Armywide initiatives instituted to promote respect and thus enhance esprit de corps in an increasingly diverse force have been ridiculed by critics of the Hackworth school as "sensitivity training" inimical to the warrior spirit, as if a more thorough understanding of his troops couldn't enhance an officer's combat readiness. Today, the cadets who reportedly made their sister-in-arms bite the head off a chicken would not recognize the atmosphere at West Point, but military culture remains "resistant," as Pat Hoy puts it, "to women's influence." When, at certain parades, that metaphorical Long Gray Line, as the graduates of the Academy are collectively known, becomes real, it materializes as a procession largely of men stretching into the distance.

Women at West Point must make their way in a culture historically charged by machismo and fraternity. There are certain enclaves of women within that world—more and less formal associations of cadets, staff and faculty, military wives—but to live or work within military culture is to exist in a world, to borrow a phrase from Virginia Woolf, of "unmitigated masculinity." When I asked a lieutenant I've known since she was a plebe, and whom I'll refer to as Margaret, what it was like to make her way through West Point, she responded with a lengthy e-mail. She had just returned from a scouting mission to Iraq, where she was scheduled shortly to deploy with her unit:

> They were both the darkest and brightest days of my life. I liken it to the agony a world class sprinter feels in her legs as she crosses the finish line to win the gold medal. Always agony and triumph intertwined. It must be so. Just as the blacksmith creates a gleaming sword by taking first dirty steel and burnishing it, so too that institution takes from you weakness, burning you ever deeper and deeper, again and again, until your body, your mind fits the mold. And if, along the way, you happen to break, as clay in the kiln so often does, you're simply swept aside. No weakness really is a tolerable weakness. There is no "weakness" in war . . . It must be so. In war you can either choose to be strong or you can

choose to be dead. Taken as that, I suppose, there truly is a method to the pain, a formula, a design to the grind.

If there is one sentence that would [encapsulate] my experience: agony and triumph always in the same breath.

Margaret responded to West Point's challenge by cultivating her capacity for leadership, endurance, and judgment. I see no shortage of warrior spirit in this particular woman, only a knowledge of the price it exacts. The highest form of courage, according to Aristotle, isn't the headlong rush of the berserker but the determined charge of the citizen-soldier who knows exactly what he—I mean *she*—fights for.

Our experiences in Iraq and Afghanistan have demonstrated that technology has not yet obviated the need for "boots on the ground." Many of those boots are filled by women, yet even as they find themselves in combat situations, these women are still barred from the Army's combat branches, including Infantry, Armor, and Field Artillery, its oldest and still its most prestigious. It remains difficult, moreover, for society at large to imagine war as anything but a male enclave. When he went to observe the Spanish Civil War, Saint-Exupéry concluded: "The absence of women seems to me right. There is no place here for mothers who bring children into the world in ignorance of the faith that will some day flare up in their sons." If when you look at a woman you see a mother, it becomes extremely difficult to dress that woman in ACUs, arm her with an M-16, and send her off to battle. If you recognize a woman's capacity for heroism, it is more likely the self-abnegation attributed to the Spartan women, who purportedly responded to news of the deaths of their sons by saying they wished they had more to give: "Let there be weeping for cowards," declares one mother at the death of her son in Plutarch's collection of Spartan sayings, "but you, child, without a tear do I bury: you are my son, and Sparta's too."

As recently as 2002, one could find a symposium on American

citizenship and military service recommending that "in a society in which male adolescents find it increasingly difficult to discern what it means to be a man or how to become one, we should *promote military service as a rite of passage to manhood.*" This attitude presents an almost insuperable psychological bar to the full integration of women in combat: women, it is feared, will disrupt the cohesion of male units and make them less effective. Other countries have managed to negotiate this terrain, but many Americans don't seem ready. Take, for example, the case of Paul—the same plebe for whom Agamemnon's day of glory rescued the *Iliad*. Toward the end of his plebe year, Paul came to my office to discuss an essay. Before he left, he delivered a confession: he wasn't all that comfortable with the idea of women in the workplace and certainly not with women in the Army. Paul fought routinely over this issue with members of his company, some of whom, obviously, were women. "Really," he announced, "they ought to be at home." He supposed that it was "okay" for a woman to teach. He had watched me for an entire semester, and I seemed competent.

"Why," I then allowed myself to wonder, "are women so unfit for the public arena?" "It is well known," he replied, "that women are less emotionally stable than men." "Really, how often do I swoon in class?" I asked. "Um, never, ma'am, not you." "What about women who must work? How do you judge them?" Paul paused and then recounted a moving story about an aunt, who had had to provide on her own for her young children. Her toughness had clearly won Paul's admiration. "My aunt is a rock," he concluded, "and I have a lot of respect for what she's done." When I proposed that this story seemed to put the lie to his theory about the emotional instability of women, he admitted that it might. He had never thought about it that way, and he seemed rather startled at the extent of his confession.

This is not necessarily one of the "teaching moments" of which I once dreamed. Cadets occasionally make confessions ranging from the grossly impolitic to the deeply personal. To make things even more complicated, not long after my arrival, Errol Flynn— one of the colonels from that first visit—to whom I had expressed my surprise at a male cadet's wholly unprompted (and immediately regretted) emotional revelations, told me: "You are the closest thing to a mother they have around here, scary as that sounds." It did sound scary. And while I refused to accept this interpretation, now that the whole mother-thing was out there on the table, it could not be so easily cleared away. First of all, I hadn't signed up for that: I was a teacher, and while the best mothers also teach, they do other things of which I wanted no part. Second, no one had ever mistaken my classroom demeanor for maternal, and even if the parental affect did come most readily to me, I would work to suppress it as being inappropriate. Cadets cannot afford the luxuries of indulgence and cosseting—of being reassured that everything will be okay. It won't, and they, perhaps more than their civilian counterparts, need to know that it won't. Besides, West Point's mission exhorts us "to educate, train, and inspire the United States Corps of Cadets." Nothing in there about mothering.

Mothers and battlefields have an uneasy relationship (outside of Sparta, that is). When in *War and Peace* Nikolay Rostov finds himself in combat for the first time, he thinks in his misery of his mother's love:

> He gazed at the approaching French, and although only a few seconds before he had been longing to get at these Frenchmen and to cut them down, their being so near seemed to him now so awful that he could not believe his eyes. "Who are they? What are they running for? Can it be to me? Can it be they are running to me? And what for? To kill me? *Me*, whom every one's so fond of?" He recalled his mother's love, the love of his family and his friends, and the enemy's intention of killing him seemed impossible. "But

they may even kill me." For more than ten seconds he stood, not moving from the spot, nor grasping his position.

When mothers and war collide, as they do in Robert Olen Butler's wonderful "Mother in the Trenches," strange things happen. In this short story an American mother journeys to the trenches of France during World War I to find her son. Their meeting is fraught with tension. How could it not be? The soldier's two worlds have smashed into each other. But the story ends with the mother comforting another soldier, a stranger who accepts from her the maternal comfort he can get in such a place only from a woman *not* his mother.

The conceit that soldiers are fighting for those mothers and wives waiting moist-eyed on the ramparts has long been integral to the mythology of war: it is what gives Hector's valedictory in the *Iliad* and the hero's belated homecoming in the *Odyssey* their power. For all their attention to fathers and sons, however, both Homeric epics yield remarkable insights into the lives of the women left behind: of the Trojan women in their anger and grief preparing Hector's body for burial and of Penelope waiting for Odysseus at Ithaca and warding off the rapacious suitors. Twenty-first-century military spouses—they are not exclusively women anymore—also feel invested, as indeed they should, in the mission, and they organize themselves into their own unofficial but nonetheless powerful units. Headed by the commander's spouse, these groups coordinate a unit's social functions and contribute greatly to its morale. This is especially true for deployed units. A retired colonel's wife once spoke to me of their first posting to Okinawa in the mid-1960s. Her husband was sent to Vietnam almost as soon as they arrived, and she told me that without the support of the commander's wife she doesn't know what she would have done alone in an unfamiliar place.

Although the current inclusive phrase is *Army Spouse*, the mystique of the *Army Wife* lingers powerfully on in the military community: take, for example, an advice-filled website like Army-Wives.com. The *Army Wife* is a figure of the utmost seriousness, but she sometimes provokes caricature, most often by a member of the class: "Oh, don't get me started. You can spot an Army Wife a mile away," a colleague's wife assured me. "A real 'army wife' drives a green mini van, wears white Keds and denim jumpers, and considers Longaberger basket parties a religious experience. She has Stivers prints and large wedding photos—husband in uniform—on her living room wall.   She has a good lasagna recipe and a set of bamboo trays." My own contact with these women is intermittent. The wives of the three commanders for whom I have worked have all been inordinately gracious, and part of their welcoming philosophy is the extension of invitations to all women new to the department: wives of officers as well as female civilian and military members of the faculty. I have, whenever I could, attended coffees and potlucks and been rather overwhelmed by the warmth of these gatherings; yet nothing can kill a conversation about the quality of an elementary school at Fort Hood or the impact of a husband's deployment faster than the mention of your latest scholarly monograph on obedience in American fiction and political prose. This is emphatically their world, not mine. I am a guest.

Army families and the neighborhoods in which they live at West Point look like something from the 1950s. Each housing area has a sort of mayor, who singles residents out for the best-kept yard of the month and similar accomplishments. With manicured lawns, identical houses, and safe streets full of happy children, the post seems a cross between Stepford and the Magic Kingdom. "What you must understand," a wise major informed me when I first arrived, "is that West Point is a place about a place, a meta-place." He was also fond of saying, whenever I apologized for darkening his office door with yet another question, "It is only when you stop asking questions—when it all starts to make sense—that you need worry." Water and electricity are paid for, and you need only leave a little red flag in the window on the appropriate day for the engineers to stop by to address any maintenance issues from a bum fuse to a flooded basement. West Point's self-image as a place perpetually on display manifests itself nowhere more clearly perhaps than in the polished perfection of its neighborhoods.

If the history of the military profession presents certain obstacles to women's ambitions for meaningful service today, women in uniform likewise destabilize a military culture founded on essentially chivalric traditions. One linguistic solution to this problem attempts to obscure the presence of women by referring to them clinically with the noun *females*. Imagine a cultural history that boasted Euripides' *The Trojan Females*, D. H. Lawrence's *Females in Love*, and the Stephen Sondheim gem "The Females Who Lunch." Already drilled in the replacement of *women* by *females*, my students don't recognize how jarring it is to hear the term in the middle of some astute literary analysis. It completely ruins the mood.

Such terminology appeals especially to those cadets and officers most disquieted by the presence of women in their ranks. Ironically, this desexualizing term coexists with another attribute of the military's chivalric patrimony, the highly sexualized urge to protect women, even women in uniform: witness the dramatic rescue of Jessica Lynch by Special Forces operatives and subsequent controversy over initial reports of her capture and treatment. Lynch herself may have resented being turned into a "symbol," but it was a symbol immensely attractive to the American public.

When I first arrived at West Point, several of my new colleagues made a point of telling me I would always find that my best students were women. Surely, I thought, that can't be possible: some will be brilliant, others undistinguished. What sense did such a claim make? Well, it makes a lot of sense if you are a man who feels responsible in a different way for women than for men. This kind of thinking inhibits equitable treatment: at best, it is paternalistic. I once worked as an adviser to a team with an officer who liked to make a big show of understanding the athletes by saying things such as "I'm still trying to figure the girls out" or "Women athletes are just different. I'm learning how to deal with them." He went on in this vein for so long that his wife finally rolled her eyes and shot back: "I'm a woman and an athlete. You don't know how to deal with me?"

Cadets are often far less concerned about such matters than are their older, less progressive superiors. Once, it took a section of all-male plebes most of the semester to realize the composition of the class: one of them suddenly looked around and said: "Hey, ma'am, do you realize that you are the only woman in the room?" "Yes," I said, absolutely delighted that he hadn't said "female," and we got back to whatever we were doing. Yet stereotypes of masculinity and femininity die hard, nowhere harder perhaps than in a military culture long celebrated as a repository of manly virtues of honor, courage, and endurance. In *Manliness*, his 2006 book on the buffeted virtues of masculinity, Harvey Mansfield suggests that one of the problems of feminism is that it teaches women that they can "have it all" but that they can't be women, too. This conclusion stems from a belief that true femininity is antithetical to the hard edges of public life and that women themselves must be warm, soft, domestic, and available to the chivalric impulses of men. It therefore regards feminism as an abdication of definition and responsibility that is to be condemned as much for what it does to men as for what it does for women.

You don't need to subscribe to the Men Are from Mars / Women Are from Venus school to recognize the challenges women face in the military. When it comes to these topics, however, I have lately discovered that I am extremely naïve. Meditating on these issues at all is in fact a rather novel experience for me. When people learn where I teach, often the first question they ask has to do with women at West Point, a subject about which they find me woefully uninformed. I can tell them approximately the percentage of women in the Corps (15 to 17 percent), but I don't know offhand the percentage who graduate or the number of women on the faculty. These are interesting statistics, no doubt, but not to me, and I think people find that a little odd. It is also odd, I suppose, that West Point, with all of its alien, baldly masculine militancy, has been to me a most hospitable place. To understand this claim perhaps you need to know a bit more about those formative years at the Winsor School.

Like West Point, the Winsor School is energized by its traditions. It also has a mission located in a sense of community: "to develop competent, responsible, generous-minded women." Founded in 1886, it is an institution proud of its history, determined to uphold traditions but supple enough to adapt itself to a rapidly evolving world. I remember an atmosphere characterized at once by determined anachronism and risk-taking flexibility. Having sent its graduates to college for the first time in 1895, Winsor was obviously committed to the fulfillment of women's educational and professional ambitions, but personal and professional success had corresponding obligations. Students were told that they also owed something to others. In the short term this took the form of service projects and community outreach, but it was typical of the school's philosophy that its director and faculty refused to define the nature or delimit the scope of the long-term service it expected. Graduates would have to figure that part out for themselves.

There is another strange similarity between West Point and Winsor: both indoctrinate as well as educate. I graduated thoroughly imbued by an ideology: I learned to take being a woman for granted. Indeed, the school was so dedicated to empowering us that I wearied of its message: I get it, I get it, I would think as I listened to one liberating lecture after another. One year, for example, the graduation speaker happened to be Gloria Steinem. I was almost entirely ignorant, as the successfully indoctrinated usually are, and knew nothing of *Ms. Magazine*, glass ceilings, restrictive divorce and abortion laws. I knew only what I was told, that my possibilities were unlimited, and I believed it. What were the struggles of Steinem's generation to me?

It was only at Harvard that I got glimpses of the trepidation and insecurity under which so many women yet labored. I learned that classmates who had come from coeducational schools were afraid to contribute to classes full of men. Only then did I begin to realize that Winsor had inoculated me against precisely this kind of intimidation. "Do you understand the material?" I would ask my friends. "Yes," they would reply, "as well as anyone else in the room." "Then what's the problem? Speak up!" I still feel that way, and for this reason I am perhaps less understanding than I might otherwise be of the special challenges women in West Point classes face. I think, to the extent that I think about it at all, that the example of a woman unafraid to speak in front of men ought to be enough. And, for some, it is.

It is also true, perhaps to a degree remarkable given institutional history, that my being a woman is immaterial to many of my colleagues—or so it seems to me. In my department, if an opinion has merit, if an idea can help us better to accomplish the mission, then it doesn't matter from whom it comes. The only thing that matters is your investment in and commitment to that mission. It is for this reason a rewarding environment in which to work: the Army, after all, prides itself on being a meritocracy. On those rare occasions when I have met with resistance, my first reflex is to attribute it to my being a civilian. A colonel stunned me one day by telling me that the hostile vibe I had received from a particular officer might have less to do with my being a civilian than with my being a woman. I told you I was naïve.

So it never occurred to me to become involved in the various women's groups, formal and informal, at West Point. I feel no instinctive sisterly solidarity and often resent the assumption that I should. Several women I know from Steinem's generation have chastised me for not making more of an effort to mentor women. One, a high-powered corporate executive, was especially critical. She feels a responsibility to lead in a particular—maternal, nurturing—way because of her sex, and it is clear that she regards my lack of a coherent gender-based teaching philosophy a kind of failure.

While I understand the argument, I remain convinced that mentoring is best conceived of as an equal-opportunity proposition; perhaps some of my female students have felt overlooked as a result. I can think of one case in particular: let's call her Ingrid, the overachiever. Writing with pride in her memoir about being dubbed "Jane Wayne" by her first platoon, Carol Barkalow reveals a pressure to outperform men at their own game—a pressure that some cadets undoubtedly still feel. Perhaps this same compulsion lay behind Ingrid's attitude. She struck me as unnecessarily tough, demanding, and stubborn. When she didn't get all the praise she thought she deserved, Ingrid became even more strident, until I finally lost patience one day during a meeting about her work, which wasn't as good as she thought it was. I watched her eyes tear up and her lip begin to quiver as I told her, in essence, that she needed to grow up. Suddenly, she ran out of the office and down the hall, "shoulders heaving," a colleague informed me, "sobbing all the way." I still don't know what to make of this incident: Would it have happened in a male colleague's office? Behind the carapace and the arrogant swagger, was Ingrid presuming an automatic solidarity that simply wasn't there? Did she feel a sense of betrayal of which I was unaware?

Military culture is obsessed with the concept of role models, but the ideal of a woman warrior is far more elusive than that of her male counterpart. My discipline doesn't provide a great deal of help in this area. Literature, like history and sociology, tends to reinforce for cadets the idea that their chosen profession is a masculine one.

In a discussion of the limitations of two of the "greatest" writers of her age, Galsworthy and Kipling, Virginia Woolf proposes:

> Do what she will, a woman cannot find in them that fountain of life which the critics assure her is there. It is not only that they celebrate male virtues, enforce male values and describe the world of men; it is that the emotion with which these books are permeated is to a woman incomprehensible . . . With Mr. Kipling's officers who turn their backs; . . . and his Men who are alone with their Work; and the Flag— one blushes at all these capital letters as if one had been caught eavesdropping at some purely masculine orgy. The fact is that neither Mr. Galsworthy nor Mr. Kipling has a spark of the woman in him. Thus all their qualities seem to a woman, if one may generalise, crude and immature. They lack suggestive power. And when a book lacks suggestive power, however hard it hits the surface of the mind it cannot penetrate within.

It is in precisely such a world—a world of men accustomed to being alone with their work and the flag—that cadets who happen also to be women must make their way. I ought to be able to help them, but while it's no trouble to find alternatives to Galsworthy and Kipling on a syllabus, it isn't so easy to find stories about women, work, and the flag.

Tales of war are designed to make women fall in love with soldiers not with soldiering. Think of Dido, who, having welcomed Aeneas along with the rest of the Trojan refugees to Carthage, promptly falls in love with him after he narrates the story of his suffering and escape: *"Quem sese ore ferens, quam forti pectore et armis!"* she declares to her sister Anna, in a phrase that the Colonel used to like to translate "What a guy!" when we taught the poem together. Robert Fitzgerald, whose translation we used, renders the line "How princely, how courageous, what a soldier." After the banquet ends and everyone else has gone to sleep, Dido watches, haunted by Aeneas's countenance and his words (*voltus verbaeque*). His war story (and a little help from the gods) reawakens in her an erotic desire she thought had died along with her first husband. How many of the male cadets with whom I read these lines envisioned a brilliant romantic future? Girlfriends left behind would become newly enchanted, while strange women met along the way would succumb to their stories of a harrowing summer spent in the hostile, sweltering jungles of the Hudson Valley.

It isn't unusual, on asking cadets how they spent a holiday weekend or spring leave, to hear them report that girlfriends back home have dumped them. Women are more reticent: I've never heard a cadet confess that her boyfriend dumped her. Plebes often seize on a practical use for sonnets: "I'm going to try that one on my girlfriend, ma'am." No wonder, when we read *Othello* together in March 2002, the cadets' future trajectories so recently diverted by the events of the previous autumn and news of Operation Anaconda in Afghanistan, they brightened at Othello's words to his outraged father-in-law, Brabantio, who has accused him of using witchcraft to steal Desdemona's love. Othello strikes the pose of the gruff, inarticulate soldier: "Little of this great world can I speak / More than pertains to feats of broils and battle." Yet of these he speaks with such eloquence—of "disastrous chances" and "hairbreadth scapes"—that Desdemona "with a greedy ear / Devour[s] up" his conversation:

> And often did guile her of her tears,
> When I did speak of some distressful stroke
> That my youth suffer'd. My story being done,
> She gave me for my pains a world of sighs;
> 'Twas pitiful, 'twas wondrous pitiful.
> She wish'd she had not heard it, yet she wish'd
> That heaven had made her such a man. She thank'd me,

And bade me, if I had a friend that lov'd her,
I should but teach him how to tell my story,
And that would woo her. Upon this hint I spake:
She lov'd me for the dangers I had pass'd,
And I lov'd her that she did pity them.
This only is the witchcraft I have us'd.

Events prove that this may not be the best foundation for an enduring marriage, of course, but the woman hungry for the fabulous stories of soldiers is a frequent figure in literature.

Most of the exemplary women of epic poetry—Penelope, An-
dromache, Hecuba—listen, watch, and wait; alternatively, they
tempt, as in the cases of Helen of Troy and Circe, the sorceress
who turns men literally into swine. The ode in which Horace proposes that it is sweet and proper to die for one's country not only
portrays the disciplined young Roman warrior marching off to ter-
rify the nasty Parthians but also conjures the picture of a virgin
with her mother atop the enemy's ramparts praying for the safe
return of the man she is to marry. Only rarely do literary women
fight: the Amazons, and Camilla, the warrior queen of the *Aeneid*,
who goes into battle with breast bared for more efficient fighting,
are exceptions.

One semester, before the war, I found myself reading about
some of those exceptions in Antonia Fraser's *Warrior Queens*. The
subtitle of Fraser's book, *The Legends and Lives of the Women Who
Have Led Their Nations in War*, suggests that it is a story of the few
and the proud. Its protagonists range from the early Celtic figure
Boadicea to Margaret Thatcher. We read the book along with
Plutarch's *Lives* in a class for juniors that revolved around the
theme of military leadership. Fraser notes the difficulties such
women have confronted and details their sophisticated negotiation
of power. Often they have used chastity or maternity as a source of
strength; at other times they have succeeded because they were
perceived as transcending the habitual weakness of their sex by cul-

tivating masculine virtues. Witness Zenobia, queen of Palmyra, who is compared by Edward Gibbon—the historian Fraser most often invokes as a foil—with Cleopatra, whom she "far surpassed . . . in chastity and valour . . . Her manly understanding was strengthened and adorned by study." The cadets' biggest complaint was that they could find no logic to the book's organization: "You don't want us to write like this, do you?" they asked. The book is not conventionally linear; it circles back on itself just as the legends it chronicles tend to do. But I wonder if their discomfort stemmed as much from the alien nature of its subject as from the presentation.

Of the important exceptions Fraser treats, none has been more important to my own understanding of women and power than Elizabeth I, whose speeches, poems, and letters always form a part of my syllabus when I teach British literature. What a magnificent concatenation of manipulation and subversion produced her speech to the troops at Tilbury preparing to meet a Spanish invasion in 1588. Elizabeth, in ceremonial helmet and breastplate, circulated fearlessly among her troops despite the warnings about assassination plots, and she didn't hesitate to let her audience know exactly what she was risking:

> I am come amongst you, as you see, at this time, not for my recreation and disport, but being resolved, in the midst of the heat of the battle, to live and die amongst you all; to lay down for my God, and for my kingdom, and for my people, my honour and my blood, even in the dust. I know I have the body but of a weak and feeble woman; but I have the heart and stomach of a king, and of a king of England too, and think foul scorn that Parma or Spain, or any prince of Europe, should dare to invade the borders of my realm; to which, rather than any dishonour shall grow by me, I myself will take up arms, I myself will be your general, judge, and rewarder of every one of your virtues in the field.

I get more of a charge reading that speech to a class of cadets than is probably fair. I can think of no better example of a woman unafraid to speak in front of men. Here was a woman who told Parliament to butt out when it started inquiring about her marriage plans: "A strange thing that the foot should direct the head in so weighty a cause." Here was a woman who told off a Polish ambassador who dared to complain that her quarrels with the Spanish king were disrupting his country's trade: "It was one of the best answers in extempore Latin that ever I heard," Lord Cecil wrote to the Earl of Essex. "As for yourself," the queen told the Polish diplomat, "you give me the impression of having studied many books, but not yet of having graduated to the books of Princes, rather remaining ignorant of the dealings between Kings." Afterward, the queen reportedly turned her back to the ambassador and told the court, "My lords, I have been forced this day to scour up my rusty old Latin."

I first encountered Elizabeth when I was a child, in an illustrated history of the kings and queens of England. A gift from my mother, the book saw me through every childhood illness; Elizabeth provided a model long before I knew I needed one. I shared this story with Renée when she came in one day brimming with excitement about her thesis topic. Renée is impressed with Elizabeth's courage, but it is the queen's *esprit d'escalier* that has seized her imagination. Finding themselves in a world that prizes the laconic and the physical, cadets retain a great deal of admiration, albeit a sometimes grudging one, for verbal prowess, a quality that finds a more contemporary embodiment in what Maria DiBattista has called the "fast-talking dames" of screwball comedy, a genre to which I introduce them in my film course. In her preface to *Fast-Talking Dames*, DiBattista, recalling her encounter "with a breed of woman, variously shaded in black and white, shimmering with a life more vibrant than any garish Technicolor goddess," explains the source of their appeal:

These women were sexy, but they were sassy, too. Most of all they were sharp and fast with words. They were quick on the uptake and hardly ever downbeat. They seemed to know what to say and when to say it; they were never, except in extreme and exceptional moments, at a loss for words. The American language seemed to be reinventing itself with every word they spoke. They weren't afraid of slang nor shy of the truth. They called things as they saw them, and even if they were wrong—and often they were—they knew how to correct their mistakes, how to find new words for the changed state of their feelings. In their fast and breezy talk seemed to lie the secret of happiness, but also the key to reality.

In the characters brought to life by Claudette Colbert, Irene Dunne, Barbara Stanwyck, Rosalind Russell, and Katharine Hepburn, DiBattista discovers, as I do, an *"empowering* model for American womanhood," and an antidote to the inarticulate female characters—she cites the "dithering maiden" roles offered to Meg Ryan as her prime example—who populate many of today's cinematic comedies.

When the conversation is as fast-paced as it is in *His Girl Friday*, it offers an opportunity for the cadets to discover an interplay between the sexes radically different from what they are used to. When I screen that film for them or introduce them to a marvelous scene full of the double entendre necessitated by the production code—Eva Marie Saint and Cary Grant in the dining car of the *20th Century Limited* in *North by Northwest* or Stanwyck and Fred MacMurray bantering about fast driving and speed limits in *Double Indemnity*—fast-talking women prove a revelation, while the elegance and quick-wittedness of Cary Grant thrills them, accustomed as they are to Stallone and Schwarzenegger. These old films reveal an unexpected alliance between words and cool for students submerged in a world of efficient abbreviation. One cadet has become a Preston Sturges devotee: "I made my roommates watch it with me," he said of *The Lady Eve*, an invitation about which they were uniformly skeptical, "and they all ended up liking it, too."

Calling attention to the romantic comedy as one of Hollywood's great achievements, Stanley Cavell claims that these films take up issues of moral and philosophical weight such as individual responsibility and one's place in society. Moreover, in a phrase borrowed from Milton, he proposes that the ideal of marriage they hold up is "a meet and happy conversation." So often, of course, the conflict in these comedies between a woman's independence and the prospect of marriage or remarriage reflects the cadets' own preoccupations. According to the regulations, cadets cannot be married or have dependents, and there is an unofficial "2 Percent Club" made up of those cadets who end up, quite soon after graduation, marrying the girlfriends or boyfriends they had when they came to West Point. Some cadets get married immediately after graduation, and I mean immediately. One year I attended graduation in the morning and a wedding at the Cadet Chapel that afternoon. If one lieutenant marries another, they must navigate the bureaucracy to be assigned to the same post, and they often make compromises over their branch in order to be together. But the prospect of a life of unsettlingly frequent moves, of extended periods in the field, and of imminent deployment makes the idea of marriage a great comfort to many lieutenants, both men and women, and this at a time when the median age for first marriages in the United States is closer to thirty than to twenty.

His Girl Friday usually sparks the most furious debate about the sexes among cadets. They find provocative DiBattista's conclusion: "Hildy finally gets to go on her honeymoon, to spend her time in the only way that really matters to her—with Walter, who treats her not as a woman but as a newspaperman." The cadets debated whether Hildy had really gained independence; whether she was in fact a triumphant fast-talker, or, as one male cadet put it, a shrew and a bitch. When cadets confront women on-screen who compete in the public arena of the 1930s and 1940s, they cannot help but reflect on their own participation in a community that is in some ways a throwback to an older masculine universe.

At about the same time that we were debating the merits of *His Girl Friday* and other important matters in film class, I was invited to address a volunteer organization of women in Boston that was honoring my mother as its Woman of the Year. When helping students learn to write more effectively, English professors love to repeat the mantra "Know your audience." They don't always know exactly what they mean, but they love to say it. As I contemplated speaking to this audience of bright, generous, and socially conscious women, I somehow felt as if I no longer really knew them, and so I returned to Virginia Woolf's *A Room of One's Own*. A book based on a series of lectures delivered to women's colleges at Cambridge in the 1920s, in the aftermath of World War I, it has become a touchstone for the situation of women speaking to women. At a dinner party a few weeks before I was scheduled to give my talk, a woman mentioned that *A Room of One's Own* was the most important book she had ever read. It is a text that attempts to explain the dearth of women in the British literary tradition. To write, Woolf insists, "a woman must have money and a room of her own." Money, of course, enables independence and the luxury of devoting hours to one's craft, while a room of one's own ensures the necessary privacy.

When I first read Woolf's book at Winsor, I didn't get it—the marginal notes in my old copy tell me that. This was not a world I could conceive. Now, however, I, too, regard it as one of the most important books I have read. It took West Point to make that true, because now I read its account of women's particular deprivations as an allegory for the situation of my students, and not only of the women among them. Privacy is not a value especially respected by an army. If you want to get a roomful of plebes excited, ask them how much privacy they have at West Point. The usual response is "Are you kidding, ma'am?" The more successful the esprit de corps and sense of fellowship—the stronger the unit cohesion that makes armies fight more effectively—the more restricted the sphere of the personal becomes.

I thought this book might help me to reacquaint myself with an audience that seemed to me far stranger than it need have done. One of the things that interests Woolf in that book is the sound of different kinds of talk. And on the day of the luncheon honoring my mother, I was especially aware of the unfamiliar din of women's voices during hors d'oeuvres and mimosas. "I'm exhausted," I whispered to my mother, and we hadn't even sat down to lunch yet. I looked to my father, who seemed aware of but not necessarily uncomfortable at being the only man in the room that day.

When I first heard the name of the award my mother was being given, my initial thought had naturally been the 1942 Hepburn-Tracy film. Like so many of the movies of that period, *Woman of the Year*, directed by George Stevens, explores through fast-talking the rights, roles, and values of the sexes. Katharine Hepburn's Tess Harding is a globe-trotting columnist, while Spencer Tracy's Sam Craig is a sportswriter for the same newspaper. The focus, of course, is all on Harding. Her prominence makes her at once a woman to be reckoned with and a figure of fun: one of Sam's colleagues, on hearing that she has been called "the number two dame in the country" behind Eleanor Roosevelt, quips, "So now they give 'em numbers like public enemies." Tess smokes, wears trousers, and has no time for or interest in domestic life: "How could *I* have a baby?" she demands. Before meeting Sam she didn't seem to feel a lack, but she loves him and agrees to marry him. When their marriage disintegrates, however, Tess is made to see the emptiness of a life without it. When she wins her own prize as "Woman of the Year," Sam observes that people would be very interested to learn that the "Outstanding Woman of the Year isn't a woman at all."

While Sam is frequently embarrassed and emasculated by her success, in the end, to satisfy the sensibilities of the audience, as well as those of the parochial Louis B. Mayer, it is Tess who must be humiliated by going through the farce of trying to make Sam breakfast using the cookbook her mother-in-law had given her as a wedding present. The film ostensibly ends in compromise when Sam explains that he doesn't want to be married to Tess Harding or Mrs. Sam Craig. Instead, he suggests, she might be Tess Harding Craig: "Why," he asks her, "must you go to extremes?" This ending always makes me uncomfortable. What most disturbs me about it is the fact that it is Sam who must set things right. Despite Tess's penetrating intelligence and worldly sophistication, despite the fact that she is clearly a competent professional, she knows herself not at all.

There was a powerful irony in the fact that I found myself speaking on June 6, the anniversary of D-Day, at a luncheon with the theme "A Bridge to Peace." Since 2001, my classroom had felt more like a bridge to war. That war has done much to blur demarcations between home fronts and front lines and between men and women in uniform: IEDs refuse to make nice distinctions. In *Regarding the Pain of Others*, a book prompted in part by the September 11 attacks, Susan Sontag poses a provocative two-part question: "Is there an antidote to the perennial seductiveness of war? And is this a question a woman is more likely to pose than a man? (Probably yes.)" I have thought a lot about Sontag's parenthetical answer because of my own increasing preoccupation with the consequences of war's seduction, but I'm not sure whether I'm asking the same question because I'm a woman or simply because I'm a human being with an emotional and intellectual investment in the people who fight.

In the spring of 2002, I embarked on the *Odyssey* with the plebes. One of the things that surprised me about this group was their impatience with Odysseus, in particular their anger at his sojourn with Calypso, the beautiful nymph who effectively imprisons him on an island for seven years, thus delaying his homecoming. This isn't what good soldiers do, they insisted with a ferocity I couldn't account for, and it isn't what good husbands do. To the extent the poem awakened their sympathies at all, they seemed to be drawn to the hapless young Telemachus, searching for his father, and to Penelope. Odysseus's wife wards off the greedy suitors feeding off Ithaca's treasure in her hall with the ruse of the tapestry. Promising to marry one of them once her weaving is done, she sits alone each night undoing the day's work and thinking about her absent husband.

Given that we were newly at war, it is likely that the cadets would have preferred the exploits of Achilles and Hector to the meandering of the disillusioned Odysseus. They weren't feeling disillusioned then, and their eyes were on the voyage out, not the coming home. If those plebes, some of whom are now no doubt in Iraq, ever think about the *Odyssey* today, perhaps its vision seems more explicable. Back then, they just wanted the poem to end. The war has also placed me in a new relation to Homer's ambivalent epic, for I have awakened, after all, to find myself a woman like Penelope, who sits at home waiting for news of soldiers who have gone to war. I can tell myself I'm not a mother—not a listener and a watcher left behind—I can weave that tapestry every morning, but at night it all unravels to reveal that the fates have conspired to cast me in the most ancient woman's role of all.

4

To Obey or Not to Obey

———◆———

It was Old Redneck Al who introduced me to the riches of Ambrose Bierce. I have before me as I write a 1927 Modern Library edition of Bierce's Civil War stories, *In the Midst of Life*, which Al gave me in the summer of 2002. These tales are full of shrewd, grim insights into military culture. Anthologists usually favor "Incident at Owl Creek Bridge," but I prefer another, even more bizarre, story. "One Kind of Officer" addresses a subject that has been one of the central preoccupations of my professional life for the past decade: the nature of obedience. The story opens in the middle of an argument between two Union officers, General Cameron and Captain Ransome, the commander of an artillery battery, as they prepare for battle: "Captain Ransome," Cameron declares, "it is not permitted to you to know *anything*. It is sufficient that you obey my order."

The longer I teach at West Point, the more fascinated I become by parables of obedience such as this one, for they illuminate the inescapable tension between "knowing" and "obeying" within military culture and the fear of commanders that subordinates who know too much might choose not to obey. Americans have never been in love with obedience. It isn't a virtue that sits easily with the national mythologies of rebellion, liberty, and self-reliance. But at West Point, I find myself in a place where Americans order other

Americans around for a living. How could obedience not become something of an obsession? What, I began to ask myself, did a soldier's willingness—my own willingness, for that matter—to conform her conduct to a specific set of rules and regulations signify? How did the drama of command and obedience shape the personalities of the actors issuing and receiving orders? Where, within a culture that insists on and often receives unquestioning obedience, could one carve out a space for the independence of mind that our national principles encourage, even demand?

People used to laugh when I would tell them I was working on a book about the dynamic of command and obedience in American literature: "Of course you are," they said. In my research for that book, I discovered the degree to which American officers, schooled in the history and customs of European conscript armies, had to adjust their styles of command to their soldiers' expectations about personal liberty and autonomy. At Valley Forge, George Washington found himself in the position of defending the troops' right to send letters of complaint to Congress. Without it, he insisted, "reason is of no use to us; the freedom of Speech may be taken away, and, dumb and silent we may be led, like sheep, to the Slaughter." In the Civil War, the autocratic William Tecumseh Sherman was frustrated by the fact that every private thought he knew best how to win the war. Sherman's friend Grant was less troubled by this independent spirit. Praising the efficiency of Sherman's own army on its celebrated March to the Sea, he said, "He had sixty thousand as good soldiers as ever trod the earth; better than any European soldiers, because they not only worked like a machine but the machine thought. European armies know very little [about] what they are fighting for, and care less."

Grant's model of the thinking machine, as distinct from the shuffling automatons of *Metropolis* or the "perfect machines" Henry David Thoreau pictured blundering to their deaths at Balaklava, helped me to understand more fully the people I taught and to imagine with greater clarity my own potential contribution to the development of future officers. A disciplined, obedient officer is a fine thing, indeed an essential thing for the nation's defense, but a blindly obedient robot who struggles to suppress his own conscience in the face of mounting piles of contrary evidence is an anachronism from old imperial (or more recent fascist) armies: "In the army of the old Austro-Hungarian Empire," the trusty *Army Officer's Guide* explains, "the emperor or empress had a medal that was awarded to officers who, by *disobeying orders*, turned the tide and won important battles. In the U.S. Army, of course, there is no such medal; this sort of judgment, wrapped within a full, disciplined understanding of the legal and moral impact of decisions, is *expected*. It is the essence of the U.S. Army officer corps." Perhaps, then, one could find ways to obey yet still "know" something.

It is a nice theory, but in practice it never feels quite that easy. Plebes, after all, must ask permission even to use the latrine. Moreover, as I know from experience, there is a deep comfort in obeying the orders of an officer in whom you have implicit trust. Obedience is a duty in military culture; war turns it into a sacred duty. Bierce's Civil War stories are replete with examples of that duty's power to deform the individual: Carter Druse, the Union sniper in "A Horseman in the Sky," kills his own father, who happens to be a Confederate, out of a sense of duty. Captain Coulter, an artillery officer, reluctantly obeys the order to fire on his own home in "The Affair at Coulter's Notch." When Coulter is later discovered in the ruined basement cradling his dead wife and child in his arms, he "civilly deliver[s]" to his superior the news that he has killed his own family with the barrage. Then there is the extraordinary Captain Ransome, who, after being reprimanded for presuming to know too much, decides to obey absolutely and pathologically.

Ransome's quarrel with the general, the reader discovers, concerned the position of his artillery battery, the imprudence of which becomes clear later in the story, when Ransome's command ends up firing on a friendly unit. A lieutenant brings the news to Ransome, but the still-seething captain simply parrots the general's earlier rebuke to him: "Lieutenant Price, it is not permitted to you to know *anything*. It is sufficient that you obey my order." When you are insulted by someone more powerful than you are, there is always a temptation to make a hapless subordinate pay for your humiliations. The tormented becomes the tormentor. I've seen the propagation of petty tyrannies and resentments down the chain of command. Sometimes when I encounter a yearling in the fall, I discover that he has become a new man. Now responsible, as a "team leader," for a plebe of his own, he might complain: "Ma'am, my plebe is so messed up, you wouldn't believe it." "Was your own plebe self the model of a modern major general?" "Well, no, ma'am, but I mean this kid is *unbelievably* dorked up. He's just broken, and I've got to spend all my time fixing him." *Fixing*—the term suggests the subtlety of the method.

I introduced Captain Ransome to the plebes, together with that wonderful parable of civil disobedience, Melville's "Bartleby the Scrivener," in the spring of 2003, while the nation watched the case for war in Iraq being made on the news. That spring the entire plebe class also read an anthology of war poetry, Tim O'Brien's *If I Die in a Combat Zone*, and Hemingway's *A Farewell to Arms*. There was an unsettling counterpoint in my head as I prepared to teach Bierce and watched Colin Powell deliver his now notorious briefing on Iraq's weapons of mass destruction to the United Nations Security Council. By the time the ground war began in late March, we had started O'Brien's memoir about Vietnam. O'Brien pulls a Wilfred Owen in this book by repudiating "Horace's old do-or-die aphorism." *Dulce et decorum est* is a sentiment that may have sustained the soldiers of World War II, O'Brien notes, but by the time of Vietnam it had become "an epitaph for the insane."

The plebes had understandable difficulty bending their minds around O'Brien's assertion that he was a "coward" for going to Vietnam to fight a war he didn't believe in instead of running away to Canada. They were, to my discomfort, far more understanding of the ease with which American soldiers grew to hate Vietnamese civilians. When the conversation turned to My Lai, where O'Brien's company fought, "boiling with hate," about a year after the massacre orchestrated by Lieutenant William Calley at My Lai 4, one plebe admitted that he understood how such things happened— come on, he said, they were bound to happen. He was right, of course, as the crimes in Iraq and Guantánamo have shown, and while such a recognition can be a sign of precisely the kind of vigilance required to prevent such incidents, I read it instead as a too-easy surrender to brutality.

Teaching the literature of war to individuals who could imagine themselves fighting a war in progress against a specific, identifiable enemy was still a new experience for me. Our conversations no longer had the air of academic abstraction, and I worried that permitting ambiguous speculation to go unchallenged might have very real consequences. Nevertheless, I think I overreacted. Suddenly a group of cadets I already knew to be humane and thoughtful metamorphosed in my imagination into budding war criminals. Thinking that a careless word or missed opportunity for moral instruction would allow these plebes to become Calleys, I risked crushing all subsequent discussion under the weight of my reproofs. I don't think I trusted them quite enough. It wasn't what I did but the righteous fervor with which I went about it that I now regret: I stopped teaching and started preaching.

Then I took the class to a lecture by Hugh Thompson and Lawrence Colburn, the helicopter pilot and door gunner who put a stop to the My Lai massacre. Thompson, who died in 2006, is today held up (by the military especially) as a hero, but for many years he was vilified for his actions: for turning his guns on fellow Americans and thereby protecting the Vietnamese. When Lieutenant Calley gave the manifestly illegal order to fire on women and children, his soldiers were duty-bound to disobey, but they didn't. Thompson and his helicopter crew, by contrast, chose not simply to refrain from participating in the slaughter but actually to put a stop to it. A colleague's meditations on his own operations in the My Lai area, which I also shared with the plebes, offer one reason why.

Like the plebe whose comment launched my crusade, this officer believes that abuses are bound to happen: "The fear and violence of warfare incite brutal and inhumane actions," he writes, recalling that Calley's platoon "was not an aberrant group of psychotics" but "a cross-section of America." Atrocities, he continues, "*will* occur without strong leadership and focused training." "To the extent that national militaries emphasize adherence to the laws of war," he insists, "these humanitarian principles will influence the actions of soldiers." Military officers, even when operating in exigent circumstances full of necessary compromise, always retain the capacity to exercise moral choice.

Several years later, a few months after those plebes had graduated and pinned on their lieutenant's bars, I was struck during a general's briefing by a slide on which the following headlines appeared: MY LAI, TIGRIS BRIDGE, PAT TILLMAN, HADITHA, ABU GHRAIB. With the exception of the first, of course, all of these incidents occurred in the context of the War on Terror, and they have undermined the credibility of the military and the nation. To this list of scandals we can now add the suspected rape and murder in Mahmudiya. West Point is a leader in the Army community in matters of moral and ethical development: not only does it teach just war theory to all cadets, but it also has a Center for the Professional Military Ethic, which generates material used throughout the Army. The general, like so many officers, was outraged by the succession of scandals and even more by the attempts to cover them up. Now more than ever, he insisted, officers are responsible for speaking out when they witness negligence, abuse, and criminal conduct.

The outspokenness insisted on by the general is inconceivable in the army depicted in Bierce's stories. In "One Kind of Officer" Ransome's grim determination to continue firing on his own side leads to an inevitable confrontation with his superiors after the battle. General Cameron himself is dead and can take no responsibility for his orders regarding the emplacement of the guns, but when another general races to the scene demanding to know why Ransome has been firing on his own men, the captain replies with lethal literalism: "That I am unable to say. In my orders that information was withheld." Asked whether he had known at the time that he was attacking his own side, the captain replies: "I knew that, general. It appeared to me none of my business." With Cameron dead, and the sulking Lieutenant Price in no mood to help his commander out, Ransome resigns himself to a court-martial: "He heard the sound of the earth upon his coffin and . . . the song of a bird above his forgotten grave."

Ransome's aggrieved literalness poses a savagely ironic challenge to those who would hold up absolute obedience as an ideal. Ransome sacrifices himself and his fellow soldiers to his pride, but the reader's response to him is complicated by the fact that he was right all along about the dangerous position of the guns. Ransome's obedience is witting, but it parodies the mindless obedience associated with disastrous consequences. The American Army prides itself on the soldier's ability to recognize immoral or unlawful orders: "I was just doing what I was told" isn't a satisfactory excuse. That is why the abuses of Guantánamo and Abu Ghraib, for example, have been such a crushing betrayal to military professionals, especially, perhaps, to those who teach ethics at West Point.

Captain Ransome's court-martial is occasioned by what could be called a criminal obedience, but it is *dis*obedience that is the more frequent cause of disciplinary action in an army. Disobedience is also immensely appealing, however, while duty isn't always a sufficiently attractive virtue, especially when its performance doesn't culminate in acts of heroic sacrifice. Thus, within an institution explicitly committed to venerating obedience there coexists an enormous weakness for defiance—a slightly illicit love for those who refuse to obey. Appreciating the rebel is one way the American soldier convinces herself of her own liberties. Who are West Point's heroes? Washington? No, his apotheosis as a national father has made us forget that he was a rebel. Grant, Eisenhower, Bradley? They are figures of respect certainly, but all the love goes to the arrogantly defiant MacArthur, the renegade Patton, and above all to the man the historian Bruce Catton calls "the courtly Lee," who defied the iron fist of federal oppression by choosing the native soil of Virginia over the more elusive principle of Union.

Lee was himself occasionally victimized by disobedient subordinates. On the eve of Gettysburg, Jeb Stuart's cavalry was nowhere to be found: "Can you tell me where General Stuart is?" Lee supposedly asked anyone he came upon in Shetter's Woods. "Where on earth is my cavalry?" When Stuart arrived at the end of the battle's second day with a captured Union supply train, Lee was infuriated. Shelby Foote re-creates the scene:

> Reddening at the sight of his chief of cavalry, the gray commander raised one arm in a menacing gesture of exasperation. "General Stuart, where have you been?" he said. "I have not heard a word from you in days, and you the eyes and ears of my army." Jeb wilted under this unfamiliar treatment and became so flustered that he played his trump card at the outset. "I have brought you 125 wagons and their teams, General," he announced: only to have Lee reply, "Yes, General, but they are an impediment to me now." Then suddenly Lee softened. Perhaps it was Stuart's obvious dismay or his somewhat bedraggled appearance after eight days in the saddle; or perhaps it was a recollection of all the

service this young man had done him in the past. At any rate, a witness recalled years later, Lee's manner became one "of great tenderness" as he added: "Let me ask your help now. We will not discuss this longer. Help me fight these people."

Like a father who loves his son too much to punish him, the over-fond Lee forgave Stuart. But running off with the cavalry isn't quite the same thing as taking the car without permission. The impetuous Stuart's death—he was killed in a subsequent engagement by a sniper while fighting in the front lines in his customarily ostentatious plumed hat and silk-lined cape—was of a piece with his earlier behavior and robbed Lee of an experienced commander. It also epitomized the kind of noble gesture to which officers are so partial: Stuart was attempting to defy nothing less than death itself.

Cadet defiance and disobedience manifest themselves in all sorts of informal ways. Dragging the heels of their highly polished shoes, slouching, or refusing to comb the hair they have been made to cut so short helps cadets feel like Bonnie and Clyde. During exam week, various cadets, all of whom are referred to as "Naked Man," have been known to streak across the cadet area. If they are caught, they are disciplined severely. I remember the "primal screams" and mostly unpunished outbursts that accompanied exams at Harvard: at West Point similar outbursts are decried as riots.

There are also institutional mechanisms designed to provide outlets for defiance. Among the sanctioned rituals of misrule is something called the "Sosh Run," an event connected with a course offered by the Department of Social Sciences. The run occurs on the afternoon on which the course's major paper is due. Cadets don outlandish costumes—superheroes, ninjas, rock stars—for the race from the barracks to the department to turn in their papers. One year I watched a bright orange safety barrel making its way along the road. Among the careful planners who have likely labored as much on their costumes as they have on their papers and have calculated their "run" so as to arrive in plenty of time, you can spot the genuinely harried few, usually in their gym uniforms, running madly with papers still warm from the printer in their sweaty paws. The week that leads up to the Army-Navy game likewise has a carnival atmosphere. Cadets devise "spirit missions," one of which, legend has it, involved a plan to abduct the Naval Academy's pet goat. They make clever "spirit videos," the best of which run on the stadium Jumbotron during the game. Perhaps the most important moment of misrule, however, is the senior-class revue, written and performed by cadets. It is called *The 100th Night Show* (the name indicates the number of days that remain until graduation). Throughout the Army, in skits performed at unit Christmas parties and other gatherings, soldiers transgress the normal boundaries by mocking one another and their commanders. These skits, which sometimes involve cross-dressing as well as other forms of travesty, are an integral part of war movies such as *The Bridge on the River Kwai* and *Grand Illusion*. Both of these films have the added frisson of being set in prisoner-of-war camps, where the tension between discipline and rebellion already palpable in military culture acquires even greater force.

The occasional hour, day, or week of misrule punctuates a line-toeing life "too much i' the sun," to borrow Hamlet's phrase. West Point is no prison, even if cadets like to call it one, yet in recent years, against the backdrop of NSA wiretapping and the Patriot Act, the feeling that we are all under constant surveillance has grown more intense, and not just at West Point. When, in the context of the course on London in 2004, the seniors encountered Foucault's theories of disciplinary mechanisms in the Victorian city, they saw a parallel to their own lives. Arthur Conan Doyle's stories and Charles Dickens's *Bleak House* provided fictional accounts of watching and being watched that prompted them to reflect on their own status as disciplined bodies. One senior fond of reminding me that cadets are "national treasures" also knew that valuable things tend to be kept under lock and key. When he read in *Bleak House* of poor Jo the crossing sweeper, who believes that the eyes and ears of the police are always upon him and that Inspector Bucket is "in all manner of places, all at wanst," the cadet announced, "That's us, ma'am, they are always watching us." People who believe themselves under surveillance begin to understand life as a performance.

I don't think I fully recognized the thoroughness of the officer's habituated performance until I found myself, one afternoon in 2006, in the labyrinthine basement of the Metropolitan Opera with a colleague, a major named Todd, and his wife, Missy. Anthony Minghella, whose new production of *Madama Butterfly* was to debut in about a month, wanted the tenor playing the American naval officer Pinkerton, Marcello Giordani, to learn military movement. Thanks to the generosity of a West Point graduate who believes in expanding cadets' cultural horizons, we have organized several trips to the opera, and the administrator at the Met who coordinates these excursions thought that an officer might be able to help Minghella. Todd was an excellent choice. He started his career as an enlisted soldier, which means that he has not only seen his share of drill and ceremony but also performed a wide variety of roles in the Army.

With its gray walls and narrow passages, its mysterious trunks and compartments, the basement of the Met resembles the hold of a ship with disembodied arias eerily floating through it. When we arrived at the rehearsal room, Minghella explained to Todd, "Marcello is a wonderful Italian tenor, but we want him to look like an American military officer. Like you," he added, admiring Todd's posture and calling his own wife, the choreographer Carolyn Choa, over to do the same. "You look like a major general. Are you?" "No," said Todd, "but I am a major." Giordani had wandered over by this time, and he asked Minghella to translate something into English. "Off duty," Minghella said. "Are you off duty?" Giordani asked

Todd, who was wearing casual civilian clothes, as if he couldn't quite believe it. When Todd said that he was, Minghella told him, "But you look fabulous." Then he sent us away to another practice room, where Todd began to teach the amiable tenor, who slouched a bit and stood with his feet slightly turned out and his hands in his pockets, how to "look military."

At first Giordani looked more like a windup toy soldier than a real one as he marched stiffly back and forth across the room trying to imitate Todd's movements. Todd explained that the walk ought to be more natural: "It's a swagger," he said. "Be confident. You're in charge. Walk into a room as if you own it." Giordani still couldn't believe that Todd wasn't on duty: "You are always like this?" he asked. Todd had to think about it for a minute; it all felt so natural to him. "Yes," Missy piped up, "he's always like that, always." Todd is a big, imposing guy with a shaved head and a weight lifter's chest and arms, but he is kind and patient, a good teacher, and before our eyes Giordani gradually turned into a plausible Pinkerton. He was especially good with the hat. He carried it under his left arm and put it crisply on his head, fitting it two fingers' width above the bridge of his nose, just as Todd had instructed. "How do you sit?" "Can you cross your legs?" "How do you kiss a woman? The woman I must kiss is very little." Missy was once again invaluable: "He never slouches. When he reaches down to kiss me—even if I'm sitting down—he always bends from the waist." Todd and Missy demonstrated. "You should feel confident in this department, too," Todd said. "Ah!" said Giordani.

The salute was the trickiest. With his wrist cocked and his palm out, Giordani had the jaunty air of Claude Rains's Captain Renault in *Casablanca*. "No," said Todd, "Americans never show their palms to anyone!" He insisted on this point with unusual vehemence while he taught Giordani how to salute American-style. There are all sorts of explanations for the differences among military salutes. The American salute was probably adopted from the British Royal

Navy. Sailors, whose palms were often dirty from their work, sup-posedly rendered the palm-down salute as a sign of respect for offi-cers. Some mythologists, however, have manufactured a more symbolic justification: Americans never show their palms, the leg-end has it, because we have never surrendered to an enemy. What-ever the case, Giordani finally got it right. At the end of the session, he smiled gratefully and asked Minghella whether Todd could come back for the stage rehearsal, just to make sure he had the walk. Be-fore we said goodbye, Giordani gently asked Todd whether he had been to Iraq. "No," Todd said, "I've been lucky." The two men viewed each other's ways and gifts—their performative selves—with mutual respect and perhaps a renewed self-consciousness about the roles of tenor and soldier, but I got the sense that neither would have changed places.

Cadets, of course, are still learning their parts. One of the most frequent responses I receive when I tell people that I teach at West Point, sometimes from teachers who find the civility of their own students lacking, is that my students must be, if nothing else, ex-tremely polite and well behaved. Indeed, to the untrained ear, they all sound like the Earl of Chesterfield, solicitous to the end, insist-ing from his deathbed that his visitor be offered a chair. Cadets are polite—polite with a vengeance—and they perform courtesy ex-pertly. Doors swing open for you; packages and books are whisked out of your hands; out of the mouths of plebes come sentences prefaced, punctuated, and terminated with volleys of "ma'ams." The observance of military courtesy is predicated on a belief in the fundamental value of civility. As the *Army Officer's Guide* puts it, "Courtesy is essential in human relationships. It stimulates the harmonious association of individuals, smoothes the conduct of affairs, and adds a welcome tone to all manner of human contacts, civilian as well as military . . . *An officer is expected to be a lady or a gentleman, and ladies and gentlemen have been defined as persons who are never intentionally rude.*" Such courtesies also reinforce the hierarchy that structures military culture. They are expressions that reveal exactly where everyone rates in the grand scheme and signal in the speaker an awareness of her place. Reflective of a deeper system of values, they are perhaps best described by the French *moeurs*, a word that embraces both manners and morals and that might be construed as external tokens of the principles by which one human being regards, trusts, or values another.

There is another way to interpret such courtesies, however; Thomas Hobbes refers to those behaviors that might be internalized by an automaton—"how one man should salute another, or how a man should wash his mouth, or pick his teeth before company, and such other points"—as "small morals." These manners, he suggests, should not be taken as definitive proof of any deeper human decency. Upon General Cameron's departure, Bierce tells us, Ransome, still smarting under his rebuke, salutes "slowly, gravely, and with extreme formality." And it is at this point in the story that Bierce articulates one of the great truths of military culture: "One acquainted with the niceties of military etiquette would have said that by his manner he attested a sense of the rebuke that he had incurred. It is one of the important uses of civility to signify resentment." Military etiquette sometimes signifies the resentful obverse of what it seems; at other times, it simply reveals effective Pavlovian conditioning. Forms and formulas are deeply ingrained in the West Point graduate, but it was one of my colleagues' wives who warned me not to make too much of her husband's manners: "Everyone thinks he's so polite, but he's just well trained."

There is a confused and confusing relationship between a soldier's surface courtesies and inner life. This isn't to say that soldiers are deliberately insincere. On some level they emphatically mean what they say. To the uninitiated, however, they have funny ways of talking. There is a tendency toward platitudes and superlatives meant to assuage (or preempt) discontent and to rally the troops. (Members of units refer to events designed to boost their morale as "mandatory fun.") There is also what could be called a relentless optimism. Officers, cadets, and Army civilians not infrequently thank me "for my time" and for what I do "every single day." Officers exhort others to "know what right looks like"; soldiers strive for the "band of excellence"; and the adjectives *world-class* and *premier* crop up in many a conversation. Soldiers want everyone to be "on the same sheet of music," a phrase I first heard from a colonel interested in the status of a star basketball player whose skills of composition didn't measure up to her jump shot: "I just want to make sure," he said, "that we're on the same sheet of music. I know," he thought to add, "that I'm preaching to the choir." Amen.

To anyone whose business is language, the reflexive usages of military culture are a subject of deep fascination. My own conversations and e-mails are now often full of abbreviations and argot: I can write memos that conform to the standards outlined in Army Regulation 25-50: Preparing and Managing Correspondence. I can recite the phonetic alphabet and have learned how to render my last name as SIERRA ALPHA MIKE ECHO TANGO. I've even been known to tell my own mother to meet me at 1800 instead of 6:00 p.m. But if certain locutions and inelegant abbreviations have long ceased grating on my ears, I still cannot brook the most pervasive linguistic offense of all: *hooah!* The origins of this exclamation, sometimes spelled *hoo-ah* or *huah*, are shrouded in mystery. Some say it dates to World War II or to Vietnam, while others claim it was borrowed from Russian, Turkish, or Australian English. Whatever *hooah's* actual derivation, it is generally interpreted as an affirmative expression of the warrior spirit.

The exclamation's manic repetition by Al Pacino's character in *Scent of a Woman* ushered it into the lexicon of popular culture. Whenever I hear a *hooah* in class, where it is sometimes accompanied by what is called "an elbow drop" (the banging of an arm on the desk that is meant to supplement verbal enthusiasm), I hear the Dies Irae, the last gasp of the inarticulate, the herald of a wordless end. *Hooah* is only the latest incarnation of a military inclination toward enthusiastic response that Tolstoy captures in his depiction of the czar reviewing the troops before the battle of Austerlitz in *War and Peace*:

> "Hurrah! Hurrah! Hurrah!" thundered on all sides, and one regiment after another greet the Tsar with the strains of the march, then hurrah! . . . then the march, and again hurrah! and hurrah! which growing stronger and fuller, blended into a deafening roar . . .
>
> There was but one desire in all: under the Emperor's leadership to face the enemy as soon as possible. Under the command of the Emperor himself they would not fail to conquer any one whatever: so thought Rostov and most of the officers after the review.
>
> After the review they all felt more certain of victory than they could have been after two decisive victories.

All of this exhausting enthusiasm, an almost ecstatic zeal, proved useless when the Russian Army broke and ran only days later. In the Civil War, Captain Ransome's war, General Sherman expressed his frustration with similar expressions of mindless enthusiasm after he watched the Union rout at first Bull Run. When President Lincoln subsequently paid a visit to his camp, Sherman told him that he needed "cool, thoughtful, hard-fighting soldiers—no more hurrahing, no more humbug."

I have found that a West Point classroom needs few explicit rules to ensure the maintenance of good order, general civility, and intellectual rigor. But one day I found it necessary to prohibit *hooah*. "No more *hooahs*," I announced funereally. "The next person who utters *hooah* during class will be asked to leave." "But why, ma'am?" demanded my enthusiastic plebes. "What's wrong with *hooah*?" I then asked them what they thought the word really meant. That posed quite a problem, for none of them could dispute my claim that its all-purpose applicability has rendered it essentially meaningless. At a briefing I once heard a colonel ask an audience of cadets whether there were any jumpmasters among them. This was unlikely, even though it was just possible that a cadet with prior enlisted service could have earned this parachute badge before coming to West Point. But at the mention of the word *jumpmaster*, the colonel heard a loud *hooah* from somewhere in the crowd. "Where?" he asked excitedly. "Where's the jumpmaster?" When he received no response, he looked perplexed: "Someone said *hooah*. Doesn't that mean *yes*?" No response. "What *does* it mean?" Disappointed, he carried on with the briefing, which was punctuated several more times by shouts of "Hooah" from the crowd.

Hooah, that everlasting *nay*, resounds throughout the Army. Adam wrote to say that he was deluged at flight school: "I think I have determined that the word 'Hooah' is the rally cry of all green-clad grade-three thinkers. I really wish it would go away. Unfortunately, it seems to be a staple of the cavalry community to which I now belong. With any luck, I can remove it from the vocabularies of the soldiers within my small sphere of influence. It's something to shoot for at least." In an English class the replacement of words by grunts, no matter how impassioned and heartfelt, seems especially bad form: "When I ask you at the end of the hour whether you can hear the difference between iambic and trochaic meter, 'Hooah, ma'am!' just isn't going to cut it." Once, as penance for his unruly tongue, a cadet wrote a fable about the origins of the wicked "Hooah Monster," the Pandora of his new mythology (and mine).

A full year after the ban, a cadet entered class on the first day and said, "You're the one who doesn't like *hooah*, right, ma'am?" "Correct." "Is there ever a time we can say it to you?" he asked hopefully. "Yes," I replied. "If you see me engaged in any athletic activity, you can feel free to shout it out." For it's true, I have been glad for a *hooah* precisely once: running up the interminable hill that leads to one of the gates at West Point in the early hours of a snowstorm, I met an officer who had already completed the climb coasting downhill: "Hooah!" he shouted from the other side of the street, and the warm feeling of solidarity got me up the snowy hill in record time. One day, the eager cadet who had prompted this revelation looked especially disappointed when he arrived in class. "Ma'am," he said, "when I saw you at the gym this morning, I could have said the word, right? I forgot. I guess I missed my chance."

Cadets also learn early on the ironic potential of *hooah* and other ritual expressions. Those ubiquitous "Yes, ma'ams" that seem to the outsider like hypercourtesy can in truth mean anything from "Thank you, ma'am, right away" to "Fuck you, ma'am, and the horse you rode in on." I've heard both and a great deal in between. The differences are as subtle as Mandarin tones.

In 1999, a few years after arriving at West Point, I was faced with a section of rambunctious plebes, many of whom were athletes. Plebes who play on teams are allowed to interact in more normal ways with their older teammates; as a result, they tend to be somewhat less intimidated than their peers by the system. I like jocks: they are often bright and always lively, but they can also be immature and self-important. When you can harness their energy, such classes are immensely enjoyable and satisfying. But this section seemed to be filled with every wiseass in the class, and they were determined to derail my attempts to focus them on the material. The "chemistry" on this team was all wrong: the large, loud cadets intimidated the smaller, serious ones, who, in turn, resented the clowns to the right and the left. The lone woman in the section held her own but seemed initially content to sit back and roll her eyes at the juvenile delinquents with whom she found herself.

There have been only a few classes I haven't in some way enjoyed at West Point. I dreaded going to this class. The prospect of that after-lunch day-care session was enough to ruin the whole morning. As classes at West Point are taught on an every-other-day schedule, rather than on the Monday, Wednesday/Tuesday, Thursday split or weekly basis common to most colleges and universities, you see the same class twice or three times in any given week. That's a lot of time to spend with obnoxious strangers, a feeling I'm sure the cadets shared when they contemplated seeing me every other afternoon. I became so disgusted that one day I handed the cadet in charge a new seating chart and told him to implement it.

Classes at West Point are technically military formations: a cadet named the "section marcher" takes the roll, calls the section to attention, and renders a report and a salute at the beginning of the hour. This was one of the customs that initially gave me pause. Among the preoccupations of many new teachers is "the entrance." The moment and manner of arrival, I felt, would set the tone for the rest of the class, and I didn't know how I was going to repair the atmospheric damage inflicted by the cadets suddenly standing up en masse while one of them saluted me and shouted that all were present. Overeager plebes have the habit of calling attention at the stroke of the clock whether or not you've given them the signal: when you are elbow-deep in chalk dust, perched on a chair adjusting the overhead projector, or on your knees behind the computer trying to find out why it won't work. Like so many other customs, however, this practice that once seemed so intrusive has become almost invisible to me; I learned, furthermore, to take advantage of the fact that there is a cadet ready and waiting to take charge of things.

I would return, I told the troublemakers' section marcher, once he finished rearranging everyone. I had separated the oversize football players—two were now exiled to the ends of rows, while two more were sandwiched in the cramped middle with small, resentful kids on either side. Now when the jocks wanted to communicate with one another, they actually had to gesticulate or shout across the room, something they weren't quite willing to do. When I returned, I overheard one of the more obstreperous, Daniel, who turned out to be the linchpin of the class, saying, "We must have been really bad to bring her to this. A seating chart? That's like junior high." We were a quarter of the way through the semester by this point, and I had succeeded at least in reducing the noise level. Once they actually listened to one another, the cadets became more thoughtful and patient. They began to want to hear more about someone else's interpretation, and to offer their own by way of rebuttal. The considerable energy they had wasted in goofing off was now being applied to the task at hand. They didn't all become Lionel Trillings overnight, but they gave a good-faith effort to learn new concepts and to understand difficult texts.

I didn't notice the transformation right away. I was already conditioned to gird myself for the worst, and it took me several more weeks to realize that I was starting to have a lot of fun every other afternoon. While the energy of the students in my other classes started to flag, the out-of-control men-children (and one woman) began to get interested and interesting. Reciting poetry in front of one another certainly helped take the starch out of a few. Their discomfort with the ambiguities of literary language, which had provoked much of their resistance in the first place, faded away. They became more disciplined thinkers and writers, while I became more adroit at praising linemen for a sensitive reading of Emily Dickinson or a nuanced insight into *Antony and Cleopatra* without provoking embarrassment. One day near the end of the semester, they got me laughing about something until I couldn't stop. I lost it, and as the tears rolled down my face, Daniel clapped his hands and cried, "We did it! We finally broke her." The ship of fools had turned around. Whenever I saw Daniel and his classmates later in their West Point careers, our conversation would always turn to that hopeless class that had made such an improbable recovery.

Those plebes taught me something about the vagaries of obedience, and they also helped me to become enamored of rebels, especially rebels such as Andy. Scion of a military family, with a general for a father, Andy knows better than most what it means to obey. An American politics major and the best writer I've ever taught, he was a firecracker sent my way by a friend who taught political science. Working on a senior thesis on Tocqueville and Emerson, Andy decided he ought to take a course on American literature, and he ended up enrolling in a second course with me on poetry. One day Andy was scheduled to give a presentation on Thoreau's *Civil Disobedience*, but he sent his paper in with a classmate and didn't make his appearance until near the end of the hour.

One does not blithely skip class at West Point. If they are absent without an excuse or even late, cadets pay for the infraction with what are called "hours." You might remember Errol Flynn's George Custer, marching back and forth with his rifle as punishment for some misdemeanor at the beginning of *They Died with Their Boots On*. Cadets can still be found marching back and forth "on the area," and they describe it as a mind-numbing experience. I've put more than a few of them there. "How was your weekend?" I asked Joey one Monday morning. "Well," he said impishly and without resentment, "I spent most of it walking hours because I was late for your class last week." And thus one finds oneself connected—implicated—in strange ways with different facets of the cadet experience. One doesn't simply teach English; there is a convoluted chain of causes and effects. Wallace Stevens supposedly composed his poetry while walking to work. For some cadet out there, the fascinating rhythms of Stevens's "The Idea of Order at Key West" or Marlowe's "mighty line" of iambic pentameter might be forever linked to the experience of wearing through the soles of her shoes "on the area."

In his absence, I read Andy's paper, an eloquent parody of Thoreau's argument that reproduced its twists and turns with painstaking fidelity: in short, Andy refused to subject himself to my arbitrary tyranny by writing the essay I had assigned. Instead he submitted a manifesto on civil disobedience, and, like Thoreau condemned to the Concord Jail for a night, Andy proved willing to incur the state's punishment for his rebellion. It was a masterstroke that took guts, and it was exquisitely written, pitch-perfect. I don't think every professor at West Point would have been similarly delighted by this paean to disobedience, its elegance notwithstanding, and I admit to being initially disconcerted by his failure to appear, until I read the paper. This was an intellectual exercise not a field exercise, and I knew that Andy could recognize the difference. Not to acknowledge the paper's brilliance—to interpret the gesture as menacingly insubordinate—would have been to demonstrate a remarkable absence of humor and common sense. Andy wasn't mocking the entire system, but his mastery of Thoreau brought into focus the dynamics of surrendering obedience.

If it is true that there would be no freedom without the knowledge of slavery, no virtue without the knowledge of sin, so, too, would there be no obedience worth the name without an appreciation of disobedience. In Iraq—it came as no surprise to me—Andy was strictly a law-and-order man. He was there at the beginning of the invasion, stayed during his first deployment through the president's "mission accomplished" moment on the USS *Abraham Lincoln* on May 1, 2003, and returned for a short deployment in 2005. In the letters we traded, I heard a young man coming to terms with a sometimes ambiguous mission.

Unlike many soldiers in Iraq, Andy had no e-mail access, and our correspondence had a distinctly old-fashioned feel. Anticipating a shortage of paper, he planned ahead by taking a lot of blank notebooks to Iraq. Writing, short stories but especially poetry, provided an escape and "something to fuss over" whenever he was not conducting police patrols and raids, building desks for schoolchildren, or defusing land mines. Andy's letters are funny and finely crafted, just as his essays had been: "The Fertile Crescent," he reports in one, "is fertile compared to the desert, but not compared to, say, France or Ohio. In this way I think it is a misnomer." In another, he meditates like some mad lexicographer for pages on the word *gasket*, which inexplicably pops into his head one morning. Soon, however, Andy ran out of both writing paper and books: he had more time for both in Iraq than he did back home. His family kept sending him new supplies, and I mailed a collection of Aeschylus, a short story anthology, and several months' worth of *Poetry*, along with a writing journal that would fit in a cargo pocket.

After receiving the first carton, Andy wrote, "I don't know if the soldiers in my platoon will want to pass around *Poetry* in the same enthusiastic way they pass around other magazines, but I will surely try to get them started." Perhaps, I replied, he would forge an entire platoon of warrior-poets. Remembering a newspaper story about the desert being littered with water bottles and the wrappers from meals ready to eat (MREs) after the First Gulf War, I shared with him my fantasy that in this war, along with the usual detritus, the desert will swallow up a few books that might resurface one day to puzzle an archaeologist.

The next letter was smudged, dirty, and water-stained. Andy's unit had moved. For a time they guarded weapons stockpiles, and then they shifted to western Iraq to patrol the porous Syrian and Jordanian borders. The next few letters were alternately farcical and dispirited. In one he sent drafts of poems with the caveat "The author wishes to reiterate that these are the musings of a man who has little else to do with his time than sit around." Then one day he wrote, "The Iraqi people have grown tired of waiting for improvements to public infrastructure, tired of unemployment, and tired of military occupation, so it seems."

Andy divided the population into two categories: "the violent and the listless." I tried to divert him with lines from unnamed poems. Correctly identifying a quotation from Wallace Stevens, his favorite, he added, "I wish I had brought my collected Stevens along, but I didn't want to get it dirty. Alas." So I sent him a paperback that would take some abuse, unlike the expensive cloth edition he left at home. The Stevens proved "a great poetic oasis in the desert. Its pages are a little sand-worn by now, but that was the whole point, wasn't it?" Underneath the humor, the urgency came through: "It's a good thing I have lots of books, because reading is the only bearable alternative to boredom other than sleep, which in itself becomes boring after many hours." Stevens seemed to give Andy a way of imposing discipline on his "dust-infused mind." In "The Idea of Order at Key West" Stevens writes of the "Blessed rage for order." It is a phrase that captures the military love of form and measure: squared corners, straight gig lines, synchronized hands and feet, everything "dress right dress." What Andy confronted in Iraq had none of this soothing regularity, and in Stevens he found someone else wrestling with a language that might shape unruly experience.

Not every shipment contained heady poetry: I also sent James M. Cain's *Double Indemnity* and J. M. Coetzee's *Waiting for the Barbarians*. Cain turned out to be as big a hit with Andy's platoon, which evidently had a taste for the hard-boiled, as he had been with my father in the Second World War. Coetzee, however, seemed to make a particular impression on Andy, who read it while stationed in the Sunni Triangle, at Habbaniyah. He credits me in one of his letters with careful planning—with not choosing this book "at random" from the shelves—but I can't claim that it received any more thought than the other selections. Habbaniyah, he reported elsewhere, is the site of a long-abandoned air base built by the British after the First World War. Across the highway sits another more modern base, "where the runways have been bombed neatly at the intersections" and half-buried planes, which "survived our Shock and Awe" but not the looters, "scatter the vast landscape [like] giant mechanical skeletons." Andy was confronted simultaneously with the dynamics of invasion and with traces of the complex imperial history that preceded American occupation. Given the view from Habbaniyah, he found Coetzee's "comments on the will and fate of

'Empire'" especially provocative. One letter ended with a long quotation from the novel about "the submerged" imperial "mind" and its telltale "pyramids of bones, acres of desolation."

On the ground in Iraq, Andy had been able to keep in view not only his mission and the welfare of his soldiers but also the need for fair and just treatment of the civilian population. He posed honest, vexing questions to himself and worked through mature, judicious responses. The experience left him with a desire to repair the damage done by detainee abuse and other misdeeds and motivated his decision to apply to the Army's law school program. He believes that we need new laws to suit new kinds of engagements, and he has cultivated the analytic skills and creativity that will enable him to provide guidance for the next generation of soldiers. He wants to ensure that the laws of war followed by our military will continue, whatever the murky wars in which we find ourselves, to be informed by humanitarian principles.

Oliver Wendell Holmes once told a meeting of his old Civil War regiment, "A great trial in your youth made you different—made all of us different from what we could have been without it." Great trials always make people different what from they would have been; sometimes, as in Andy's case, they make them better, stronger, more resilient. At a time when complicated missions and counterinsurgency continue to blur the lines between combatants and noncombatants, the Army needs principled people who aren't shy about expressing their opinions, and no one could accuse Andy of being diffident—of remaining silent, like Captain Ransome, when he ought to speak up.

Officers such as Andy, who was selected to be the editor in chief of his law review, vindicate the hopes of the deeply ambivalent and mistrustful Adams and Jefferson that West Point could effectively educate young men into republican principles (and—this was important to the founders—out of their apparent affinity for the absolutism of kings). About the courage of Continental Army officers,

Adams "had no doubt," but he found them lacking in the kind of knowledge needed by the free citizen of a republic—"I was too well informed that most of the officers were deficient in reading: and I wished to turn the Minds of such as were capable of it, to that great Source of Information." The military preoccupation with surfaces led Adams to wonder about the depth of thought of which soldiers were capable. The possible disjunction between a scrubbed, pressed, and shined exterior and an ambiguous character within worries thoughtful cadets and officers attuned to the nuances of seeming and being just as it did the Academy's civilian founders. Adams regarded military custom itself as inimical to republican virtue, and he professed not to understand it. On a diplomatic mission to Lord Howe in 1776, he beheld two lines of grenadiers "looking as fierce as ten furies, and making all the Grimaces and Gestures and motions of their Musquets with Bayonets fixed, which I suppose military Etiquette requires but which We neither understood nor regarded."

Adams's belief in the pernicious "dazzle" of military glory was typical of late-eighteenth-century republican attitudes toward standing armies. Observing the perfect manners of officers, Mary Wollstonecraft drew a provocative analogy between soldiers and women in A Vindication of the Rights of Woman. Arguing that women and soldiers share a weakness owing to their acquisition of manners before morals and resulting in their blind submission to authority, Wollstonecraft perceived nothing more at odds with the rightful exercise of citizenship than absolute obedience: "If they [soldiers] have any sense, it is a kind of instinctive glance, that catches proportions, and decides with respect to manners; but fails when arguments are to be pursued below the surface, or opinions analyzed." According to Wollstonecraft, the myopic soldier never penetrates beneath the physical surface—polished boots, creased uniforms, shining swords, waxed mustaches, impeccable manners— to the moral pith of things. Inordinately concerned with his body as a sexual and an athletic asset, Wollstonecraft's officer never gets much beyond the dramatic surface of his own potential heroism.

In *Civil Disobedience*, Henry David Thoreau would recruit the Enlightenment image of the soldier as blindly obedient automaton for his argument about antebellum America's "undue respect for law." From the moral freedom of his prison cell, to which he was condemned for not paying his poll tax in protest against the Mexican War, Thoreau envisioned the political and moral enslavement of "a file of soldiers, colonel, captain, corporal, privates, powder-monkeys and all, marching in admirable order over hill and dale to the wars, against their wills, aye, against their common sense and consciences, which makes it very steep marching indeed." "Visit the Navy Yard, and behold a marine," Thoreau suggested, "such a man as an American government can make, or such as it can make a man with its black arts, a mere shadow and reminiscence of humanity." The notion that obedience dehumanizes those who render it is a popular cry of the philosophers of radical individualism, such as Thoreau, who are so important to America's myth of itself. The rebellious counterculture of the 1960s reanimated Thoreau's attitudes and helped to make the American soldier come to seem a rather strange and exotic creature to many civilians: an anachronistic conformist in a more knowing modern world or Huntington's Spartan lost in Babylon.

Every so often, however, the most outrageous, uncompromising individualists find themselves in the midst of Sparta. In 2003, while the plebes and I wrestled with O'Brien and Hemingway, one of West Point's arch-rebels was moving across the Iraqi desert with his unit. Max, who wrote and directed his senior-class revue, is the cadet I know who has come closest to rebelling his way right out of West Point without actually getting "separated," as expulsion is called. For his offense he received 120 hours on the area and was sentenced to room restriction—West Point's version of solitary confinement—which meant that when Max wasn't in class, at a meal, or walking through the soles of his shoes on the area, he was in his room. He finished his hours only just in time to graduate. I have noted that *The 100th Night Show* provides a sanctioned outlet for relatively harmless transgression. What had Max done to bring down the wrath of the administration? To get the Corps revved up for the show, Max made a very crude joke (comparing the painful experience of West Point to a particular sex act) in the Mess Hall one day at lunch in front of several senior officers and a few VIPs who just happened to be there. It was a stupid thing to do, and Max knew it. This was the last shot he fired in a longer battle with his censors, who had repeatedly told him to modify his script.

Before his senior-year calamity, Max had revealed his cleverness with spirit videos such as *Temptation Barracks*, a riff on the then-popular television show *Temptation Island*. He took drama and Shakespeare classes with me, but his real love was always film, and I still remember the montage he edited to illustrate the dynamics of on-screen violence. That connection between violence and cinema would come back to him years later in the middle of the desert. To some it may have seemed that Max struck something of a Brando pose, but the cool outsider was at his impassioned best when he had the opportunity to show his encyclopedic knowledge of cinema. During one of the conversations we used to have after class, I learned of his ambition to make movies. Max had started to create short films in junior high to entertain his friends, and before coming to West Point, as an enlisted soldier with the Rangers, he used to amuse his comrades with lines from movies such as *Rambo*, *Conan the Barbarian*, *Patton*, *Heartbreak Ridge*, and *The Karate Kid*. At West Point he arranged a screening of *Jaws* for his cadet company in the swimming pool, and he put the audience in the pool.

In Max's rough-and-tumble childhood, comic books and movies were his lifeline: he was a Brooklyn Truffaut. *Casablanca* is his favorite film. It used to be his test for potential girlfriends. If they didn't get it, the relationship was over. Not surprisingly, he has an abiding love of the gangster genre. I'm not talking Coppola and Scorsese; he has memorized large chunks of *Little Caesar* and *The Public Enemy*. We share this love of films. For me they were the natural companions of the only child in the house, for him a "saving grace" and "an escapist balm" in a household of drinking, infidelity, and daily "knock-down, drag-out fights" between his parents. As he prepared to apply to film school, he articulated his relationship to the movies and described a cinematic pantheon filled with loners, outsiders, and radical individualists who find themselves at war with the system:

> In junior high and high school, movies evolved from my babysitters to my instructors. I learned self-sacrifice from both Humphrey Bogart in *Casablanca* and James Cagney in *The Roaring Twenties*. Clint Eastwood, Steve McQueen, and John Wayne taught me to be tough. Paul Newman taught me that it's okay to have nothing, because "sometimes nothin' can be a real cool hand."

In the Army, Max's West Point reputation followed him. He had become a legend. Strangers greeted him with "Are you the guy . . . ?" When he got to Iraq, he found himself in demand by his fellow platoon leaders because they knew he could make troops laugh. In addition to his stand-up routines, Max, armed with an enormous collection of DVDs and a portable player, rigged up a movie screen, scrounged some speakers, and borrowed a projector from Battalion Headquarters to create the "dog-faced soldier drive-in movie theater, located just on the other side of the Euphrates River . . . We were proud of it."

When I asked him how he came to have all those movies, Max told me that his deployment priority list included "weapon, body armor, holy water, cigars, portable DVD player, hundreds and hundreds of DVD's." He used to show one black-and-white film followed by a contemporary blockbuster. He wanted to entertain, but he wasn't going to lose the opportunity to give his audience a little taste of Hollywood history: "As time progressed and other units learned of what we were doing," he explained, "different unit commanders began coordinating 'movie nights' so their soldiers could visit our base camp in order to watch a movie or two." One day Max learned that "a high-ranking general" wanted him "to report to his office right away." It is unusual for lieutenants to be summoned in this way: "So off I went not knowing what he wanted. Well, long story short, I report to him," Max recounted, "and all he wanted was to go through my movie collection because he 'heard I had some good ones.' He still owes me three or four movies that he 'borrowed' and I never saw again."

Max seized the opportunity to become the David O. Selznick of Iraq only after surviving the initial ground war. Days into the invasion, as an officer in the 3rd Infantry Division and a leader of his battalion's Quick Reaction Force, Max had engaged the enemy for the first time on an overnight mission to protect the perimeter. Here's how he tells the story:

> Using his Night Vision Goggles (NVG's), one of my soldiers spotted a platoon-sized element of enemy infantry slowly advancing towards our perimeter. Looking through my own NVG's to confirm my soldier's observation, the hair on the back of my neck stood up. My heart began to pound uncontrollably. And all I could think of—the only thought that came to mind at that particular moment in which life and death hung in the balance—was "*Jacob's Ladder* is the most realistic war movie of all time." That's right. Not, "God protect us." Not, "What should I tell my soldiers to do?" Nope, my only thought was, "*Jacob's Ladder* is the most realistic war movie of all time." Quickly realizing this was neither the

time nor the place for a cinematic analogy, I forced it to the back of my mind. I then quickly confirmed identification of the enemy and contacted my higher headquarters on the battalion frequency, letting them know what was about to take place. I placed a second radio message to a friendly nearby Bradley unit, knowing that, as an armored unit, they'd stand a much better chance than my small patrol did of fighting against a superior number of dismounted infantry. And while we were waiting for the local Cavalry to arrive . . . , we engaged the enemy with my Humvee's M-2 .50 caliber machine gun. By morning, I had survived my first enemy engagement. But more important than my own survival, I hadn't lost a single friendly soldier in the firefight.

It was while sitting on his HMMWV the next morning that Max allowed his thoughts to return to *Jacob's Ladder*, the 1990 film directed by Adrian Lyne in which Tim Robbins plays a Vietnam veteran subjected to psychotropic drug experiments. When, "a lifetime ago," an officer at West Point had described it to him as "the most realistic war movie ever made," Max had been skeptical. Combat made him see "the truth" of this assessment:

The uneasiness, fear, anxiety, confusion, and absolute horror felt just before fighting for one's life can be "summed up" only as follows: watch a horror movie, and by a horror movie, I mean the scariest movie you've ever seen. Watch it alone, and watch it in complete darkness. Now just when you positively know something horrible is about to happen or jump out and scare the absolute hell out of you, put your life on pause. Hold onto that feeling and stay at that insanely heightened state of your senses. Chaos is about to ensue, and there's not a thing you can do to stop it. That's what being in a war zone feels like.

Atop that HMMWV Max also saw clearly for the first time that he had a choice. He had what it took to be a successful career soldier: he could continue to serve, or he could pursue the thing that meant most to him—the thing that helped him to explain the world he saw and the emotions he felt, the thing that helped him to make his soldiers' lives just a bit easier—film. At that moment Max realized, "there was only one thing that I *wanted* to do. Only one thing I felt *compelled* to do. Only one thing I *needed* to do: become a filmmaker."

I learned all of this only after Max got back from Iraq. On leaving West Point, he had promised to send me a copy of his favorite movie, *The Roaring Twenties*. About four years later a DVD arrived in the mail with the message "A promise is a promise." We have carried on a correspondence ever since. An unconventional cadet like Max can bring unusual gifts and energy to the Army, but he also tends to become restless with military life. Max's screenplays are wonderfully inventive, and he has not lost his affinity for gangsters, but now his gangsters operate in a world of supernatural influences: devils that talk like Tarantino and angels that fight like Schwarzenegger. War shapes his artistic vision in subtle ways.

Max and his Harley have recently made their way to Florida State, where he has started to realize his screenplays on film. Leaving the Army and its steady paycheck means that he will no longer be able to help his two younger brothers out whenever they need his assistance. They do get cameos in his short films, however. It also means that he carries, as so many who leave the Army do, the guilty feeling of having abandoned the soldiers with whom he has served. A final conversation with one officer, who, though he had not been to Iraq, saw fit to accuse Max of disloyalty and cowardice, didn't make his departure any smoother. But Max has seen his elephant, heard his owl, and been to the other side of the mountain. Over there, he discovered that he owes something to himself as well as to his country. Now he is a rebel *with* a cause.

5

Bibles, Lots of Bibles

◆

On that first visit to West Point in 1996, sitting next to the mysterious elephant-foot planter in the Colonel's office, I began to imagine that such a talisman might serve the larger than life the way a rabbit's foot does the rest of us. Soldiers who have "seen the elephant" don't have to tell war stories; it is enough for the rest of us simply to know they have lived them. Of course, some soldiers thrive on reliving the day of battle. Their cinematic model might be *The Four Feathers'* General Faversham, who ritually reenacts Balaklava by deploying ranks of after-dinner walnuts along the table against a thin red line of port. The Colonel, however, resisted the temptation to strip his sleeves and show his scars. In fact, he never told war stories per se; his narratives were always oblique.

Once, returning to Central America from the United States, he had concealed an anniversary gift from his wife, a beagle puppy (Humbert Humbert), in a duffel bag under the seat. While waiting for his plane in the airport, he had stared at an enormous sign illustrating contraband items on which the picture of a beagle assisted travelers having trouble with the word *Animals*. On arrival in Panama, he saved Humbert from a stint in quarantine by simply walking through baggage inspection and hailing a taxi. Humbert ended his days joyfully at Boys Town of Costa Rica. Recently returned to Saigon from some remote outpost in Vietnam, the Colonel had been invited to a python's daily feeding, a summons he felt he couldn't decline. Watching in silence as a rat made its way through the guileless serpent, he smiled as he thought of the soufflé he would eat that night on the lost French frontier, "after months," he mused, of "not eating well."

In his storytelling the Colonel reminds me of Lieutenant Ford, the protagonist of Henry James's "The Story of a Year." Ford, on a walk with the woman he will ask to marry him, looks up at the clouds to discover "the semblance of a battle" and to find in their "opposing squadrons" "an allegory . . . of the war." It was in Vietnam that the Colonel had first turned to a steady diet of James. As this is a man who knew where to find the best French food in Saigon, I can easily conjure him relishing the machinations of Gilbert Osmond and Madame Merle in Southeast Asia. He reported finding these books in cartons full of Bibles—"lots of Bibles"—sent either by an innocent or by someone possessed of an exquisite sense of humor. I often think of him in Vietnam coming to terms with James: the beast in the jungle indeed.

The Colonel was part of a generation of officers—Colin Powell is perhaps its most visibly influential member—who gave a distinct character to the post-Vietnam army. He helped to design the plan for the all-volunteer force that emerged when the draft ended in 1973. When I first arrived at West Point, many of the senior colonels there had served in Vietnam. They had the presence and poise won of experience and wore their authority gracefully and easily. Several also possessed a stoic restraint I associated with the betrayal of their professional principles and ideals by the protracted conflict in Southeast Asia and by the lies that fueled it. Their commitment to military service had miraculously survived that betrayal, and they had chosen to stay in an army whose morale had been badly damaged. It is fashionable to draw analogies between our failures in Vietnam and Iraq; not all of them hold. In the future, however, if today's lieutenants and captains stay in the Army, these wars may share a legacy, namely that of a generation of senior officers whose sensibilities were formed in an ambiguous conflict that did not go according to plan, soldiers whose youthful idealism and certainty have been tempered by reality and disappointment at the beginning of their military careers.

Devoting several decades of your life to an army demands not simply obedience but also a kind of faith: faith in the institution's ethos, in your commanders, in the military as an effective political instrument, in the cause for which you fight, in the nation you serve, in the nobility of dying in battle, and, for those who endorse the canard that there are no atheists in foxholes, in God. Military culture is permeated by a rhetoric of religiosity: even an ambivalent soldier like Al can tell you without irony that the Army "saved" him, and I have heard many soldiers describe their relationship to the Army in just that way. "Duty—Honor—Country," MacArthur told the Corps in 1962, "are your rallying points." The incantation of these "three hallowed words" would, according to MacArthur, help the West Point graduate "to regain faith when there seems to be little cause for faith." In his poem "Pearl Harbor," Robinson Jeffers suggests that in a country that has no language, race, or religion of its own, *nation* itself has become a sort of faith: "nation or nothing." Another term for this phenomenon, popularized recently by the journalist Anatol Lieven and others, is *national messianism*. "It has been our fate as a nation," the historian Richard Hofstadter once wrote, "not to have ideologies but to be one."

The lexicons of faith and politics have always intersected in powerful ways in the United States and in colonial America before it. In the nineteenth century, one need only think of Lincoln's use of the term *political religion* to describe what he regarded as a necessary "reverence for the laws" and his co-option of the apparatus of religion to serve this manifestly secular end: "Let [political religion] be preached from the pulpit, proclaimed in legislative halls, and enforced in courts of justice," he told an audience at the Springfield, Illinois, Lyceum in 1838, "let the old and the young, the rich and the poor, the grave and the gay, of all sexes and tongues, and colors and conditions, sacrifice unceasingly upon its altars." Today, the conflation of faith and politics is far more provocative. President Bush concluded his "Mission Accomplished" speech in May 2003 by suggesting that American soldiers bear the message of the Old Testament prophet Isaiah:

> All of you—all in this generation of our military—have taken up the highest calling of history. You're defending your country, and protecting the innocent from harm. And wherever you go, you carry a message of hope—a message that is ancient and ever new. In the words of the prophet Isaiah, "To the captives, 'come out,'—and to those in darkness, 'be free.'"

The rhetoric of the War on Terror has been from the first deeply inflected with a messianic vocabulary that makes it easy for soldiers to conflate military and spiritual missions and that complements the military's own sense of itself as a noble profession and a higher calling.

The Colonel chose Henry James those many years ago in Vietnam, but many officers would have reached for one of the Bibles. An officer who served on a general's staff in Baghdad in 2005 described bulletin boards filled with "Christian adverts . . . all with an underlying theme of the importance of witnessing." In the edition of *Stars and Stripes* distributed in the Middle East she read advertisements entreating soldiers to become "active-duty missionaries." This officer reported finding pictures of Knights Templars hanging in various cubicles in her section. The owners of the pictures knew very well the significance of displaying such material, yet they were "truly offended" when the officer asked them to remove the various pictures of knights and crusaders to avoid giving offense to the local nationals who cleaned the office.

The Army's most celebrated warfaring Christian is probably Lieutenant General William G. Boykin. As Richard T. Cooper reported in October 2003, in the *Los Angeles Times*, the general has been a vocal enthusiast for "the army of God." Boykin, who served in the Special Forces in several hot spots, including Somalia, said confidently about his battle with a Muslim warlord, "I knew my God was bigger than his. I knew that my God was a real God and his was an idol." Of the current War on Terror, Boykin has affirmed, "We're a Christian nation, because our foundation and our roots are Judeo-Christian . . . and the enemy is a guy named Satan." Boykin's sense of mission has all the earmarks of a crusade: "We in the army of God, in the house of God, kingdom of God have been raised for such a time as this." Because of this record, his 2003 appointment as deputy undersecretary of Defense for Intelligence was troubling to many. Cooper makes the point that President Bush's religious rhetoric and "references to God" are "nonsectarian," while Boykin's are emphatically not. He also quotes one retired officer as saying: "For the Army, the issue of officers expressing religious opinions publicly has been a sensitive problem for many years."

On the very day of the "Mission Accomplished" speech, as they thought about their own futures as desert warriors, the juniors and seniors in my British literature elective were reading *Seven Pillars of Wisdom*, T. E. Lawrence's account of his participation in the ultimately failed Arab Revolt of 1916–18. Lawrence operated in the region to which the cadets imagined themselves deployed and later helped to create its current map. Despite its difficult style, the book had seemed, when I was choosing texts in the fall of 2002, an appropriate end to a course focused on literature, nation, and empire. The invasion made its narrative even more resonant. Now *Seven*

Pillars is on many soldiers' reading lists. According to a 2006 *Esquire* profile by Thomas P. M. Barnett, General David Petraeus, appointed ground commander in Iraq in 2007, is "a devoted student of T. E. Lawrence, whose ideas and tactics he teaches to his own commanders," and he "appears to know [*Seven Pillars*] by heart." In February 2006, moreover, the authors of the Defense Department's Quadrennial Defense Review, in one of their only references to the history of the region, called attention to Lawrence's successful attack on the Turkish-held port of Aqaba from its "undefended desert-side" as a prime example of taking "the indirect approach" that "physically and psychologically . . . unbalances the enemy."

The longer I spent with Lawrence, however, the more forcefully I felt that the most provocative lesson of *Seven Pillars* has nothing to do with tactics and strategy and everything to do with a crisis of faith: "Some of the evil of my tale," the first chapter begins, "may have been inherent in our circumstances. For years we lived anyhow with one another in the naked desert . . . The everlasting battle stripped from us care of our own lives or of others'." Compounding the corrosive effects of prolonged campaigning was Lawrence's insight that Europe's promises to the Arabs "would be dead paper" once the Turks were defeated and the war won, and he considered himself a "trickster" and a "fraud": "Instead of being proud of what we did together, I was continually and bitterly ashamed." The "triumph" of the Arab Revolt won Lawrence celebrity but left him with the belief that he had been trapped in the peculiar position of betrayer and betrayed.

By 2004 it had grown increasingly difficult for many in uniform and out—even those initially enthusiastic about the war in Iraq—to keep the faith. April, the deadliest month of the war to that point, closed with Seymour Hersh's *New Yorker* exposé of prisoner abuse at Abu Ghraib and the airing of the notorious photographs on *60 Minutes II*. This was a year, almost to the day, after President Bush's declaration of "Mission Accomplished." The Long War grew even longer, and by 2005—the year of the plague, as I came to think of it—the seniors had begun their disillusioned refrain: "What's the difference, ma'am? I'll be in Iraq within a year anyway." In the spring, a season that ended with the suicide of my colleague Ted Westhusing, the plebes read Robert Fitzgerald's translation of Virgil's *Aeneid*, a text the Colonel and I had taught together in an elective on Augustan Rome several years before. Fitzgerald himself first turned seriously to the *Aeneid* in the Army to alleviate the excruciating boredom of a staff job while stationed on a tranquil island in the Pacific in 1945. Later, as a participant in the Allied landing on Honshu, he records in the notes to his translation: "More than literary interest, I think, kept me reading Virgil's descriptions of desperate battle, funeral pyres, failed hopes of truce or peace." Opening with its storm-tossed hero's wish that he had died at Troy, Virgil's poem combines deep ambivalence and chronic loss with examples of enduring faith and moments of messianic prophecy.

For centuries Virgil's poetry held, as the classicist Bernard Knox explains, "a semi-religious stature. It became an oracle known as the *Sortes Virgilianae*, the Virgilian lottery: you took a passage at random and it foretold your future." Hadrian and England's Charles I, among others, consulted the lottery; Knox himself had recourse to it while serving as a U.S. Army captain with Italian partisans in World War II. Finding an old copy of Virgil on the floor of a bombed-out villa near Modena, he opened to a passage from the *Georgics* that described "a world in ruins." Despite Virgil's use as an oracle, however, and despite the fact that the plot of the *Aeneid* is driven by an unstoppable national destiny, its hero is preoccupied from the first by feelings of failure and regret. Dutiful and subdued, *"pius Aeneas"* is, as many commentators have noted, a rather difficult hero to embrace.

It was the quality of restraint, distinguishing Aeneas from the more zealous warriors who most often grip our cultural imagination,

that the Colonel found so compelling. Over dinner at his kitchen
table, he also revealed a special affinity for the Carthaginians—for
the doomed Dido and for Hannibal, that spectacular failure, an un-
deluded overreacher who never quite reached Rome but nonetheless shook its foundations in the second century B.C., about 150
years before Virgil's birth. Hannibal kept the Punic faith, reprising
a war his father couldn't finish until, after years of prowling the
pale, he finally took the poison he supposedly carried with him in
his ring, outfoxing to the end the nervous Romans who pursued
him. Destiny, mused the Colonel, is nothing in the face of self-
possession. He, too, had learned to read the entrails in a distant,
difficult place.

Whenever Aeneas hesitates, a divine messenger—often his
mother, Venus, but sometimes Jupiter's errand boy, Mercury—
appears to set him straight, to tell him what to do. Today's soldier
can rely on no deus ex machina, but his faith, like any other, has
both articles and creeds. Aeneas takes his household gods with him
from Troy and prays to them for guidance; American soldiers tote
the Seven Army Values—loyalty, duty, respect, selfless service,
honor, integrity, personal courage—on cards worn on dog tag chains
or slipped into wallets like talismans. In addition to these values,
there is the Soldier's Creed. Crafted in 2003, to encapsulate a newly
revitalized warrior ethos, it has four tenets:

I will always place the mission first.
I will never accept defeat.
I will never quit.
I will never leave a fallen comrade.

These articles bind soldiers to one another and to a professional
code. They assure individuals of the institution's belief in them and
extract a reciprocal promise of fidelity.

In the months after September 11, my former student Nick
wrote to me from flight school at Fort Rucker, Alabama—"Mother

Rucker," as the aviators cleverly call it. Nick felt he lacked the zeal of his classmates, some of whom had turned bloody-minded after the attacks. They liked to throw around the term *rag-head* a lot, for one thing, and they seemed a little too eager to wreak vengeance. Usually Nick's correspondence has the tinge of marvelous lunacy; his exploits and predicaments sometimes call to mind the misadventures of Guy Crouchback in Evelyn Waugh's Sword of Honour trilogy. When the invasion of Iraq began, however, his tone took a more serious turn. Too few of his classmates, he reported, seemed interested in "considering any deeper political or moral issues." Still firm in his commitment, grateful for the liberties his country had afforded him, full of "an overwhelming sense of obligation," as he wrote, "to support it," he nonetheless could not feel a similar fervor. Was this failure of feeling, he asked me, this lack of faith, disloyal?

When I decided to teach English, I did not anticipate that I would be in the business of dispensing this sort of advice—on scanning Alexander Pope, perhaps, or on unpacking a metaphor in an Elizabethan sonnet—but not this. In reply, I suggested to Nick that circumspection, even skepticism, is not inconsistent with responsible service. I revealed to him that the officers I most admired were at once loyal and thoughtful; I had in mind some of those colonels who had fought in Vietnam. They had distinguished themselves on the battlefield but also gone through periods in their careers when they wondered whether they ought to stay the course. In short, they knew when to fight and when to think, when to have faith and when to doubt. When Aristotle meditated on courage, I added, he juxtaposed the headlong charge of the reckless with the steady calm of the citizen-soldier who knows what he fights for and understands fully the dangers he faces on the battlefield.

Nick was an Army brat—his father retired as a colonel—and he knows how things go. Yet he decided on a military career for a perhaps unconventional reason: he found the idea of the Army as a peacekeeping force, an idea briefly alive in the 1990s and anathema to some warriors, immensely appealing. After our exchange about loyalty, Nick's messages began to sound more hopeful. Noting that flight school limited his reading to a few hundred pages a week, he nevertheless managed to work through Michael Talbot's *Holographic Universe*, Howard Zinn's *A People's History of the United States*, and Victor Hugo's *Les Misérables*. On arrival at his first assignment in Korea, he reported with his characteristic appetite for the new that he had "the most diverse group of soldiers a leader could ask for." Some of the cadets in our program go out into the Army expecting to appear a bit eccentric, but Nick and his new chief of aviation maintenance had discovered a shared interest in the poetry of William Blake. He noted that they were both rereading *The Marriage of Heaven and Hell* in preparation for their next field exercise. Ever attuned to oddities, Nick told me of a pilot in Korea who requested an exorcism of his Chinook helicopter along with the usual maintenance before every flight. Yet Nick's playfulness coexists with ferocious loyalty to his soldiers and gravity about his increasing responsibilities as a commander. To Nick, the actions of the troops under his command are his own; everything that happens on a flight is his responsibility. This ethos keeps many doubting officers in the Army: no matter what they think of any given war, they do not wish to abandon their soldiers.

When he had occasion to pass through New York in 2006, Nick and I had a long conversation. It was the first time I had seen him since his graduation. We discussed his tour in Korea and the Army school he had just finished as a captain. Nick was frustrated. Even in the wake of Abu Ghraib and Guantánamo, the curriculum seemed to him to include insufficient instruction in just war theory and the laws of land warfare. He was also nonplussed by the fact that even a few of his instructors referred to the Iraqis as "hajjis." Especially now, he thinks, this education needs revamping and enhancement, and he hopes to publish an essay he wrote for the course advocating for change. It begins with an epigraph from Tennyson's "Charge of the Light Brigade" and ends with a call to re-structure the moral-ethical education soldiers receive: "In the wake of the events at the Abu Ghraib prison, the necessity of providing our soldiers with comprehensive education in the laws and ethics of land warfare has never been clearer . . . This instruction should aspire, not merely to teach rules and consequences, but to train officers to use ethical reasoning to arrive at a specific decision. This is vital when no set rule clearly defines right . . . from wrong."

It is a neat trick to admit to such doubts while carrying on. As Nick is fond of saying, "Not everyone thinks the uniform prevents free speech." He is perfectly capable of announcing in the same breath, "I want my country back" and "I'm staying in the Army." It isn't everyone who can balance such contradictions. In the character of Nikolay Rostov, Tolstoy reveals what can happen when the first stirrings of doubt awaken to disturb the faithful soldier. A young officer inspired by his love for the czar to die in the war against Napoleon, Rostov becomes acutely confused when the czar suddenly decides to make peace with the French. At supper with his comrades, Rostov explodes in anger:

> "We are not diplomatic clerks, we are soldiers, and nothing more," he went on. "Command us to die—then we die. And if we are punished, it follows we're in fault; it's not for us to judge. If it's his majesty the Emperor's pleasure to recognize Bonaparte as emperor, and to conclude an alliance with him, then it must be the right thing. If we were once to begin criticising and reasoning about everything, nothing would be left holy to us. In that way we shall be saying there is no god, nothing," cried Nikolay, bringing his fist down on the table. His remarks seemed utterly irrelevant to his companions, but followed quite consistently from the train of his own ideas. "It's our business to do our duty, to hack them to pieces, and not to think; that's all about it," he shouted.

Rostov emphatically slams the door on reflection. To negotiate with doubt requires more finesse than this young officer, gallant as he is, can muster. The czar's word must be good enough.

Like Rostov, cadets have chosen a particular path of service. They have done nothing short of answering a call, and not all of them can find within themselves the extraordinary capacity to criticize and reason, on the one hand, and to retain their faith, on the other: to reconcile duty with the apparent fact, for example, that there are no weapons of mass destruction hiding in the Iraqi desert. For many it is safer not to reason why. With its mechanisms for careful deliberation, its system of checks and balances, the nation's civilian leadership is supposed to make it possible for soldiers to take a lot of things, including the reasons they go to war, on faith. After Vietnam this faith became increasingly difficult. Recent tensions between civilian and military leaders—especially between the office of former Defense Secretary Rumsfeld and the group of retired flag officers who spoke out against him in April 2006 in the so-called Revolt of the Generals—over troop levels, strategy, and rules of engagement haven't made things any easier.

Take, for example, my colleague Dan, who volunteered for a tour in Afghanistan yet contemplated resigning his commission when we invaded Iraq. As a warrior and a theorist of just war, he received the news of prisoner abuse and other war crimes as a personal and professional affront, but his sense of duty would have taken him to Iraq if he had been asked. Junior officers came to Dan because they respected his military credentials—Infantry, Airborne, Ranger—but also because they knew him to be a soldier with a conscience. They sought his advice at a time when they wondered about what this war has done and is continuing to do to the people who fight it.

Dan and I had a long conversation about the Revolt of the Generals. I asked whether these flag officers would have made a greater impact had they spoken up while still in uniform and then resigned in protest, but Dan insisted that resigning would have betrayed a responsibility to protect as best they could the soldiers under their command. Dan anatomized the officer's peculiar circumstance: the fear is that if you lay down your command, someone who doesn't have your knowledge and your experience, or who lacks the same loyalty to your soldiers, will come along to snap it up. Staying enables you to take care of those soldiers, even if going along with a plan you believe to be flawed may also consign them to the very fate from which you hope to preserve them.

As David Margolick reveals in "The Night of the Generals," which appeared in the April 2007 issue of *Vanity Fair*, many soldiers and civilians believe that these generals should have kept silent in retirement as well. In uniform, they argue, these senior leaders bore a responsibility privately to inform the chain of command about their doubts; once retired, however, they were obligated to keep their mouths shut. Some critics, Margolick reports, believe that the generals have done irreparable damage: "imperiled civilian control, undermined military mores and morale, jeopardized the military meritocracy and the trust between senior and junior officers." Others are more sanguine. For example, I heard one officer propose that the next time civilian authorities contemplate ignoring the advice of military leaders, the memory of the generals' revolt will make them think twice.

As the situation in Iraq continued to worsen in 2005, and Dan's letters to his congressman continued to go unanswered, doubt invaded his sleep to produce an extraordinary dream. He was drunk and quite responsibly decided that he couldn't drive home. He therefore surrendered his keys to a designated driver, his drahthaar, a German wirehaired hunting dog. He had been assiduously training this dog, still a puppy really, and was extremely proud of her progress. Dan invests himself in the training of dogs and people with equal devotion, and he values the same things in both: loyalty and an ability to hunt. So there he was in the passenger seat with the wonder dog at the wheel. The dog, however, hadn't quite gotten the hang of steering, and it ended up running a few people over on the way home. Dan now found himself in a quandary: he had to report the accident, that much was clear, but he was unsure about the right course of action. Should he tell the police that he and not the poor dog had been driving? Or should he admit that he had tried to do "the responsible thing" by letting his carefully trained dog drive home? When he told me about this dream, I was at once amused and saddened, because its significance seemed so cruelly obvious. Here was a man who had been for several years now wrestling with his conscience and trying to determine the just course, a man whose unambiguously good and successful project of training his dog had now also collapsed in a wreck by the side of the road.

Twenty-year-olds, whose relationship to military service is still forming, aren't as prepared as Dan might be to wrestle in this way with their consciences. Brad, a sophomore who had been in my literature class the year before, came to see me. He was upset about a conversation with a civilian friend. Over coffee one day, she had declared, "I don't understand why you want to kill people." That is not at all, of course, what Brad *wants* to do, even though he knows he might one day have to. At the time of this conversation, Brad was nearing the end of his second year at West Point. Cadets take an affirmation oath at the beginning of their third, or cow, year. Before the oath, they can leave the Academy free and clear of any obligation; afterward, they are required to fulfill a service obligation in exchange for their education. His friend's assumption about his bloodlust so distressed Brad that he contemplated leaving. He started to wonder if he understood what being an officer really entailed. Having served some enlisted time before coming to West Point, he knew that being an officer would require a different measure of commitment and responsibility.

Nothing makes you grow up faster than being asked to help someone to decide whether to stay in the Army. More than once it has been a cadet who has displayed uncommon potential—who is scrupulous and courageous, more mature than her peers, always on the lookout for the welfare of his classmates—who has ended up confessing to doubt. When that happens, I ask myself what a particular officer with whom I used to work would have done, for he had an extraordinary facility for illuminating the possibilities without pushing you into the decision he might have made in your shoes. That takes a lot of discipline, something of which he had an apparently inexhaustible reserve. That day in my office I tried to do for Brad what this officer had done for me on a number of occasions: I tried to present the case from as many angles as I could.

Several months after our conversation, I checked in again with Brad. While reading *War and Peace* that summer, I had been struck by the passage in which Prince Andrey's friend Pierre asks him what he is "going to war for." "'What for?'" responds Andrey, "'I don't know. Because I have to. Besides, I'm going' . . . He stopped. 'I'm going because the life I lead here, this life is—not to my taste.'" Like Brad, Andrey didn't have a ready answer for his civilian friend. After going to war, moreover, his motivations become even more complicated, indeed almost impossible to articulate. Andrey loves glory yet knows its emptiness. He bears a deep responsibility to the men of his regiment, a love of country, and a full recognition of the waste of war. All of these causes and desires battle within him even as he fights the enemy. I told Brad the story of Prince Andrey. What I guess I wanted him to understand was that no thinking soldier can ever rid himself of periodic ambivalence.

I have become increasingly preoccupied with Prince Andrey as the war drags on. I worry that Tolstoy's book might have become my own Virgilian lottery or oracle. While writing to Brad, I hadn't forgotten what fate awaits Andrey at Borodino, where he receives the wound that eventually kills him, but even as I know that fewer wars would be fought if the Andreys of the world stopped feeling that primal urge to go to battle, I also realize with breathtaking selfish-

ness that even more wars would be lost, and that on occasion we
might be lost, if the Brads of the world decided to sit them out
rather than to serve. Once again I have retreated—or advanced—to
literature perhaps because I'm more comfortable analyzing it than
I am my own relationship to war and to the people who wage it. I
suppose I hope that the world of imaginative literature I have
grown so accustomed to inhabiting and through which I feel that
my own horizons have been enlarged might provide the same rich
vein for someone like Brad, who is trying to figure out nothing less
than how to live his life.

A summer out in the woods in charge of some new cadets
turned out to have renewed Brad's commitment to the Army. He
described his experience to me:

> I got along wonderfully with my New Cadets. The interac-
> tion that I had while leading them this summer was truly en-
> lightening. I know that if my soldiers are like New Cadets I
> will probably never leave the military. I finally have a good
> understanding of what my job is going to be, and as far as I
> am interpreting it right now it is to take care of these people.
> The mutual respect we built was quite amazing. I know that
> my New Cadets would follow me anywhere and do anything
> that I asked of them, and in return they understood that I
> was there to teach and to take care of them. I cannot express
> the feeling that springs from this type of relationship, it is
> just wonderful . . . I have begun to come into a place in
> which I am comfortable; I just don't know exactly where that
> place is.

The Army is a difficult church in which to worship; it damns
even as it saves. Brad has faced the darkest of doubts in order to get
to a comfortable place, even if that place is still a little obscure. He
knows what his job requires, and he has, as he puts it, "embraced"

his responsibilities. I expect he'll continue to have moments of doubt; indeed, I hope he does, because those doubts will help to keep his judgment honed and his conscience vigilant.

The lack of understanding on the part of Brad's civilian friend— her automatic assumption that every soldier must be a bloodthirsty killer—seems to be at least in part a consequence of a volunteer army. When I hear a tale like Brad's, I understand how easy it is for my students and colleagues to mistrust, and in some cases to have contempt for, the very civilian population they have sworn to defend. In the absence of a draft, a defensive rhetoric of insular professionalism has unfortunately intensified. The belief held by many West Pointers that the Army is one of the last repositories of honor, selflessness, and virtue in a fallen world is a troubling one in the light, for example, of the revelations from Abu Ghraib. The marvel of it is that there are still moments—while reading a letter from Adam or Nick, while meeting with Brad—when this proposition seems to me to contain a shred of truth. The risk is that the military officer's idealism can morph into triumphalism and into what the journalist Robert Kaplan has called a willingness to go on "moral crusades."

Richard H. Kohn and others have called attention in recent years to the "diminished . . . ideological diversity" of the all-volunteer officer corps. With homogenization comes an increased willingness to vocalize political and religious affiliations: at the office, in the classroom, on the playing field. This is a radical departure from the mid-twentieth-century model of the disinterested soldier embodied by George C. Marshall or Dwight D. Eisenhower, both of whom refused even to vote while in uniform. A vote for one party or another or a faith in one god over another can easily be annexed to those more perceptibly secular, nonpartisan faiths of duty, honor, and country. After doing a study of political and social attitudes at West Point, two officers who taught in the Department of Social Sciences, Jason Dempsey and Craig Cummings, concluded "that pressures may exist" for cadets to identify with certain political positions.

Insofar as it can be disentwined from politics, the matter of religion is even more fraught. According to Major Jason Riley, who completed a master's thesis, "For God or Country? Religious Tensions Within the United States Military," at the Naval Postgraduate School in 2006, the conflict "being waged among religious groups" and "between religious and secular groups" in the United States in recent years is now manifesting itself within the armed forces. "The threat of religious conflict," Riley concludes, "is a direct challenge to the foundation of the military's values and beliefs." He calls attention to the presence of proselytizing senior officers in all of the services and cites in particular the reports of gross religious intolerance at the Air Force Academy that first surfaced in 2005.

West Point's leadership has been extremely hospitable to religious pluralism and scrupulous about constitutional freedoms: moral fitness may be the command's business, but the spirituality of cadets and faculty remains, at least in official eyes, a matter of private conscience. Individual officers, however, are not always so careful. It is probably easier to find an atheist in a foxhole than to find one at West Point. Nick recalled more than one of his professors beginning the semester by enumerating the things most important to him, usually in this order: God, family, country, and the United States Army. In matters of politics and religion, Nick tends to fight fire with fire. Not only does he carry his ACLU card in his wallet, but he also displays a Darwin fish and an Amnesty International sticker on the back of his Jeep. The latter proved a subject of some consternation for one of his superiors, who called Nick into his office to ask him whether he thought it was appropriate to ride around with a sticker from an organization that has been critical of U.S. policy. Nick replied, "Sir, would we be having this conversation if I had a W '04 or a CHARLTON HESTON IS MY PRESIDENT sticker on my car?" The officer chewed this over for a good long time. "Will there be anything else, sir?" Nick asked. "No, get out of here."

One day a plebe—let's call him Mark—came to my office ostensibly to discuss a paper. It turned out, however, that he really wanted to talk about something else. This cadet, who had what I can best describe as a slick Elmer Gantry charm, mentioned to me in passing that the barracks were "a real cesspool." Mark had convinced himself that he was under siege, assaulted in particular by the foul language of his peers. Mark had once had a filthy mouth, he confessed, but he had made a vow never to use any language that he wouldn't use in front of his mother. (A vow like that would do almost nothing to clean up my vocabulary, I'm afraid.) Yet if they mocked him for his clean living, it was also the case that the sinners, as he put it, "all come to me in the end."

It still hadn't dawned on me that sitting in my office was a twenty-year-old with a messiah complex, but all was soon revealed. Why, I asked, miserable as he was, had he chosen to stay? "Because," he replied, "the Army is the best vehicle through which I can spread the word of Jesus Christ." This may have been his mission, I told him, but it wasn't the Army's. In keeping with its constitutional mandate, the Army was not in the business of spreading particular faiths. And this time I gave some definite advice, as I had refrained from doing with Brad: I reminded Mark of the allegiance he had sworn to the Constitution and of the officer's need to reconcile his or her personal mission with that of the Army. Growing up in the People's Republic of Massachusetts did not adequately prepare me for this kind of conversation, nor did Harvard and Yale prepare me for working with a colleague who based important life decisions on signs from God. At least as he has described them to me, these were not answered prayers but portents as arbitrary as the entrails of a sheep or the flight path of a bird studied by Roman augurs.

After Mark left my office, I started to wonder where he had gotten his rhetoric. It was too canned to be spontaneous. It most

likely came from an organization active throughout the Army called
the Officers' Christian Fellowship (OCF). The OCF's ultimate goal,
posted on its website, is "a spiritually transformed military, with am-
bassadors for Christ in uniform, empowered by the Holy Spirit, living with a passion for God and compassion for the entire military
society." There is nothing nonsectarian about this mission. Where
are Jews, Muslims, and Buddhists, to say nothing of atheists, in this
picture? Members of all of these groups have served honorably in
the armed forces, some have died honorably, yet they are nothing
but fodder for conversion in the OCF's vision. Furthermore, although there are several women on the organization's board, its attitude toward them is, not coincidentally, archly traditional. Much of
the material devoted to women on the site celebrates motherhood
and offers guidance on how to become a better Army Wife.

With guidelines, pamphlets, posters for Bible study, and a "pray
and plan" program to assist with professional as well as personal decisions, the organization reaches into every part of a member's life.
Its first spiritual pillar provides an important clue about the way the
OCF understands its relationship to military authority: "While we
gladly embrace the participation of military chaplains and other or-
dained individuals, we seek to capitalize upon the unique opportunity God gives to all officers to witness to and spiritually encourage
their comrades-in-arms in the military society." Scripture, not the
Constitution, is the OCF's guiding authority, and it seems to view
the Army as an instrument not of national policy but of divine will.
The group's "strategic vision" contains the most explicit statement
of a mandate to proselytize: "Expand the corps of Christian officers
who are prepared for a lifetime of integrated professional service
and spiritual leadership within the military society by more effectively evangelizing, discipling, and mentoring officers, officer candidates, cadets, and midshipmen."

Nick, who first called my attention to this particular document,
offered his layman's opinion about it:

Most people tend to look at me a little cross-eyed when I suggest that the "mission" of OCF is inconsistent with the very Constitutional precepts we are sworn to defend. I have no problem with people who want to be Christians, but I cannot stand having it thrust onto me. If they left me in peace, I think I would be more likely to turn a blind eye to some of their activities, but . . . THE ARMY IS NOT THE PLACE FOR EVANGELISM!

The particular context for his capitalized outrage was that Nick had just overheard a captain trying to persuade a young soldier to attend Bible study. Nick has been on the receiving end of such invitations as well, and he has had the courage to refuse even a former commander's insistence that he attend church: "I'm not going, sir." But a young, inexperienced private, at the very bottom of the food chain, isn't necessarily in a position to resist such a suggestion, and any officer who uses her rank to urge her faith on another soldier is abusing her power. Soldiers are not normally confused on the subject of rank. Al is fond of quoting an old expression: "Senior never remembers; junior never forgets." The same officer who expects an order to be carried out when she gives it is running away from the question of rank if she thinks that in discussions of faith in class or in the halls she is speaking simply as a Christian rather than as an officer. Even out of uniform, a colonel is never anything but a colonel to his subordinates. Junior officers who work for a commander who desires them to go to a particular church with her or cadets who are told that voting for a certain political party is the act of a traitor may be forgiven for thinking that their right to privacy has been grossly violated. The First Amendment guarantees the freedom of the battalion commander to go to church, but it also ensures the right of the private to go to his mosque or to stay home without feeling that he has made a career choice.

Fundamentalists who agitate for narrowing the separation of

church and state like to point to the religiosity of the founders and to the many references to God in their speeches and writings. The OCF's executive director, Retired Air Force Lieutenant General Bruce Fister, was quoted by Alan Cooperman in *The Washington Post* as saying, "'The people around a military leader ought to see the characteristics of Christ in that leader.' It is a national tradition reflected in 'hundreds of writings and proclamations issued down through the ages by American leaders who claim divine protection for our nation, place our nation's trust in God and claim God as our source of strength.'"

A less selective perusal of founding texts suggests the capaciousness of the founders' attitudes toward religion. When Moses Seixas, warden of Touro Synagogue in Newport, Rhode Island, invited George Washington to visit in 1790, Washington responded with an address in which he asserted his fundamental reluctance to make private matters of conscience the preserve of the state:

> The Citizens of the United States of America have a right to applaud themselves for giving to Mankind examples of an enlarged and liberal policy: a policy worthy of imitation. All possess alike liberty of conscience and immunities of citizenship. It is now no more that toleration is spoken of, as if it was by the indulgence of one class of people that another enjoyed the exercise of their inherent natural rights. For happily the Government of the United States, which gives to bigotry no sanction, to persecution no assistance, requires only that they who live under its protection, should demean themselves as good citizens.

Members of the armed services may surrender much of the privacy that citizens enjoy. They do not, however, lose "liberty of conscience."

It is little wonder within a community shot through with so many official and unofficial dogmas that doubt is often taken to be the worst of sins. Doubt creeping into the minds of the faithful looks to a commander's eye like an epidemic ravaging a trench: rot from top to bottom. Cynicism is usually regarded as an undergraduate rite of passage—doubt and suspicion certainly marked my own college experience and that of my friends—but at West Point, it is regarded as a cancer to be rooted out. Cynicism is the dreaded fifth column of military culture, but a healthy suspicion and a cold-eyed understanding of what you are being asked to do isn't the same thing as a cynic's outright contempt for the system. It is difficult to see how a thoroughgoing cynic could remain at West Point or in the Army for very long.

In *The Devil's Dictionary*, Ambrose Bierce offers the following definition: "*Cynic, n.* a blackguard whose faulty vision sees things as they are, not as they ought to be." It is customary to regard armies, to borrow the language of anthropology, as traditional shame cultures, but I think it is truer to say that they are cultures of complaint. Grousing, griping, sniveling, and pissing and moaning— these are military arts, and there is always an element of performance involved. *They*, whoever *they* are, are usually the villains in cadets' tales of misery; from *them* come all the arbitrary, unwise, imprisoning rules and regulations. "Who are *they*?" I once asked a cadet: "You know, ma'am, 'The Man.'" This is a clever parody of disaffection and sometimes the thing itself, but it stops well short of mutinous rebellion. Every organization, no matter how apparently conformist, needs its own version of an anarchist fringe. Cadets' joking references to The Man, their ability to mock themselves as "national treasures," and their deep suspicion of herds are simply the normal and natural expressions of college students. Some old soldiers, on reaching that last sentence, will shout: "Cadets *aren't* just college students. They are more than that." True enough, but they are also eighteen, nineteen, or twenty years old, and you can either beat them into submission or allow them more gracefully to make their way toward the institutional goal of lifelong service. "The discipline which makes the soldiers of a free country reliable in battle is not to be gained by harsh or tyrannical treatment," Major General John M. Schofield told the Corps in 1879. "On the contrary, such treatment is far more likely to destroy than to make an army." That little gem can be found in *Bugle Notes*, among other places; Schofield said it when he was the superintendent.

What worries me far more than any cynicism I see on the part of cadets is a certain cynicism *about* cadets—the cynicism of Brad's friend, for instance—on the part of those people who respond to the news that I teach English at West Point with an openmouthed stare of disbelief. My mother reports that on more than one occasion when the subject of what I do has come up in conversation, acquaintances have exclaimed: "You mean they read?" She thinks that such responses stem primarily from ignorance about the nature of the Academy's comprehensive undergraduate curriculum; she's more generous than I am. "Oh, they can read? That's a relief. What do they read?" asked an incredulous clerk at a bookstore one day, holding my bag of purchases out of reach until I gave him a satisfactory answer. As the Army, in the wake of Vietnam, became more profoundly isolated from certain important sectors of the civilian society it serves, the impression grew in certain quarters that the military was, to borrow a phrase from Tim O'Brien, a "jungle of robots." In the context of today's conflict, moreover, the transformation of robots into martyrs, heroes, and other symbols of sacrifice has done little if anything to rehumanize soldiers. It is precisely in their ability to wrestle with faith and doubt that cadets most effectively refute the accusation that they are nothing but automatons or victims.

One finds conflicted soldiers throughout the literature of war: in Homer and Virgil, in Tolstoy, and in the favorite author of many cadets, Hemingway. As the plebes who read Hemingway along with Bierce and O'Brien in the spring of 2003 discovered, sometimes bitter cynicism and fervent belief can be entwined in the same psyche. O'Brien suggests that the great appeal of Hemingway's soldiers lies in the fact that they are "resigned to bullets and brawn . . . They are cynics. Not quite nihilists." In *A Farewell to Arms*, for example, Lieutenant Henry reports himself "embarrassed by the words sacred, glorious, and sacrifice." Regretting his inability to feel the power of these words, he nevertheless understands them and betrays a lingering admiration for those who can respond to their call. When he hears them uttered by his friend, the Italian soldier Rinaldi, Henry thinks back to all the times that he has heard them before:

> We had heard them, sometimes standing in the rain almost out of earshot, so that only the shouted words came through, and had read them, on proclamations that were slapped up by billposters over other proclamations, now for a long time, and I had seen nothing sacred, and the things that were glorious had no glory and the sacrifices were like the stockyards at Chicago if nothing was done with the meat except to bury it. There were many words that you could not stand to hear and finally only the names of places had dignity. Certain numbers were the same way and certain dates and these with the names of the places were all you could say and have them mean anything. Abstract words such as glory, honor, courage, or hallow were obscene beside the concrete names of villages, the numbers of roads, the names of rivers, the numbers of regiments and the dates. Gino was a patriot, so he said things that separated us sometimes, but he was also a fine boy and I understood his being a patriot. He was born one.

To a cadet like Kevin the Musketeer, the attraction of heroes such as Henry is that they do not ultimately reject honor: they redefine it while appearing to keep their distance from larger causes.

Kevin's thesis focused on those masculine loners of American fiction and cinema—the modern incarnations of the self-reliant hero of Thoreau and Emerson—who operate according to a strict individual creed. Hemingway articulated the cynic's code in various ways throughout his work: "About morals," he writes in *Death in the Afternoon*, "I know only that what is moral is what you feel good after and what is immoral is what you feel bad after." His meditations on bullfighting in this book also gave rise to the oft-quoted aphorism "There is honor among pickpockets and honor among whores. It is simply that the standards differ."

The heroes of hard-boiled fiction by Raymond Chandler and Dashiell Hammett evince a similar amalgamation of honor and unsentimental self-preservation. At the end of Hammett's *The Maltese Falcon*, Sam Spade turns over Brigid O'Shaughnessy, who is convinced that he loves her, to the police for having murdered his partner. By way of explanation, Spade offers her an ambivalent version of a professional code: "Listen. This isn't a damn bit of good. You'll never understand me. When a man's partner is killed he's supposed to do something about it. It doesn't make any difference what you thought of him. He was your partner and you're supposed to do something about it." After a lengthy enumeration of practical considerations, Spade concludes with a refusal to play "the sap" for her: "If that doesn't mean anything to you forget it and we'll make it this: I won't because all of me wants to—wants to say the hell with consequences and do it—and because—God damn you—you've counted on that with me the same as you counted on that with the others."

Bogart's Sam Spade is of a piece with his Harry Morgan, the fishing-boat captain in *To Have and Have Not*, a film based on Hemingway's novel of the same name. Both men manage to stand outside the codes to which they end up subscribing. When his friend Frenchy, played by the marvelous Marcel Dalio, asks Morgan why he has sided with the Free French against the Vichy authorities in Martinique, Harry replies by recasting ideological struggle as personal preference: "I don't know. Maybe 'cause I like you, maybe 'cause I don't like them." This is a prime example, of course, of knowing morality only by how it makes you "feel." But it is another Bogart role, that of Rick Blaine in *Casablanca*, that is the American ne plus ultra of the type. Rick may claim to stick his neck out for no one, but we know that an attenuated sentiment we could call patriotism if we needed to will win out in the end: "There are certain sections of New York," he tells the German Major Strasser, "I wouldn't advise you to try to invade."

In the stoicism of Hemingway's heroes and of the on-screen personae of Bogart and Gary Cooper, Kevin discovered some of the same qualities fostered by the cadet culture of West Point. In particular, he noted that culture's inescapable combination of ritual and physicality: "Cadets will fight hard. You are weak if you don't fight hard. You cannot be afraid . . . Cadets learn much at West Point that is not in books. They learn strength of spine and grace under pressure. They are almost all cynics, yet almost all will fight hard for their manhood. Your worth here is how you measure up against your peers . . . Competition is healthy; destruction is heroic."

Hemingway's cynicism also hinged on physical competition, and he was quite capable of accusing others, John Dos Passos among them, of being cowards for not fighting. Dos Passos, for his part, as George Packer noted in an article in *The New Yorker*, traveled to Spain "to see . . . workers and peasants struggling to create a more just society—not to drink *anis* with Russian commissars in range of enemy artillery . . . Hemingway's romantic fable [*For Whom the Bell Tolls*] is in almost every way more compelling. But Dos Passos, in his dispirited and unblinking realism, was the one to convey what it meant to be alive in the nineteen-thirties." It is one of the great paradoxes of the Hemingway hero, Kevin found, that his cynicism is sustained by heroic fantasies. The appeal of such a sensibility to cadets believing themselves underappreciated by civilians who construe their military service as an uncomplicated desire "to kill people" is understandably potent.

Several years ago I took to reading Brigit Pegeen Kelly's poem "Wild Turkeys: The Dignity of the Damned" in class the day before Thanksgiving. The poet had visited West Point the year before I arrived, and my friend Scott had passed on a copy of her book with this poem marked. In it Kelly makes the most of the birds' awkwardness: their ungainly flight; the ridiculous-looking wattles hanging from their necks like "shriveled, lipstick red hearts"; their bluish heads. Over the course of the poem, Kelly likens the procession of wild turkeys to skull-shaved convicts, sick pilgrims, "swag-bellied bombers," and, in the final stanza, doomed soldiers. These birds possess:

A faith beyond the last desire to possess faith,
The soldier's resolve to march humpbacked straight into death
Until it breaks like oil over him

And over all that is lost.

In 2005, for the first time, I was brought up short by the end of the poem. It was one of those strange moments when a metaphor that elsewhere would mean nothing special suddenly meant the world. For every one of the cadets in that class had it—that "soldier's resolve," that faith beyond faith—and in reading the poem I felt, superstitiously, as if I had assigned to them the same inevitable doom Kelly had imagined for those hapless wild birds.

These days the shadow of the battlefield experience bleeds through the language of literature all the time. Often the things we say in class carry different weight than they did before. Recently, I was discussing Gerald Stern's "Bullet in My Neck," an essay the poet wrote about being shot in Newark, with a group of firsties who were embarking on a personal essay project. "Your essays don't have to begin with a showstopper like that," I suggested. "Most of us don't have bullets in our necks, but if you do, that's a great story." As soon as I said it, I realized that the whole room had gone miles away, and my you-idiot voice told me that some of them might well be able to write that very essay one day. As I sustain the faith that I am equipping my students through the study of literature with the ability to read and interpret their world, one of the things I have begun to suspect is that there is no preparation—not in the Bible, not in the *Aeneid*, not in Henry James—wholly adequate to some of the experiences they may well endure.

6

The Courage of Soldiers

◆

Who knew you could learn so much from a hat? During my first year at West Point, I witnessed a scene that periodically returns to my thoughts. When class lets out, there is a mad press of sweaty cadets in the corridors of Thayer Hall making their way to the next class or to afternoon activities such as drill or team practice. Nothing, Errol Flynn had told me soon after my arrival, can prepare you for the steamy smell of plebes on a warm day in Thayer. He was right: that first blast of anxiety-soaked plebe on a humid late August day is like nothing else. One day, however, by the time I had emerged from my room after the last class of the afternoon, the halls were empty. The departing cadets' scramble to collect their hats (or "covers," as they are called), backpacks, and jackets was over. Because everyone wears the same indistinguishable uniform, cadets scrawl their names on the labels, hang their garments in a peculiar way, or devise some other trick to identify their belongings. Inevitably, there is confusion: a jacket that doesn't fit or a momentarily misplaced pack followed by a laughing exchange between parties. Walking down the hall in the wake of this tumult, you'll sometimes see an unclaimed item hanging forlornly on the racks that line the walls.

As I stood in the doorway of the classroom on this particular afternoon, I saw two plebes scurrying frantically down the hall in my direction. After unsuccessfully searching the room in which they had just had class, they stopped in front of the lone hat remaining on the rack in the otherwise empty corridor. In their distress they didn't even notice me standing across the hall. "Is it yours?" one plebe, his own hat in hand, asked the other, who was examining it for some mark of ownership. "No," said the hatless one. "What should I do?" "I don't know," said his friend, and they stood staring helplessly at each other.

The gravity of this situation may not be immediately apparent, but for a soldier, going outside without the prescribed headgear is *verboten*. When we once witnessed a colonel walking the short distance from his car to a mailbox without a hat, Al, whom no one could accuse of being a martinet, shook his head in disgust. "Damn colonel ought to know better," he said. Al loves hats: he regards a Borsalino the way other people might gaze at a Raphael. "It takes balls to wear a hat," he likes to say with typically effective anatomical confusion. "Either you wear the hat, or the hat wears you." Uniform hats, however, are more than fashion statements. When Al misplaced his own beret in his office one day as he was getting ready to walk to class, he seriously contemplated the Kevlar helmet he had used during summer training that was still sitting on his bookshelf: "I'd sooner wear that Kevlar than walk to Thayer without a hat." If lieutenant colonels give so much thought to a missing hat, imagine the consternation of a plebe who finds himself in the same predicament.

The clock was ticking, and the two friends were undoubtedly going to be late for something, but they just stood there looking at the hat as if coaxing a reluctant oracle. Then I heard the telltale scuffing footsteps of an upperclassman, and a world-weary firstie came upon the pair and asked what the matter was. He listened to their problem and said without skipping a beat: "Just take the hat." "Sir?" "You don't have a hat, so just take that one." Then, shaking his head at the obvious infirmity of these tyros, he scuffed away, leaving the plebes to stare at each other once again. "Do you want to take it? I mean, he said it was okay," ventured the friend with some hesitation. But the hatless plebe replied decisively and fluently: "If I take this hat, then the guy who forgot it won't have one. When he comes back to look for it, it won't be here." The plebe now faced the daunting prospect of running a gauntlet of upperclassmen and officers who would first demand to know why he wasn't wearing a hat and then "flame" him for daring to provide them with the requested explanation. In the short distance between Thayer Hall and the barracks, it wasn't inconceivable that he would have been stopped a number of times by an assortment of eagle-eyed predators. There would be no excuses, and he knew it. Yet when he arrived at his beautiful conclusion, his misery seemed to fall away because he had discovered within himself a particular kind of courage: the courage to do the right thing.

The Cadet Prayer requests divine assistance in pursuing a number of laudable goals, among them "honest dealing" and "clean thinking." If only that latter were a typo for "clear thinking," I would be a lot happier. As is, it reminds me of the message I once read on a church marquee: DUSTY BIBLES LEAD TO DIRTY LIVES. But the passage I hear cadets quote most often is this one: "Make us choose the harder right instead of the easier wrong." To explain both their own behavior and that of a literary character, they will often invoke the language of the prayer. "Well, ma'am," one might say during a discussion of the Weird Sisters' prophecy in *Macbeth*, "Banquo chose the harder right." And that hatless plebe whose name I never learned and whom I never saw again remains for me the definition of choosing the harder right.

Armies are overly fond of slippery slope arguments—borrow a hat today, steal the payroll tomorrow—yet there are moments in history, and this is one, when it is hard to avoid drawing such connections oneself. Choosing the harder right is not something that all American military personnel have been able to do. Choosing the harder right requires a quality beyond physical bravery. Susan Sontag, whose reflections on 9/11 in the September 24, 2001, issue of *The New Yorker* outraged so many readers, was not, after all, the first to propose that courage is "a morally neutral virtue." As Samuel Johnson noted, it is possible to admire the valor even of a highwayman: "We have more respect for a man who robs boldly on the highway, than for a fellow who jumps out of a ditch, and knocks you down behind your back. Courage is a quality so necessary for maintaining virtue, that it is always respected, even when it is associated with vice." Johnson points here to the moral slipperiness of courage: if physical valor enables both the soldier to hold his ground in the face of enemy fire and the robber brazenly to steal your money in the middle of the road, it cannot serve as a guarantee of good character.

Battlefield death has long been celebrated in the Western world as the ultimate proof of courage: in the *boulē* of the city-state, in the court of the king, on the village greens and city squares of the republic. Aristotle argued that, because death is the greatest human fear, triumphing over that fear by dying in battle is the greatest and noblest end for the courageous man. To die in battle is also to be exempted from the common run, from what Antoine de Saint-Exupéry rejected as the bookkeeper's life. George Orwell's experience as a patient in the charity ward of a Parisian hospital likewise prompted him to conclude, "It is a great thing to die in your own bed, though it is better still to die in your boots." It is the ideal of a battlefield death that lures Prince Andrey back to Borodino and that lends the touch of envy to the prevailing atmosphere of sadness at a military funeral.

The hat incident was trivial, I suppose—those plebes were confronting fears well short of death—but, perhaps because it happened so soon after my arrival, it has assumed an epic importance for me. In blue periods I read it as an allegory of failure: what makes a plebe new to the system intuit answers that someone about to graduate seems to have forgotten? In more sanguine moments, however, I remember that no system can have a 100 percent success rate. I like to think that the firstie wasn't quite as bad as he sounded and that those two plebes would emerge from their four years at West Point carrying the same perfectly calibrated moral compasses with which they had arrived. In addition to physical courage under fire, officers need the moral and intellectual courage that enables them to become, as they are sometimes called, judicious "managers of force." With such integrity alone, perhaps, can the "human spirit," to borrow the words of Simone Weil, resist deformation "by the very force it imagines it could handle." The courage I'm describing isn't the sort for which you win medals or for which you become a legend in the annals of war. There are few monuments to the prudent soldier, to the one who decided against making a bold but foolhardy charge. The term *Fabian strategy* is a tribute to the Roman general Fabius Maximus, yet his own countrymen vilified him for the very policy of delay that ultimately saved Rome from the Carthaginian army. They thought him a coward and called him "Hannibal's governess" for refusing to meet his adversary in a pitched battle.

Courage isn't something I used to think a lot about except in an abstract or a platitudinous way. The terms *courage* and *guts* (as well as the loathsome *intestinal fortitude*) are familiar to anyone who grew up, as I did, playing and watching sports. Such expressions pepper the speech of high school coaches and sports commentators just as they do the narratives of war. A clever announcer like cycling's Phil Liggett ransacks the chronicles of war to find language adequate to the athletic feats he witnesses: "Floyd Landis has come down the mountain across the Alps today, just in the style of a Hannibal of modern times," Liggett declared when Landis laid waste to the field on Stage 17 of the 2006 Tour de France. Conversely, the Victorian poet Henry Newbolt's *Vitai Lampada* depicts a soldier inspired to bravery on the battlefield by the recollection of school cricket: "His Captain's hand on his shoulder smote—/ Play up! Play up! And play the game!"

The analogy of sport and war is a very British tradition intended to celebrate at once a sense of fair play and a certain national pluck: think of Shakespeare's Henry V responding to the haughty French dauphin's gift of tennis balls by beating the mighty French army at a far deadlier game at Agincourt. In the eighteenth and nineteenth centuries, in conjunction with British imperial expansion, such analogies expressed a public school ethos imbibed by a privileged class. The Duke of Wellington's apocryphal saying that the battle of Waterloo "was won on the playing fields of Eton" is usually taken as the supreme evocation of that ethos. But it is worthwhile remembering that only the officers would ever have played on those fields. The bulk of the British Army was "composed," in the duke's own estimation, "of the scum of the earth—the mere scum of the earth."

When he studied the poetry of World War I in his senior year, Adam discovered the degree to which this clubby milieu had shaped the British officer corps and, indirectly, the fate of the millions of private soldiers who died at their direction in that conflict. On the path from preparatory to public school and thence to Oxford or Cambridge, a young man learned, as Robert Graves puts it in *Good-bye to All That*, "to keep a straight bat at cricket, and to have a high moral sense." Paul Fussell records the story of Captain W. P. Nevill, who launched an advance on the German lines at the Somme by kicking a football into No-Man's-Land. Fussell notes that a football had first been used at Loos by the 1st Battalion of the 18th London Regiment in 1915, after which the practice "soon achieved the status of a conventional act of bravado and was ultimately exported far beyond the Western Front." Yet the trench experience did much to unsettle the analogy between playing fields and battlefields. Soldiers met their deaths crawling by bloodied tens of thousands through the mud of Passchendaele and the Somme toward an enemy they often could not see.

To the extent that the U.S. Army possesses an equivalent to a "playing fields of Eton" sensibility it can be found in the Newbolt-like lines of Douglas MacArthur, West Point superintendent from 1919 to 1922, whose experiences in World War I had shown him "the value of organized group athletics in creating and maintaining morale . . . Nothing," he wrote in his 1964 memoir, *Reminiscences*, "brings out the qualities of leadership, mental and muscular co-ordination, aggressiveness, and courage more quickly than this type of competition." For MacArthur, who also made major changes to the academic curriculum, exercising the body also sharpened the mind: "Physical qualities may well determine the destiny of the intellect. To emphasize these truths I had carved on the stone portals of the gymnasium these words: 'Upon the fields of friendly strife / Are sown the seeds / That, upon other fields, on other days / Will bear the fruits of victory.'"

As he read of British soldiers taking their stiff-upper-lipped way to death, Adam was preparing for his own war in a nation still obsessed with heroism of the most romantic kind. He had chosen to devote his final undergraduate semesters to the study of the anti-heroic verse of Wilfred Owen at a time when the idea of dying for one's country was once again being trumpeted as a saving truth. The ground was seeded for our current preoccupation with heroic sacrifice by the nostalgia for the "greatest generation" awakened by the celebration of World War II fiftieth anniversaries in the 1990s, but the American fascination with heroes is as old as the country's founding, when it disturbed statesmen such as Adams and Jefferson, who regarded a susceptibility to heroes, especially military heroes, as fundamentally undemocratic. Echoing the concerns of the founders, Ralph Waldo Emerson proposed in *Representative Men* that heroism is "a regal condition." Hero worship, which comes to seem almost pathological in Emerson's writings, replaces the democratic virtue of self-reliance with the systemic dependence of aristocratic societies.

At the end of his plebe year in 2002, West Point's bicentennial, Adam had listened along with me and the thousands who filled the football stadium to President Bush's graduation speech. In it, the president had followed tradition by granting "amnesty to all cadets . . . on restriction for minor conduct offenses." Filled with allusions to World War II and the Cold War, the speech insisted on both the universality of morality—"Different circumstances require different methods, but not different moralities. Moral truth is the same in every culture, in every time, and in every place."—and the simultaneous exceptionalism of the United States and of the cadets themselves, who had the courage to answer "the calling to hardship and purpose, to risk and honor." Adam's West Point career began before September 11, and by the time he graduated, in May 2005, we knew the worst of Guantánamo and Abu Ghraib. It isn't likely that any of the War on Terror's ambiguities are lost on Adam, who is, remember, an advocate of "grade-one thinking," of discovering the truth. He brings to his profession a more capacious and courageous imagination than most of us can muster.

Adam chose to join the hard-charging "cavalry community" of aviators, which is infused with a kind of anachronistic gallantry. Today mechanized vehicles have replaced the horse as the cavalry's preferred mode of transport, but cavalrymen still wear spurs with their dress uniforms, and at places such as Fort Hood, home of the 1st Cavalry Division, Stetsons and horses retain ceremonial uses. As early as the Franco-Prussian War, the use of the improved breech-loading rifle turned the heroic cavalry charge into a suicidal gesture. Reliance on conventional tactics, notes the historian Michael Howard, succeeded only in littering the battlefield with "aristocratic corpses." Nevertheless, Howard reminds us, stubborn cavalrymen would forget this lesson by 1914. The last horse-mounted charge in U.S. history occurred in 1942, when elements of the 26th Cavalry, Philippine Scouts, led by Lieutenant Edwin Ramsey and armed with .45 semiautomatics instead of sabers, galloped into Morong to engage a unit of Japanese infantry.

The cavalry is home to some of the military's most deeply romantic myths. At West Point, there is a wonderful plaque honoring the Army Horse in Thayer Hall, which used to contain a riding ring. Devoted "To the Noblest of the Train that Wait on Man," it celebrates the history of the horse at the Academy: "From his earliest appearance at West Point in 1839 to his departure in 1947 he made his humble but important contribution to the development of those qualities of the soldier and the sportsman so necessary in the Army officer." The seductiveness of the cavalry myth can be discerned in Francis Ford Coppola's *Apocalypse Now* in the figure of Lieutenant Colonel Bill Kilgore (Robert Duvall), commander of the Air Mobile battalion that carries Willard (Martin Sheen) and a Navy river patrol boat along with its crew to the mouth of the river that leads to Kurtz.

Kilgore respects valor wherever he finds it: "Any man brave enough to fight with his guts hanging out can drink from my canteen any day," he declares when a dying Vietcong soldier begs him for water. Kilgore carries an ivory-handled sidearm and dreads the end of war: "I love the smell of napalm in the morning . . . smells like victory. Someday this war's going to end." Kilgore is an extremist, but a friend of mine who is his antithesis, an extremely gentle aviator who fought in the First Gulf War, has also confessed to me the matchless rush of exhilaration that washed over him as he piloted his helicopter into combat.

According to Willard, Kilgore has a "weird light" around him that makes everyone feel "safe," and he predicts that he will survive the war without so much as a "scratch." Imperturbability is one of the greatest assets a soldier can have, and Kilgore is utterly unflappable. As his helicopter takes fire from a village, he calmly continues to drink his coffee and muses: "Don't these people ever give up?" The potent esprit de corps that authorizes Kilgore to bomb a village back to "the Stone Age" if it means taking care of his men— be it getting the wounded to the hospital or making the beach safe for them to surf—captures the military's cultic aspects.

Perhaps no American made more effective ideological use of this cult than another old cavalryman, Theodore Roosevelt. In a 1913 speech prepared for the Boys' Progressive League, Roosevelt declared: "I wish to see you boys join the Progressive Party, and act in that party and as good citizens in the same way I'd expect any one of you to act in a football game. In other words, don't flinch, don't foul, and hit the line hard." The idea of citizenship as an endless football game sprang naturally—as anyone who grew up reading countless inspirational biographies written for children knows—to the mind of a sickly boy whose father taught him that growing up was a matter of sufficient exercise. Having learned to vanquish asthma by means of chin-ups, Roosevelt would later defeat political opponents by charging up San Juan Hill. It was, he always said, the best day of his life.

All of Roosevelt's books are studies in the seductions of the strenuous life. *The Rough Riders* portrays the Spanish-American War as a great adventure. *African Game Trails* recounts the safari on which Roosevelt stalked lions from Mombasa to Khartoum, the great hunter cradling a rifle in each arm and preaching against game butchery while he and his son Kermit took 512 animals— from aardwolf to zebra—between them. *Through the Brazilian Wilderness* tells the story of a trip to South America, undertaken in the wake of his defeat in the presidential election of 1912, up the uncharted River of Doubt. There he almost died of fever in the bottom of a dugout reciting "Kubla Khan" while Kermit paddled him home. Even after he returned to Oyster Bay from South America, a sick and broken man, Roosevelt vilified Woodrow Wilson and the cowards who wouldn't let him fight the Germans with a volunteer force of reincarnated Rough Riders. The best he could do was to send his sons to war instead. He studied the swords and flags the boys sent home and hung them up as monuments at Sagamore Hill, where he received the news about Quentin, shot down over France in a Nieuport 28. When the dynamo died, Archie cabled the news to his brothers, who were still abroad: THE OLD LION IS DEAD. STOP.

Roosevelt's energy is at once fascinating and terrifying. He regarded West Point as a wellspring of strenuous living in a largely sedentary world; it was a place, moreover, where honor could be breathed in the very atmosphere. While reminiscing about the Spanish-American War at the Academy's centennial graduation in 1902, Roosevelt told an anecdote about a cadet that evokes the gallant myth saturating his writings:

> I had at that time in my regiment as acting second lieutenant a cadet from West Point. He was having his holiday. He took his holiday coming down with us, and just before the assault he was shot, the bullet going in, I think into the stomach, going out the other side. He fell over, and as we came up I leaned over to him, he said, "All right, Colonel, I am going to get well." I didn't think he was; but I said, "All right, I am sure you will," and he did; he is all right now.
>
> There was never a moment during that time, by day or by night, that I was not an eyewitness to some performance of duty, some bit of duty well done, by a West Pointer.

The tale of the plucky cadet who talks about a life-threatening bullet wound as if it were an ankle twisted on first down is typical of Roosevelt's sensibility. The seemingly insoluble connection between physical exertion and robust Americanism that dominates his writings to this day inspirits West Point, which is a relentlessly physical place.

In addition to the compulsory athletic rituals of the Department of Physical Education—the "Department with a Heart"—all cadets play on intramural, club, and/or intercollegiate teams. They can be seen jogging from the early morning hours until lights out. Cadets bound out of the woods, they scale walls, they pound up and down the sidewalk with rifles and packs, they cycle by in a blur, they jump out of planes overhead and parachute onto the Plain. When a firstie once asked a colonel what he needed to succeed in the Army, the officer replied, "Show up on time and stay in shape." If I had not played sports for as long as I can remember, all this physicality doubtless would have felt rather alien to me. As it was, my first few years at West Point were a return to summer camp: only this time the counselors weren't bored college kids but Army Rangers.

The dreamlike quality of the place for me in those prewar days owed a great deal to its sporting camaraderie. Members of the department devoted themselves in the absence of real battles to weekly internecine football games. Mary Wollstonecraft was persuaded that the military obsession with the perfection of "corporeal accomplishment" prevented a corresponding "cultivation of the understanding." At first I, too, devoted myself to corporeal accomplishment; perhaps, after the cerebral intensity of finishing my dissertation, I was rebelling. That first year it was Art, an infantryman, who superintended my physical training (PT). Before our department softball games—he was also the coach—he would run me up and down various hills around post. While I slogged it out, Art would run backward, sometimes in circles, clapping his hands and calling out cadences to urge me on. In the steamy heat of the Hudson Valley summer, we often retreat to the woods to run on the trails. But on the hottest day of the year, it doesn't much matter where you run, and gamboling through the woods with several colleagues one day, I allowed myself to ask whether chills were a bad sign. I didn't allow myself to ask whether we could stop.

It was my friend Michael who introduced me to cycling, which, considering the inept way I ride, qualifies as an extreme sport. My first purchase was a mountain bike, but soon, thanks to Michael's contagious passion for the cycling life, I also had a road bike in my office. One day he told me it would be a good idea to ride our mountain bikes down the ski slope on post. (It was out of season.) I didn't quite believe him. But after watching him fly straight down, I began like a snail to traverse the width of the hill until, mercifully, I discovered a flat tire, which Michael then pedaled back *up* the slope to fix. On another of our adventures, I found myself at the foot of a tree crawling out from under the bike and pulling leaves from my teeth before I could finish the ride.

Cycling is only one of Michael's sports; it was also at his urging that I found myself clipped to a belay rope climbing a wall of rocks one afternoon, lying on the floor of the department conference room learning how to aim a rifle, and shooting a 9 mm pistol at the crude sketch of a burly felon with stubble on his chin and a tooth-pick hanging from his mouth at a gun club upstate. Michael prefaces each adventure with the claim "It's something you ought to know how to do." He's right, but so far I have resisted the invitation, proffered now by several of my colleagues, "to jump out of a perfectly good airplane."

Michael is a remarkable athlete and an intrepid Special Forces officer: he has cycled across the United States and climbed Denali. He has dropped with his small team into the middle of more than one hostile landscape. He has done much he can't tell anyone about, but I have no trouble imagining that, whatever it was, it took a lot of guts. You always feel safe with Michael: he's one part Sir Edmund Hillary, one part MacGyver, and the rest John Muir. The embodiment of one of his literary touchstones, Emerson's "Self-Reliance," Michael wears naturally the elemental masculinity that a lot of the guys we met at that gun club were so clearly searching for with their collectible World War II pistols and their military surplus uniforms from the Army & Navy Store.

Army officers are magnificent trainers and motivators: they make you believe in yourself and sometimes take you beyond your capacity, but you know they'll never leave you behind in all your wheezing inefficiency. Sometimes the mania for physical fitness has a bizarre edge: there was the Pattonesque colonel who used to stop and salute "the fine young Americans" whenever Art and I ran by him. The head of one department, *The Wall Street Journal* reported several months before I arrived, evidently used to walk around the office in a sleeveless shirt and spandex shorts asking people to feel his biceps. But there is also a deadly earnestness to much of the athleticism on display, and the most impressive cadets and officers I have encountered possess extraordinary will and endurance together with a near compulsion to push themselves beyond ordinary limits.

My first week in town, a colonel I hadn't met during my interview—let's call him Colonel X—crossed paths with me in the hall and without slowing his pace said simply: "Thursday, twelve hundred, squash courts." I spent the intervening days feeling like someone who had been mistaken for Wyatt Earp and told to show up at the O.K. Corral to shoot it out with the Clantons. That first showdown with Colonel X was followed by countless sessions of squash, racquetball, and tennis. These marathon games, after which I could barely move, were always a highlight of my week. One day I was told to report to the racquetball court instead of the squash court. I felt lost in the much larger space, and I soon discovered that a racquetball has a lot more bounce than a squash ball, which you have to warm up before you can get it to rebound at all. I felt as if I were in a fun house or a cartoon as I swung wildly and got tangled up like Bugs Bunny whiffing at a fastball. There was no preliminary orientation, no explanation of the rules, no easing into things: I was just told to hit the ball.

After about five minutes of trying to hit it, I found myself awaiting the first serve of a game. In self-defense, on this my very first point, I swung, and my shot hit the colonel square in the ass. One learns to take the periodic whack in squash and racquetball; I've been hit by innumerable balls and even the occasional racquet over the years. But the colonel was still a stranger, and even after you get to know him, he isn't someone you would ever feel comfortable smacking. There was an instant in which I thought quite seriously about running away and never coming back . . . to West Point. But Colonel X just turned around with his wry smile and magnificent calm, saying quietly, "That's not good form," before turning back around to await the next barrage.

Colonel X is quite simply the toughest man I've ever met—not because he can take a racquetball shot with equanimity but because he has a more powerful sense of discipline, both mental and physical, than anyone I've known. We share a love of tales of exploration and adventure, and used to trade books on Roosevelt and Ernest Shackleton. Once he returned Peter Nichols's *A Voyage for Madmen*, an account of the 1968 Golden Globe single-handed yacht race, with the note "I may have dreams about 30–80' waves. Needless to say, I was quite unaware of the race at the time, being focused on short-term survival and little else." That note told me a lot. In 1968 he had been in Vietnam. Adventure was one thing for him, war quite another. The courage required to sail a yacht around the world on your own is not the same thing as the courage it takes to lead soldiers into battle.

Colonel X has the attribute Saint-Exupéry found among the mail pilots he flew with in the early, chancy days of aviation: "There exists a quality which is nameless," Saint-Exupéry writes in *Wind, Sand and Stars*. "It may be gravity, but the word does not satisfy me, for the quality I have in mind can be accompanied by the most cheerful gaiety. It is the quality of a carpenter face to face with his block of wood. He handles it, takes its measure. Far from treating it frivolously, he summons all his professional virtues to do it honor." Saint-Exupéry met with this attribute in his friend Guillaumet, who survived a forced landing and a harrowing walk through the frozen Andes. If the quality can be given a name, perhaps it is "responsibility." Here, having recounted the march through the snow and described his rescued friend's shattered body, Saint-Exupéry attempts to capture Guillaumet's spirit:

> If I were to talk to him about his courage, Guillaumet would shrug his shoulders. But it would be just as false to extol his modesty. His place is far beyond that mediocre virtue . . . He knows that once men are caught up in an event they cease to be afraid. Only the unknown frightens men. But once a man has faced the unknown, that terror becomes the known. Especially if it is scrutinized with Guillaumet's lucid gravity. Guillaumet's courage is in the main the product of his honesty. But even this is not his fundamental quality. His moral greatness consists in his sense of responsibility. He knew that he was responsible for himself, for the mails, for the fulfillment of the hopes of comrades.

A sense of ultimate responsibility was something that Colonel X also possessed. When I asked him, after he retired, what element of his life had changed the most, he replied: "That's easy: I'm not responsible for other people anymore."

This was the same quality I had recognized in Ulysses S. Grant even before I knew what to call it. He never seemed to lose sight of the gravity of the enterprise even though he could make jokes at his own expense. Grant's term for the attribute in question was *moral courage*, and he wasn't afraid to reveal those moments when he failed to summon it up. He had seen combat as a junior officer in the Mexican War and proven himself on a daring ride across the wide-open squares of Monterrey to get a message back to General Taylor: "My ride back was an exposed one," he writes with characteristic equanimity, "Before starting I adjusted myself on the side of my horse furthest from the enemy, and with only one foot holding to the cantle of the saddle, and an arm over the neck of the horse exposed, I started at full run. It was only at street crossings that my horse was under fire, but these I crossed at such a flying rate that generally I was past and under cover of the next block of houses before the enemy fired. I got out safely without a scratch."

At the beginning of the Civil War, however, Grant had his first real command, and he lacked a knowledge and maturity commensurate with his newly increased responsibilities. Tracking Colonel Thomas Harris in the vicinity of Florida, Missouri, he faced and failed one of his first tests of combat leadership:

As we approached the brow of the hill from which it was expected we could see Harris' camp, and possibly find his men ready formed to meet us, my heart kept getting higher and higher until it felt to me as though it was in my throat. I would have given anything then to have been back in Illinois, but I had not the moral courage to halt and consider what to do; I kept right on. When we reached a point from which the valley below was in full view I halted. The place where Harris had been encamped a few days before was still there and the marks of a recent encampment were plainly visible, but the troops were gone. My heart resumed its place. It occurred to me at once that Harris had been as much afraid of me as I had been of him. This view of the question I had never taken before; but it was one I never forgot afterwards.

In this passage and the episodes that follow, one can see the unknown becoming known, the terror subsiding just as Saint-Exupéry said it does, as Grant realizes that he and his enemy shared the very same fears. Yet it is important to note that it was not the enemy but his own men that most frightened Grant at this stage. His admission "I had not the moral courage to halt" suggests that he was worried as a new commander that his men would think him a physical coward if instead of advancing blithely up the hill he had chosen the more conservative approach of calling a halt to send out scouts. Testing one sort of courage, war can paradoxically encourage a different kind of cowardice. By lacking the requisite moral courage in this instance, Grant ran the risk that his troops would be ambushed by the Confederates.

A national audience would soon learn that Grant was not afraid of enemy bullets, but the men he commanded that day in Florida, Missouri, hadn't seen him as a young lieutenant racing across the squares at Monterrey or braving the cannonballs at Palo Alto. To them, he felt it necessary to prove his warrior spirit. Later, when his sphere of responsibility became much wider, Grant was, as the military historian John Keegan notes, more careful of his person and customarily stopped "short of the end of what riflemen call 'the beaten zone.'" On those occasions when he did unexpectedly find himself in the line of fire, however, Grant displayed an absolute calm that his soldiers saw and respected.

At Yale, where I first read the passage about chasing Harris, I knew that an important recognition had occurred, but I had trouble sorting out exactly what it was. It was Colonel X who elucidated the episode's full significance. Although he didn't offer his own experience in evidence, clearly he had faced similar moments as an officer: When should I charge ahead? When, recognizing that I have all of these other people depending on me, should I reject dash in favor of prudence? Several years later, after I described a lecture I had attended by a former battalion commander in Vietnam—a cowboy who could always be found in the thick of the action but who was not especially scrupulous about the rules of engagement— the colonel said carefully: "He is unquestionably a physically brave man." This wasn't an unalloyed compliment, I realized, for the same reason that Grant's decision to risk everything at Florida was not entirely praiseworthy even though it testified to his nerve. The polar explorer Robert Falcon Scott was as brave as they make them, but dying slowly in that tent on the Ross Ice Shelf in the middle of a blizzard, Edward Wilson and Henry Bowers might have been forgiven for wishing their leader had more foresight (and luck) and less of the stubbornness that led to so many miscalculations. Anne Fadiman has written of the Arctic explorer Vilhjalmur Stefansson in similar terms: "And though he was one of the greatest solo operators in history, he was a terrible leader." While dashing after the enemy makes a far better story than calling a halt, being an adventurer and leading an expedition are altogether different propositions.

On that first reading of Grant's *Memoirs* in New Haven, it was enough for me to know that the author was the antithesis of the braggadocio with whom literature had made me so familiar. On subsequent readings, however, it became increasingly clear that Grant was quite interested in moments when moral courage comes at the expense of an opportunity to demonstrate physical valor. The reader catches a glimpse of conflicting courages early in the *Memoirs*, long before the Florida episode, in Grant's condemnation of the practice of dueling: "A majority of the duels fought have been for want of moral courage on the part of those engaged to decline." His rejection of the sort of honor that appealed to so many of his contemporaries seemed very strange to an old friend like the Confederate general Simon Bolivar Buckner, whose request for terms of surrender Grant summarily denied at Fort Donelson. "No terms," Grant wrote unchivalrously, "except an unconditional and immediate surrender can be accepted."

At West Point the careful cultivation of moral courage through instruction is an antidote to adventure's temptations and a necessary counterpoint to the tableaux of physical courage that dominate the landscape in the form of monuments, statues, and plaques. When I stop to read one of the many testaments to courage I pass in the course of a day, I am sometimes reminded of Keegan's claim in his landmark work of military historiography, *The Face of Battle*, that most accounts of battle tend to leave us with "a list of unanswered 'hows'" and "a mighty 'why.'" Wander around West Point, and you'll find yourself asking the same questions. In the halls, on staircase landings, around every corner—Medal of Honor plaques are ubiquitous. They display the winner's name, the date and place of the action, and a narrative of the award-winning deed. On occasion, I will buttonhole a cadet to hear what he or she thinks of the impossibilities recorded for our appreciation. Usually, we both end up shaking our heads in wonder.

The Army website maintains a library of Medal of Honor citations. The older ones tend to be brief and a little mysterious. Take, for example, the case of James Allen, a private in F Company, 16th New York Infantry, who, on September 14, 1862, "single-handed and slightly wounded . . . accosted a squad of 14 Confederate soldiers bearing the colors of the 16th Georgia Infantry (C.S.A.). By an imaginary ruse he secured their surrender and kept them at bay when the regimental commander discovered him and rode away for assistance." We are left to wonder exactly how Private Allen managed to outfox fourteen rebels and keep them "at bay" until assistance arrived.

During the Civil War, the Medal of Honor was the only award available to soldiers, and it wasn't instituted without controversy. As the website notes, General in Chief Winfield Scott killed an early proposal because he thought that "medals smacked of European affectation." Nevertheless, by 1863 Congress had made the medal a "permanent decoration." By the twentieth century, it was the highest of a whole series of awards for heroism. More recent citations often have a level of detail commensurate with the award's preeminence. One of the longest is that of Second Lieutenant Audie L. Murphy, the most decorated combat soldier of World War II. Because it captures so many characteristics of the genre, I'll quote it in full:

2d Lt. Murphy commanded Company B, which was attacked by 6 tanks and waves of infantry. 2d Lt. Murphy ordered his men to withdraw to prepared positions in a woods, while he remained forward at his command post and continued to give fire directions to the artillery by telephone. Behind him, to his right, 1 of our tank destroyers received a direct hit and began to burn. Its crew withdrew to the woods. 2d Lt. Murphy continued to direct artillery fire which killed large numbers of the advancing enemy infantry. With the enemy tanks abreast of his position, 2d Lt. Murphy climbed on the burning tank destroyer, which was in danger of blowing up at any moment, and employed its .50 caliber machinegun against the enemy. He was alone and exposed to German fire from 3 sides, but his deadly fire killed dozens of Germans and caused their infantry attack to waver. The enemy tanks, losing infantry support, began to fall back. For an hour the Germans tried every available weapon to eliminate 2d Lt. Murphy, but he continued to hold his position and wiped out a squad which was trying to creep up unnoticed on his right flank. Germans reached as close as 10 yards, only to be mowed down by his fire. He received a leg wound, but ignored it and continued the single-handed fight until his ammunition was exhausted. He then made his way to his company, refused medical attention, and organized the company in a counterattack which forced the Germans to withdraw. His directing of artillery fire wiped out many of the enemy; he killed or wounded about 50. 2d Lt. Murphy's indomitable courage and his refusal to give an inch of ground saved his company from possible encirclement and destruction, and enabled it to hold the woods which had been the enemy's objective.

On the subject of Murphy, a veteran of Vietnam once said to me at a party: "Soldiers hate shit like that. It makes the rest of us look bad." Hollywood, however, loves shit like that. In *To Hell and Back*, the biopic based on Murphy's eponymous autobiography, the author (at what personal cost we can guess) plays himself. Watching the climactic battle for which Murphy won his medal, we attribute his survival in part to the magic of Hollywood bullets; our sense of the improbable is mitigated by the fact that Murphy was left alive to play himself. I remember being surprised at the differences between the movie and the book, which I read as a kid one summer. The lice, misery, and filth of the written account, replaced in the film by some artfully applied mud, gave me perhaps my first real indication of the degree to which war stories are sanitized for mass consumption and made to conform to popular expectations about what heroes do and how they live. "Like a horror film run backwards," Murphy had written, in a formulation that reminds me of Max's response to combat: "images of the war flicker through my brain."

What enables actions such as Murphy's? Many of the sociological studies on combat motivation conducted in the decades after World War II suggested that soldiers fight for their own survival and for that of their comrades but only rarely for causes and ideals. Many of the lieutenants I know define victory as not losing any soldiers. "On the whole," notes Hofmiller, the cynical Austro-Hungarian cavalry officer of Stefan Zweig's novel *Beware of Pity*, "more men had perhaps escaped *into* the war than from it." Yet the monograph *Why They Fight: Combat Motivation in the Iraq War*, produced in 2003 by the Strategic Studies Institute of the Army War College, found that today's American soldiers are in fact more "politically savvy" than their predecessors. The soldiers interviewed were more likely to be "motivated by . . . idealistic notions"—specifically by the prospect of "liberating the people and bringing freedom and democracy to Iraq"—than were the now-legendary citizen-soldiers of World War II. The authors of the study link this development to the rise of a professional force. The study concludes: "Professional soldiers still fight for each other, but professional soldiers also accept the responsibility that the Army has entrusted to them."

It was Pericles, the fifth-century B.C. Athenian statesman, who turned the aristocratic virtue of courage to democratic purposes. Leading his city against oligarchic Sparta in the early years of the Peloponnesian War, Pericles differentiated Athenian courage from that of a people like the Spartans: "Others," he told his countrymen in a funeral oration for the soldiers who had died in the first year of the war, "are brave out of ignorance; and, when they stop to think, they begin to fear. But the man who can most truly be accounted brave is he who best knows the meaning of what is sweet in life and of what is terrible, and then goes out undeterred to meet what is to come." Far from partaking of the tragic, dying for Athens and the democratic dignities it conferred seems in Pericles' rhetoric a privilege: "Make up your minds that happiness depends on being free, and freedom depends on being courageous," Pericles instructed. "Let there be no relaxation in face of the perils of the war."

By allying courage with reason and with the *duty* of an Athenian citizen, Pericles effectively muted war's powerful connection to primitive passions and obscured the possibility that combat might also provoke pleasures unconnected to a noble end. He taught the Athenians to regard their enemy's aggression as primal but to dress their own belligerence in the most sumptuous philosophical garb. Yet precisely because war provides the best forum in which to exercise the virtue of bravery, the battlefield becomes attractive to some as a redemptive end in itself: "All the great masterful races have been fighting races," Theodore Roosevelt declared in 1897, "and the minute that a race loses the hard fighting virtues, . . . it has lost its proud right to stand as the equal of the best." If to citizens of the ancient Greek city-state the battlefield was a sphere for the physical demonstration of political freedom and personal virtue, to others it was also inevitably home to another kind of murderous honor that, as the historian Eugen Weber observes, is nothing more than "power and the glory that comes from power."

Today the idea of war as redemption again has currency. Supporters of the invasion of Iraq believed that a war made by a free people would naturally produce the liberation of oppressed others. They illustrated their rhetoric with sentimental images of the World War II G.I. as Europe's liberator and of the modern-day first responder, contextualized it within an apocalyptic contest between good and evil, and infused it with suspicions about the worth of peacetime's sedentary citizenship. There seems little room in this world picture, however, for circumspection. The idea that democratic responsibility can be attested by the *refusal* to act prematurely remains a difficult concept for a nation so committed to the veneration of heroic action. The patient, the thoughtful, the courageously inactive, like the Roman Fabius Maximus long ago, are inevitably accused of being uncertain and cowardly by those committed to the strenuous life.

There was perhaps a time in our history when deliberative courage was more highly prized. Supreme Court Justice Louis Brandeis proposed a very different way in which the citizen of a republic might imagine his or her relationship to the exercise of courage: "Those who won our independence believed that the final end of the State was to make men free to develop their faculties," Brandeis wrote in a 1924 opinion, "and that in its government the deliberative forces should prevail over the arbitrary. They valued liberty both as an end and as a means. They believed liberty to be the secret of happiness and courage to be the secret of liberty." The near homophony of the Latin roots of the words *liberty* and *deliberation—liber* (free) and *libra* (balance or scale)—coincidentally underscores the necessity of preserving always a connection between the two.

This is precisely the challenge accepted by an officer like Captain Ian Fishback, whose desperate letter to Senator John McCain was published in *The Washington Post* on September 28, 2005. Fishback, a West Point graduate who deployed to both Afghanistan and Iraq with the 82nd Airborne Division, witnessed things that suggested to him only the murkiest understanding among some soldiers of the law of armed conflict. Dispirited by his chain of

command's unwillingness or inability to clarify the rules of engagement, Fishback attempted to figure out for himself the rules govern-
ing detainee treatment. He asked peers whom he respected, and
when they had no answer, he asked senior officers, among them Dan.

Dan helped him to understand the rules as best he could, but
Fishback remained frustrated that guidelines had not been promul-
gated throughout the force with sufficient clarity. He wrote to his
congressmen and then to Senator McCain about potential violations
to the Geneva Convention. "I am certain," he informed the latter,
"that this confusion contributed to a wide range of abuses including
death threats, beatings, broken bones, murder, exposure to elements, extreme forced physical exertion, hostage-taking, stripping,
sleep deprivation and degrading treatment." Correctly invoking the
term *tragedy* to describe what had happened, Fishback recalled
that at West Point he had resolved "that my men would never com-
mit a dishonorable act; that I would protect them from that type of
burden. It absolutely breaks my heart that I have failed some of
them in this regard." Fishback believes in the necessary connection
between a society's values and the way in which it fights its wars. He
wrote to McCain: "I strongly urge you to do justice to your men and
women in uniform. Give them clear standards of conduct that reflect the ideals they risk their lives for." Fishback could regulate his
own conduct well enough; it is the worry that he has "failed" his soldiers that marks him out as a conscientious officer.

Dan's correspondence with this young captain prompted him to
reflect on his own time in Afghanistan, at Bagram. In something he
wrote subsequent to his exchange with Fishback, you can hear the
anxieties of another troubled officer trying to find the best way
through difficult terrain:

> While I was in Afghanistan in 2002, I was told that suspected
> Al Qaeda detainees held at Bagram were . . . kept awake,
> subjected to bright lights, and interrogated by women (in an
> effort to humiliate them). I also heard that the confinement

facility was not [climate] controlled . . . The point of all this is that, even though now I am concerned that that sort of treatment was unethical, at the time, I did not raise an eyebrow. And if I, a lieutenant colonel with 20 years of service at the time, did not question the legitimacy of such treatment, it seems unreasonable [that] the burden of blame is being borne by lower enlisted personnel[. M]y experience, at least, supports [Captain Fishback's] contention that the blame rests, rather, on an unclear policy and unclear or inappropriate guidance from higher up the chain. This is not to equate the actions of Bagram, 2002, with the heinous acts of degradation at Abu Ghraib. [On the one hand,] much . . . about Abu Ghraib clearly falls outside the realm of decency. On the other hand, we must recognize that it is not always so clear . . . what constitutes torture: does sleep deprivation; does discomfort? My position now, after much reflection, is that we should be permitted to treat detainees in ways comparable to the ways we treat domestic criminals. If it is permitted in the domestic arena, it is probably okay with respect to detainees. If it is not permitted in the domestic arena, then we should not permit it towards detainees.

Dan's anxieties are shared by many soldiers: "War is the place of the passions," an officer about to deploy to Iraq told me, paraphrasing Clausewitz. "I worry about that." This is precisely the kind of worrying that works against the recklessness prompted by the passions and prevents the loss of control that leads to various kinds of tactical, strategic, and moral disasters. What soldiers prevent being done is often at least as important to the outcome of war and the potential for peace as what they accomplish. The initially hostile reaction to Hugh Thompson's intervention at My Lai, however, illustrates the obstacles faced by the morally courageous, by those who possess what Zweig's Hofmiller calls "individual courage."

Hofmiller laments that such courage is "dying out in these times of progressive organization and mechanization. During the war," he explains, referring to World War I,

> practically the only courage I came across was mass courage, the courage that comes of being one of a herd, and anyone who examines this phenomenon more closely will find it to be compounded of some very strange elements: a great deal of vanity, a great deal of recklessness and even boredom, but, above all, a great deal of fear—yes, fear of staying behind, fear of being sneered at, fear of independent action, and fear, above all, of taking a stand against the mass enthusiasm of one's fellows.

And so it happens that those "other fields" of which MacArthur spoke seldom bear much resemblance to "the fields of friendly strife." The rules aren't clear, and you don't get thrown out of the game for fouling someone. You may get killed, of course, and you may get others killed, but in the end victory and defeat are rarely as definitive as they are on the scoreboard after regulation has expired. There are no whistles, except those of incoming rounds, and there are no referees except the one within. Yet on the walls of Michie Stadium appear the words of General George C. Marshall: "I want an officer for a secret and dangerous mission. I want a West Point football player." If that West Point football player is someone like Donald Holleder, this seems sound policy. Holleder, a 1954 All-American tight end noted for his selflessness on the football field, carried that same attribute to the battlefield when he landed his helicopter under fire in Vietnam in an attempt to rescue wounded soldiers and was subsequently shot by a sniper.

Yet if you had in mind another football player, Nathan Sassaman, quarterback of the 1984 squad that defeated Michigan State at the Cherry Bowl, Army's first-ever bowl game, the choice might give you pause. Dexter Filkins reported Lieutenant Colonel Sassaman's story in a *New York Times Magazine* article on October 23, 2005. Filkins emphasizes the point that Sassaman's exploits on the gridiron added considerable luster to his reputation in the Army: "For much of the season, Sassaman played with three cracked ribs. 'That's the kind of leader he was,' says his coach, Jim Young." It was the same warrior's determination that would prompt Sassaman during a mortar attack in Iraq to "rac[e] to his Bradley to hunt down the guerillas," and under "machine-gun and R.P.G. fire to drag one of his wounded soldiers from his vehicle. Then he chased down the insurgents and killed them." In emergencies Sassaman led from the front with evident fearlessness, but what of those moments that required deliberation rather than action? "Sassaman took the concept of non-lethal force to its limits," suggests Filkins. Although many of Sassaman's tactics "had been explicitly ordered or at least condoned by senior American officers," his career was ultimately destroyed because, despite his evident battle prowess and many successes as a commander in Iraq, he told his subordinates to hush up an incident in which some of his men had thrown two Iraqis into the Tigris River. One of them, an Army investigation later revealed, had drowned.

My friend Scott was Sassaman's teammate, and I have found myself wondering what he would have done if confronted by a similar situation. I have no way of knowing for certain, of course; not even Scott can be sure, but my confidence in him stems from having watched him evaluate various moral puzzles. I have gone to him for advice about how to handle certain situations involving cadets because I perceive in him a rare judiciousness. As a result, I like to think that he would have imagined another solution, one consistent with the principles both men had imbibed at West Point. Judgment is the key to moral courage, and I believe that a recognition— perhaps an unconscious sense—of the importance of cultivating such judgment in cadets inspired Scott's decision to organize the plebe literature course around the topic of defiance in the spring of 2006.

Among the various texts cadets read were *Antigone*, *Prometheus Bound*, and *Narrative of the Life of Frederick Douglass*. What these texts taught them, among other things, was the value of deliberation and the moral cost that both obedience and disobedience can sometimes exact. Cadets in several sections, including my own, also read the memoir of Simha Rotem, known as Kazik, a leader of the Jewish Fighting Organization, which battled the Germans in the Warsaw Ghetto Uprising of 1943. After the destruction of the ghetto, Kazik led the surviving fighters out through the sewers to safety. Many hid in the forest, but Kazik, whose appearance and unaccented Polish allowed him to pass as a Christian on the Aryan side of Warsaw, lived out the rest of the war as a courier for the underground. Kazik's story is remarkable, all the more so because he was only nineteen, the age of many of the plebes, and had no military training when he found himself the leader of a ragged band of rebels defying the seemingly unstoppable force of the Third Reich.

As press coverage of the Revolt of the Generals continued in April, the class gravitated toward Kazik. They respected his frankness and his guts. "Ma'am," one of them said, "Kazik is a bad ass." But they responded even more keenly to his moments of selfdoubt. His anguished meditations on courage prompted them to reveal that they worried about the same issues in the barracks: "We like to think that when the time comes we'll find the courage," one volunteered, "but we'll never be sure until it happens." To accompany the memoir, I screened *Night and Fog*, Alain Resnais's film about Auschwitz, and another documentary, *Prisoner of Paradise*, about the great German cabaret star and film director Kurt Gerron, who was compelled to make a propaganda film for the Nazis before being sent to Auschwitz on the last transport from Theresienstadt. The latter film presented them with a protagonist who faced impossible choices, and they debated Gerron's decisions with the urgency and commitment of those who can imagine themselves in exigent circumstances. Those sixteen plebes were the most interesting and the wisest people in my life that semester. They seemed to understand that courage isn't simply a matter of leading charges: sometimes it consists in speaking up, sometimes in stoic silence, sometimes in forging ahead, sometimes in circumspection, and sometimes in nothing less than preserving our own humanity. As Kazik said of a Polish policeman who ran great risks to help the Jews, "He was a human being—and that wasn't a simple thing in those days."

7

Anatomy of Sacrifice

◆

I wasn't consciously reflecting the prevailing mood when, in the spring of 2005, I selected Defoe's *A Journal of the Plague Year* and various other chronicles of disease, fire, and chaos for the senior seminar on London I was to teach the following fall. We had focused on New York City the previous year and had found ourselves alluding frequently to the events of September 11 in our discussions of the city's relationship to national identity. That course, filtered through such a recent cataclysm, bore rich educational fruit with Adam's class, who had been plebes in 2001. I had introduced the course with the proposition that the attacks on the World Trade Center effectively turned New York into a synecdoche for the entire nation. Moving from John Winthrop's metaphorical city upon a hill through the Gilded Age New York depicted in Edith Wharton's *House of Mirth* and E. L. Doctorow's *The Waterworks*, we explored the centrality of the idea of the city to America's self-imagining. Cadets from New Jersey, Oklahoma, and Mississippi began to examine the sources of their own understandings of national identity and patriotic feeling.

We scrutinized the competing pressures of regionalism and nationalism in American history, the clashes between urban and rural sensibilities, and the literary trope of the innocent's arrival in the "mysterious city" about which she has dreamed such "wild dreams," in the words of the novelist Theodore Dreiser, and about which she will suffer such brutal disillusionment. *The Crowd, Rear Window, Dog Day Afternoon*, and other films, together with theorists of the city such as Le Corbusier, Jane Jacobs, Lewis Mumford, William Julius Wilson, and Kenneth Jackson, also helped us to see ways in which urbanization transforms our relationship to our neighbors and potentially hardens our sympathies by presenting such frequent spectacles of misery. "In modern city life," suggests Doctorow, "you can conceivably experience revelation and in the next moment go on to something else." Our topic was literally very close to home: we took a class trip to New York, and several cadets returned on their own to work on final projects documenting aspects of city life. Our discussions were frequently impassioned, on occasion even angry, as cadets defined for themselves the America they had signed up to defend.

In choosing London, I imagined a different kind of illumination, the kind that historical perspective and geographical distance might provide. Just as the cadets and I embarked on Defoe and Samuel Pepys's accounts of plague and fire, however, Katrina struck, and we were plunged right back into the present. Long before the hurricane, I had scheduled presentations on sanitation, mob violence, slums, and pollution. The cadet who chose sanitation came to class on the day of her report with a copy of that morning's *New York Times*, on which the headline read NEW ORLEANS IS INUNDATED AS 2 LEVEES FAIL; MUCH OF GULF COAST IS CRIPPLED; TOLL RISES. She had suddenly encountered an event that made the rather distant sufferings of pustulated Londoners more explicable and immediate. She had seen Mayor Ray Nagin, caught between the Scylla and Charybdis of FEMA and Lake Pontchartrain, appealing for help on television. In him she recognized the descendant of London's hapless lord mayor, whom Pepys encounters in the streets during the Great Fire crying: "Lord, what can I do? I am spent! People will not obey me. I have been pull[ing] down houses. But the fire overtakes us faster than we can do it."

Katrina also threw Iraq into new relief for the cadets, as it did for the nation at large. The old argument about charity (and democracy) beginning at home resurfaced as the abjectness of the Lower Ninth Ward became obvious to all. But the domestic disaster had the further unfortunate effect of making Iraq and the soldiers who continued to die there seem even farther away. Iraq was, at least for a time, bumped from our collective front page. Just as imperial crises, revolution, and the rise of a global economy had prompted some of the moral and political philosophers we read that semester—Bernard Mandeville, David Hume, Edmund Burke, Adam Smith—to wonder whether we were essentially selfish or benevolent creatures, New Orleans and Iraq prompted cadets to speculate about the conditions that shape our sympathies today. Was a spectator's proximity to suffering a guarantee of generous action? Why did the spectacle of distress move some people to compassionate response but most of us only to idle demonstrations of feeling?

Most of the authors we studied had fairly clear ideas about how sympathy worked: the farther away the victim, the less sympathetic we become. Hume's claim that we are touched more nearly by the scratching of our finger than by the deaths of unseen millions encapsulated the dynamic. In a similar formulation, Adam Smith wrote: "If [a man] was to lose his little finger to-morrow, he would not sleep to-night; but, provided he never saw them, he will snore with the most profound security over the ruin of a hundred millions of his brethren, and the destruction of that immense multitude seems plainly an object less interesting to him, than this paltry misfortune of his own." This aspect of human nature was either something to be borne or something to transcend. Some authors were more optimistic than others. Burke offered one model in *Reflections on the Revolution in France* (1790): "to love the little platoon we belong to in society is the first principle, the germ as it were, of public affections . . . the first link in the series by which we proceed toward a love to our country and to mankind." As the cadets discovered, however, the illusion of proximity produced by visual media further complicated the theories of benevolence and spectatorship devised centuries before.

In Dickens's *Bleak House* (1853), the book with which the course concluded, we encountered another model of human sympathy gone grossly wrong in the satiric account of Mrs. Jellyby's "telescopic philanthropy." Mrs. Jellyby numbers herself among those "individuals anxious for the welfare of their species." She occupies her days with a project, conceived in ignorance of the misery she hopes to relieve, for educating the natives of an African community "on the left bank of the Niger," while her own unsupervised children fall down the stairs and otherwise injure themselves, and while the nearby slums of London teem with poverty and disease. Yet the cadets knew that Dickens had presented them with a false dichotomy: it is never *simply* a choice between relieving the miseries of London and relieving those of Africa, between alleviating the suffering in New Orleans and alleviating that of Baghdad. These cadets were neither isolationist nor telescopically philanthropic by nature, and they saw themselves poised on the threshold of a world in which the ubiquity of suffering and the often crossed wires of self-interest and benevolence, of sympathy and antipathy, demand far more nuanced engagement.

In contrast to the complex metropolises we studied, West Point has all the advantages and disadvantages of a very small town. The generous and very military desire to take care of others is so powerful it can occasionally overwhelm someone—including this civilian—unaccustomed to such close-knit communities. The wonderful feeling produced by unit solidarity that people genuinely care about what happens to you, and the concomitant tolerance for certain kinds of human frailty, is offset by a less attractive and more intrusive feature of small-town living: everyone's business, even one's whereabouts, is a matter of public interest. You are somehow made to feel accountable for all of those things you once thought private and inviolable; furthermore, you become interested in details of other people's lives to which you never used to give a second thought.

The Army conceives of itself as a family: its members and their dependents are referred to as the "Total Army Family," and the Army Internet home page has links to official sites, such as www .armyfamiliesonline.org, which provide guidance for families with deployed members, help for wounded soldiers, and an array of essential support services. The Army's Morale, Welfare and Recreation section is responsible for everything from the Army Library Program to after-school sports activities for military children. *Wellbeing* is the word that crops up most frequently on these sites: the Army is committed to enabling families "To Serve, To Live, To Connect and To Grow."

At West Point, this commitment manifests itself in all sorts of ways. New cadets are sponsored by families living on or near post. Many of my colleagues acquire large broods of adopted sons and daughters. Some of them run de facto hotels: cadet mothers, fathers, girlfriends, sisters, cousins, and aunts bivouac in their quarters on a regular basis. There are also official ways in which units dispense assistance. Each year donations are solicited for a department morale fund, which is used to send flowers to anyone who has had a death in the family and to purchase "baby cups" to present to new parents. My male colleagues' wives superintend a great deal of this caregiving. If you or a family member is sick, weeks' worth of food will appear at your door. If you have a baby, more food appears, along with baskets of infant-related paraphernalia. The members of your Army Family will deliver all this to you, and they don't even have to like you. It's simply what units do for the people who serve in them.

Participation in such a community, even as a civilian, can become all-consuming. Pat Hoy describes West Point faculty as being drawn "together in a cooperative venture, a partnership committed to service." When he taught at Harvard, he found no "common understanding about just how we ought to be educating," no harnessing of "intellectual power" for "the common good." Whereas at West Point he "had yearned for freedom and solitude," at Harvard he found himself "yearning for the gifts of community." These gifts are substantial. For eight years I lived within ten miles of post. It was not unusual for me to spend seven days a week there, working, socializing, exercising, attending athletic events or band concerts. As the years progressed, I began to understand that what I was feeling when away from my "little platoon" in the company of outsiders—at an academic conference, for example, or even at a relaxed social gathering of family and friends unconnected with military life—was profound dislocation and isolation. I know of no better description of this phenomenon than that of Nikolay Rostov's return to his regiment in *War and Peace*:

> After reporting himself to his colonel, being assigned to his own squadron, and serving on orderly duty and going for forage, after entering into all the little interests of the regiment, and feeling himself deprived of liberty and nailed down within one narrow, unchangeable framework, Rostov had the same feeling of peace and moral support and the same sense of being at home here, and in his proper place, as he had once felt under his father's roof. Here was none of all that confusion of the free world, where he did not know his proper place, and made mistakes in exercising free choice . . . There was no possibility of going from one place or to another. There were not twenty-four hours every day which could be used in so many different ways. There were not those innumerable masses of people of whom no one was nearer or further from one . . . In the regiment everything was well known: this man was a lieutenant, that one a captain; this was a good fellow and that one was not; but most of all, every one was a comrade.

During that initial interview in 1996, the colonels had asked me whether I could work in a world of regimentation, but they hadn't asked me if I thought I could live in one. And even as the work—the cadets—grew increasingly important to me over the years, the sense that some other life was passing me by grew stronger as well. One can begin perhaps to identify too closely with something to which one can never fully belong—with an organization in which one will only ever be an honorary member. And so, in the summer of 2005, I moved to New York City, downriver from the Inner Station to the metropolis.

In an essay called "Imperial Bedroom," Jonathan Franzen argues that Americans, despite their hysterical rhetoric about the right to privacy, are suffering not from a violation of the private realm but rather from a destruction of the public sphere. "A genuine public space is a place where every citizen is welcome to be present and where the purely private is excluded or restricted," he writes. "How sweet the promenading, the seeing and being seen." Franzen suggests that our culture's "fully public places"—museums, courtrooms, trains, bus stations, cafés, and "certain city sidewalks"—are rapidly disappearing. In the truly public space, we pretend not "that 'no one is looking,' but that *everyone* is looking."

I am sympathetic to Franzen's thesis: the ubiquity of iPods and cell phones suggests the degree to which people are living their private lives in public. At West Point, by contrast, the impression that everyone is looking all the time prevails. In this sense it is not partaking of the national crisis that Franzen describes. Working there gives one an appreciation for what it means to live one's life in public. By contrast, city living, especially New York City living, still boasts the wonderful advantages of privacy and anonymity. The exchanges one has with strangers, from the civil few minutes with a doorman to the full-on catfight with a woman driving her shopping cart as if it were a tank at Fairway, are discrete. You walk away, go home, and close the door—not without caring but without owing or being owed.

What happened on the day of my move, however, also brought home to me what I would be losing by joining Rostov's "innumerable masses of people." Early in the morning, a colleague and his wife, upset that I had hired a professional mover instead of asking them for help, arrived just to make sure everything went smoothly. The two of them then spent the better part of the day vacuuming, dusting baseboards, and scrubbing the refrigerator with me. Whatever I didn't think would fit in the new apartment—a bicycle and some odds and ends—they insisted on taking home with them to store in their basement. This was not the kind of interest I could expect from my new neighbors.

One of the most bizarre discoveries of those first few months in New York City was the ice cream man, whom I hadn't seen since my suburban childhood. During the summer in New York, you can find a Mister Softee truck around every corner. Of course you can also find used condoms and sauntering rats. The city's daily disorders, incongruities, and mysteries—echoes of the smaller-scale unruliness I remember from New Haven and Cambridge—are antidotes to the beautiful, manicured transparency of West Point. In repatriating me to the civilian world, the move also gave me a bit of hope that at least in certain respects the divide between military and civilian universes might not be as wide as I had begun to convince myself it was. To Victor, the man who works at the garage, my job is "cool." "It's the teacher!" he cries when I drive up in the evening. To Sammy, the electrician who spent hours in my apartment trying to solve a wacky circuit problem, the military is a subject of animated conversation. His best friend is a captain in the Marines. The account manager at my new bank had just gotten back from a tour in Kuwait with the National Guard, and we spent a sympathetic hour on a transaction that would ordinarily take ten minutes.

In the old days, before the war and the disproportionate suffering of the ill-equipped Guard, I used to hear occasional complaints about "weekend warriors" from a few of my active-duty colleagues, who periodically help to train them. I don't hear them anymore. Thanks to the soldier who put Donald Rumsfeld on the spot one day, we have all now heard of the scandal of underarmored HMMWVs. Max told me that when his column came upon a Guard unit in Iraq, they found them without basic equipment and in need of instruction on the proper maintenance of the weapons they did have. What the Guard also lacks, of course, is the elaborate support system available to active-duty soldiers returning to, say, Fort Bragg or Fort Drum. When Guard soldiers come home, they return to communities from which they feel distant—communities often ill-equipped to deal with the myriad complexities of a soldier's homecoming. They have to work much harder to preserve their Army Family.

I had an opportunity to see a Guard unit at firsthand in April 2006, when I was invited to speak at the annual military medicine conference of the Connecticut Army-Air National Guard, head-quartered in Niantic. A colonel, whose Support Medical Battalion had recently returned from a year in Iraq, had heard me talk about Jarrell's "The Death of the Ball Turret Gunner" on the radio several months before. He told me that listening to the poem "brought back memories of crouching down in the back of the HMMWV's hoping that we would neither roll over nor encounter an IED." No one is a banker, a surgeon, or a professor in her spare time, he reminded me, but these soldiers have full-time jobs in addition to their military ones. They really are "citizen-soldiers."

I reached Niantic way ahead of schedule, just as I had done so many years earlier on my first trip to West Point. I stopped in a donut shop to kill some time. When I walked in, the locals eyed me suspiciously; it was a small town, and everyone knew one another. I felt like Spencer Tracy in *Bad Day at Black Rock*. Clutching my foam cup in a corner, I waited for Ernest Borgnine to upend a chair and tell me to get out of town. Only when I rolled onto Camp Rell and the armed guard stopped me at the gate did I begin to feel welcome. I knew the drill, spoke the lingo, and had the necessary identification to navigate the terrain. I didn't even know what my host looked like, but I knew that the first NCO I found would deliver me right to him, and she did.

The conference began with a familiar ritual, a promotion ceremony. A major in the Air National Guard was being promoted to lieutenant colonel. When "Attention to Orders" was sounded, I knew just what to do. As I stood with everyone else, I could just as easily have been in Cullum Hall watching one of my colleagues get promoted under Pershing's portrait. There again was that comforting warmth of feeling emanating from strangers: from the colonel and his wife; from the indefatigable Sergeant First Class Burns, whose directions were better than a Global Positioning System; from the recently promoted lieutenant colonel who later thanked me for coming to speak, I felt—there is no other word for it—at home.

The motto of the colonel's battalion, "To Conserve Fighting Strength," encapsulates with uncomfortable irony a medical unit's mission. A doctor's perspective on war is unique; it discloses complexities that other soldiers are not as likely to note. I had watched a lot of $M^*A^*S^*H$ episodes as a kid, but I had never given much serious thought to the strange predicament of medical personnel in the war zone. At Camp Rell, I learned the many things that healthcare professionals do in theater. "I hope those slides weren't too graphic for you," the colonel apologized as he sat down next to me at the end of his presentation. The slide show was designed for the medics in the audience, who were, in addition to reconnecting with their Army Family, receiving continuing education credits. It started out harmlessly enough with photos of the peeling hands and feet symptomatic of scarlet fever.

It is easy to forget amid dramatic accounts of the extraordinary medical care given to those wounded in battle that the ailments of peace, from the sergeant's bronchitis to the general's upset stomach, persist in war. The second slide, which depicted evidence of ringworm on a soldier's rear end, provoked some laughter among the medics: its caption read "Moonin'." The unsightly papules of the pox virus and the nonhealing lesion of an infected sand fly bite that followed seemed at once more painful and less amusing. Next came the slide of a seemingly innocuous spotted rash on a soldier's palms and on the soles of his feet; for those of us who didn't know what this rash portended, the downright nasty photograph that followed, a penis covered with open sores, proved quite a surprise. Syphilis was the coup de grâce. I suddenly remembered why I hadn't gone to medical school.

The second part of the colonel's presentation chronicled diseases no longer familiar to most Americans, including American medical personnel. These are the still-extant scourges of the developing world: polio, tuberculosis of the spine (something I had always associated with Alexander Pope), the advanced stages of tetanus caused by tying off a newborn's umbilical cord with unsterile material. Finally, we watched video footage of a young girl, her legs paralyzed by polio, crawling on her knees along the floor of a hut. The muddy roads of her village would have rendered the wheelchair the docs offered to send a useless gift. The colonel's battalion, like other medical units deployed to Iraq and Afghanistan, had made goodwill visits to countless towns and villages, where they encountered conditions virtually obsolete in developed nations. When I asked the colonel if they had been able to help in any significant way, he suggested that the visits were too short and the scale of suffering too great for anyone to make a lasting impact.

The central theme of the conference was post-traumatic stress disorder, and the colonel had invited me to talk about "literature and the reality of combat." Post-traumatic stress disorder is only the latest in a series of names given to a condition that has been diagnosed since the Civil War: Da Costa's syndrome, soldier's heart, effort syndrome, shell shock, war neurosis, neurasthenia, and battle fatigue. Jacob Mendez Da Costa, who did pioneering work in the field, first encountered soldiers with dizziness, shortness of breath, faintness, palpitations, and rapid heart rates while working as a physician at a Philadelphia military hospital during the Civil War.

Only during World War I did doctors begin to consider psychological causes for these symptoms. In 1918 the British physician Thomas Lewis published *The Soldier's Heart and the Effort Syndrome*, in which he suggested that the Army had mistakenly diagnosed traumatized soldiers as cardiac patients: "Unwittingly the Army has done a monstrous thing . . . It is a first task in treating the patients under consideration to persuade them of the truth, to bring home to them the fact that their hearts are really sound." Lewis knew he was in murky territory: "If we are to raid more fully that no-man's-land, the borderland of disease which is the hunting ground of the adventuresome, this syndrome will be a foe we shall often encounter."

It was not cardiology but psychoanalysis that at last offered a new vocabulary with which to discuss the invisible damage done by war. Freud's definition of trauma in *Beyond the Pleasure Principle*, published in 1920, isn't so very different from that found today in the entry on post-traumatic stress disorder in the *DSM-IV*: "A condition has long been known and described which occurs after severe mechanical concussions, railway disasters and other accidents involving a risk to life," Freud writes; "it has been given the name of 'traumatic neurosis.' The terrible war which has just ended gave rise to a great number of illnesses of this kind." Among the symptoms that signaled traumatic neurosis were the inability to remember the event that triggered it, the incidence of distorted nightmares and flashbacks, and a general numbing of emotion. A traumatic memory resists assimilation into our consciousness; instead, too terrible to be owned, it lurks in the unconscious, threatening us with its hints and shadows. As we are once again being forced to think about trauma in a time of war, it is worthwhile to recall how strongly influenced Freud's psychoanalytic theories were by the devastation of that "terrible war" that was supposed to end them all.

Whatever I knew about trauma came from books: from the *DSM-IV*; from Freud, whom I had studied in a course on trauma theory at Yale; and from the various representations of traumatic experience I had encountered there and elsewhere—the narrative gaps of Heinrich von Kleist's *Marquise of O*, the impasses of Toni Morrison's *Sula*, the haunted character of Krebs in Hemingway's "Soldier's Home," the shell-shocked figure of Septimus Warren Smith in Virginia Woolf's *Mrs. Dalloway*, the variously maladjusted Vietnam veterans of Michael Cimino's film *The Deer Hunter*, and the "small drawn" hearts of Owen's "Insensibility." "If Freud turns to literature to describe traumatic experience," writes Cathy Caruth, who taught the course on trauma I took at Yale, "it is because literature, like psychoanalysis, is interested in the complex relation between knowing and not knowing, and it is at this specific point at which knowing and not knowing intersect that the psychoanalytic theory of traumatic experience and the language of literature meet." Literature, especially poetry, can know several truths at once.

At the conference I had planned to talk about such semantic distinctions and about the reasons trauma is interesting from linguistic and literary points of view, but I crossed my opening paragraph out as soon as the Army psychiatrist who spoke before me about combat stressors declared, "Everyone here knows what I'm talking about." I was next on the program, and I suddenly felt I had nothing to say. Even my belief in literature's potentially restorative powers seemed hopelessly callow and abstract after that. What could I tell the medics that they didn't already know? Now, and I think for the first time, I suddenly understood why my plebes clung so steadfastly to the idea that Jarrell's not having been a ball turret gunner really matters. Like the plebes who arrive at their first English class armed with the number of gallons in the reservoir, I had come to the conference armed with a species of knowledge that was seemingly of no use.

The psychiatrist spoke of the shame that still attaches to mental illness in the military and how difficult it is to get soldiers to report problems. He also told of the counseling he gave to troops following the accidental shootings that inevitably result when soldiers unused to carrying weapons with chambered rounds follow combat-ready procedures for the first time. He cited the particular challenges of treating suicidal or homicidal soldiers who came into the treatment facility with their loaded weapons. Recounting a visit to Abu Ghraib, which occurred soon after news of the abuses broke, he communicated the old and new horrors of that place. I was becoming increasingly apprehensive as the talk wore on. Toward the end, however, the psychiatrist showed a picture in which he and his team were dressed up in all-black "beatnik outfits," as he called them, the way little children might dress up as soldiers. To relax at Camp Victory, in Kuwait, they had staged a poetry reading. "It was more than a coincidence," the colonel later wrote to me, that the doctor "arranged a poetry reading session in Iraq. The ball turret gunner of yesterday stands today in the turret of the HMMWV."

The soldier-poets of Camp Victory made me feel better. The links articulated by Freud between literature and trauma seemed valuable once again. Besides, literature was all I had, and I told the medics precisely that. I spoke about Jarrell and the plebes, about how cadets by reading literature might prepare themselves for what Adam called those "far away realities"; about how they know that having their remains washed out of a HMMWV with a hose is one of the eventualities they have signed up for. I told them about Margaret, then a lieutenant in Germany awaiting deployment to Iraq, who wrote to me about the poem's new significance for her:

I am reminded of my own Plebe Year when we went over war poetry and prose in your class. What a flashback . . . my brother . . . just returned from Afghanistan and narrowly missed riding in a HMMWV that ended up being blown up by an IED and everyone but one soldier died in that vehicle—including the person sitting in the seat he was going to sit in, himself, had he gone. In the near future my unit will be deployed to Iraq . . . and . . . "The Death of the Ball Turret Gunner" [seems] fitting in times like these. Even more so knowing that two of my brother's friends had to have their own body parts washed out of their HMMWV.

Margaret's job in Iraq required her to be alone much of the time, away from her soldiers, in the indifferent company of bats and camel spiders. "All around me is dust and isolation, wind and 130 degree heat," she wrote during her deployment months later.

At night it's a stagnant heat with bats circling soundlessly and always this silence in and around everything here, when unbroken by mortar or rocket attacks. I had thought to myself that if there really were an edge of the world, if at one point you could sail a ship to where sky meets Earth and fall off . . . here is where you would land—with a big dusty plop. Right here, in the middle of absolutely nowhere, absolutely nothing. At the end of the world.

Am I ok . . . ? Well, I don't know. I think part of what is inside shuts off in you when you come to a place like this, live something like this. You can't count the days, there's too many left. You can't focus on the end, it's too far away. You can't wish for more or for different, there's no changing anything. There's no leaving. I think it's a numbness that comes over one here.

At the end of the earth time stops. Margaret's was a suspended life in which she could not afford to look forward. Perhaps it is no coincidence that the Army term for a deadline is a *suspense*, sometimes abbreviated simply S: and followed by a date. The first time I was told that I had to "meet a suspense," I didn't know where to look, but now I understand the aptness of referring even to an end by a term most of us associate with uncertainty. Uncertainty ordinarily produces in us both pleasure and anxiety, but in the case of traumatic injury it may disrupt the emotional life altogether. The Army is a life of perpetual suspense: the soldier waits for war to begin, and then she waits for it to end.

By now I have grown used to getting e-mails like Margaret's from the war zone, but that wasn't always the case. I still remember receiving my first one on September 10, 2003, the day on which my relationship to the war fundamentally changed. Neil's message sat in my in-box with the subject line "Greetings from Mosul." To me, if not to the sender, there was something odd about the kind of war in which a soldier could return from a patrol to fire off an e-mail to an English professor. Traditionally, the only safe spectators of battle have been the elite: Lord Ellenborough supposedly watched a battle in nineteenth-century India from the back of an elephant; at the battle of Crécy, Edward III monitored his army's progress from a nearby windmill and there received news of the death of his son, the Black Prince; Xerxes watched the climactic naval battle of Salamis from the shore.

Most civilians—from the Scots at Culloden to the Iraqis in Haditha—unfortunate enough to find themselves in an army's line of march or within range of its guns become subject to all manner of depredations. During the Sicilian Expedition, in the pivotal naval battle between the Athenians and the Syracusans in 413 B.C., Plutarch tells us that "the spectators suffered as much emotional turmoil as those who were taking part in it, since they could survey the whole action and see how rapidly and unexpectedly things chopped and changed." I remember watching the First Gulf War in a college dorm room: every night after dinner we would all pile onto someone's couch for the nightly coverage. It was, as the media meant it to be, entertainment of a kind, and there was no doubt more than a touch of the antique Roman in our fascination with the spectacle served up to us. The story my friends and I followed with the greatest interest was not, strictly speaking, a military one. It was, rather, the psychological disintegration of one correspondent on a rooftop amid the shelling and his replacement by a suave, slim customer who proved he could take the heat. We weren't suffering at all.

My strange relationship to the current war—my contradictory feelings of proximity and understanding on the one hand and impossible distance on the other—was brought home to me one weekend at the Tribeca Film Festival in 2006, as I watched *The War Tapes*, a prizewinning documentary about a unit of the New Hampshire National Guard. Throughout the screening I felt out of sync with much of the audience. I laughed alone when I heard a soldier make a wry observation that might have come from one of my students. Conversely, when a soldier said something I knew to be in deadly earnest—something that perhaps reminded me of a message I had received from Iraq—I was silent, while the rest of the audience burst out with laughter. I left before the question-and-answer session with the director because I could imagine only too well the tenor of the conversation.

Now the gap between my two worlds felt wider than ever, and I couldn't wait to return to West Point the following Monday to talk to someone who would understand the source of my frustration. This film, shot largely by the guardsmen themselves with handheld cameras, which they carried or mounted on their helmets and vehicles, purported to give us war as the soldier sees it. But the war we get in documentaries such as this, on network and cable news shows, only looks real. It is a kind of reality television: a neatly packaged simulacrum with a door to the outside world, which, like the one Jim Carrey's boat bumps up against in *The Truman Show*, we can find if we look hard enough. Now that I know some of the combatants in this war's digitally recorded spectacle, I no longer like to watch. It isn't because I suffer the way those old Athenians did but because of the ease with which I can still find myself mesmerized by war's violent tableau.

Television, embedded reporting, and videography have turned the rest of us into war's insulated voyeurs, the assiduous consumers of the sounds and sights of death. While technology creates an illusion of intimacy, the consumption of the war as a spectacular movie arouses our pity but does nothing to enlarge our sympathies. Paradoxically, Neil's e-mail brought war and all its suffering home to me by keeping it virtual and very far away and by telling the story in words instead of pictures. I had not heard from Neil since he finished Ranger School, when he wrote to tell me that it was hard to find time to read. He had been able to finish only Jonathan Franzen's *The Corrections* and *Choke*, by Chuck Palahniuk (whose novel *Fight Club* has become, along with the movie made from it, something of a cult favorite among cadets). From Mosul, he told me of the challenges of rebuilding a city "from the ground up." His platoon handled everything "from broken water mains, unhealthy meat markets, excessive dumpsites" to "the occasional bad guy." In his downtime Neil read more Palahniuk and a lot of Bret Easton Ellis, but also David Halberstam's *The Teammates* and James Mc-Donough's *Platoon Leader*, an account of the author's combat experience in Vietnam that is a staple of many officers' reading lists. Now all he had left was Nelson DeMille, which he considered beach reading, but it would have to hold him until the next shipment of novels showed up, as he put it, "to feed my hunger." Amazon.com delivers to Iraq, he reported, and a friend's wife back home promised to send some of Neil's old textbooks so that he could "get a little more enlightened" while he was there.

At last, here was a problem for me to solve. Soon journals, magazines, and paperbacks—*The Grove Press Reader, A Farewell to*

Arms, back issues of literary quarterlies and magazines—were flying off my bookshelves into a carton. I trolled the halls, asking my colleagues for donations. "Books for Baghdad?" they would ask enthusiastically, referring to a program that collected books for Baghdad University, to which the Military Academy faculty had contributed with such generosity that it had come to seem like a Berlin Airlift of books. "Um, no," I would say, "I've got my own thing going," and return to my office armed with more donations. "Books are coming," I tell Neil. Good, he replies. Foucault, Camus, and Pynchon won't last forever. "Everything," he declares, "will be read."

Neil continued to send messages about books and baseball, another favorite topic for both of us. He spoke so often about reading that I began to wonder what else he did in Iraq. "It probably sounds like I have too much time on my hands out here," he writes, anticipating my question, "but when we aren't patrolling we are waiting to patrol, so the schedule has been more than kind to my reading habit." In his next message he insists, "Things here are great . . . I am enjoying everything that has been thrown at me (minus grenades), and I can't complain about the amount of time that I am afforded to read and write and have to myself." What larks! I think, but I can't help interpreting much of this nonchalance as a form of self-preservation.

The phenomenon of compulsive reading and writing on the part of soldiers was familiar to me from the case of T. E. Lawrence, that other desert warrior, who wrote that to him "fiction"—reading as well as writing it—"seemed more solid than activity." Lawrence carried the Arthurian romances of Sir Thomas Malory everywhere with him in his kit, yet he felt that he lived in an antiheroic age: "The epic mode was alien to me, as to my generation." Throughout the Arab Revolt, Lawrence wrote steadily, pathologically even, using any paper he could find. In addition to the small, leather-bound pocket diaries housed at the British Library, there is an entire pad of British Army supply forms the backs of which he filled with notes and maps, the handwriting so ragged in places that it must have been done on the back of a camel.

Ultimately, Neil revealed the fundamental importance of his reading: "I have been rolling through books out here at a pretty steady clip, and anything that has provided a challenge or stimulated the mind a little more than usual has made the day, the week, go by much quicker." When Neil finally came home, he used his leave for a long, meandering trip across the country before returning to work at Fort Campbell, Kentucky, where, he confessed, "I have not been able to read as much I like to." Now he could only "slowly creep" through books. Unleavened by war, they had become somehow less urgent. Although he so obviously loves books, he was no longer reading for his life.

In speaking to the Guard about Neil, Margaret, and the other young officers with whom I had been corresponding, I realized that I had adopted the physician's language of palliation and cure. I seemed to be promoting literature as a kind of elixir, as something that had the power to bestow a particular kind of courage and a particular kind of knowing. The courage I had in mind was the deliberative variety that could withstand all the accidents that might derail the merely brave. The knowledge I had in mind consisted in an ability to know more than one truth, to rest in uncertainty when uncertainty is required, and to change one's mind when the evidence demands. It was a mature knowledge of the type Montaigne describes in his essay "On Educating Children" as enabling us to move beyond the books from which we learn: "'Knowing' something does not mean knowing it by heart," he writes, "that simply means putting it in the larder of our memory. That which we rightly 'know' can be deployed without looking back at the model, without turning our eyes back towards the book." It was that courage and that knowledge, I told the medics, that I hoped the cadets could acquire somewhere along the way.

My trip to Niantic helped to reaffirm for me the connections between what I teach and the people to whom I teach it. The visit also introduced me to one of the more eccentric and enriching perspectives on Iraq I have yet encountered. Sergeant First Class Jonathan Trouern-Trend works in civilian life for the American Red Cross. He is tall, lean, gentle, and boyish; I was startled to learn that he has five children. "He's an encyclopedia," the colonel whispered to me as Trouern-Trend began an improvised lecture on the inevitability of bird flu. Later in the day he gave another briefing on wildlife in Iraq, during which he noted that Kermit Roosevelt, who fought in Mesopotamia during World War I, called the book he wrote about his experience there *War in the Garden of Eden.* Trouern-Trend's garden had its snake, too; in his case, a Persian sand viper hiding in someone's boot. His slides depicted a wide variety of beasts: bull sharks that grew to enormous sizes after feeding well during the Iran-Iraq War; white storks and bustards perched in tamarisk trees; striped hyenas that prowled camp and were shot by vector-control agents from Kellogg Brown and Root.

In *Birding Babylon: A Soldier's Journal from Iraq*, Sergeant First Class Trouern-Trend has made what he called in the copy he inscribed to me his own "little contribution" to the literature of Operation Iraqi Freedom. The book, which originated as a blog, is a remarkable account of his time at Camp Anaconda, which, in addition to holding "a large American arsenal" and being "the target of almost daily rocket and mortar attacks," was also home to a veritable menagerie. The birds ranged from the exotic to the comfortingly familiar: from the ubiquitous house sparrow to the hoopoe (*Upupa epops*), a bird to which the Iraqis attribute magic powers. "Knowing that the great cycles of nature continue despite what people happen to be doing is reassuring, I think," writes Trouern-Trend. "There is an order we can take comfort in and draw strength from." Now, whenever he remembers Iraq, he will always think of the catalog of birds he saw there, several of them "life birds," the wonderful, one might almost say hopeful, term given by birders to species they have spotted for the first time.

After his presentation, Trouern-Trend and I talked about the birds of World War I poetry. He knew all about Isaac Rosenberg's "Returning, We Hear the Larks," in which soldiers struggle back to camp on a "night ringing with unseen larks," but he was eager to learn more about Rosenberg's contemporary Edward Thomas, whose poetry is full of nightingales, sedge warblers, and blackbirds. Birdsong seemed more congenial to Thomas than the language of men; he valued nothing so much as "a pure thrush word." Perhaps it said to him all that the desperate human voice no longer could. Nightingales and other real and metaphorical birds also feature in the literature treasured in Iraq and Afghanistan. As Annia Ciezadlo noted in a 2004 *Christian Science Monitor* article about the cultural and political significance of poetry in Iraq, beside every palm tree, a popular saying goes, you will find a poet. In *One Thousand and One Arabian Nights*, itself a tapestry of prose and verse, a falcon saves the life of a king, a parrot discloses a secret to his master, and "a bird of Eden" with a body of pearls and emeralds sings the praises of Allah. Among the Persian poems Al read with the Afghan colonel were Rumi's "The Parrot of Baghdad" and Attar's "Parliament of Birds," in which the magic hoopoe itself appears as a divine emissary.

All of this bird talk made me think of Joey. The week before his graduation, he had come to my office carrying an enormous box wrapped in newspaper. When I opened it, I found the metal sculpture of a rooster. "I hope you like ugly roosters," he said. My rooster is less ugly than whimsical, with a tail so voluminous that I had trouble finding a place to put it. It perches proudly atop a wardrobe in my office as a reminder of its slightly eccentric giver. One afternoon in November 2004, about a year after Joey graduated and shortly after he reported to Fort Hood, Texas, he left a voice mail saying that he would be on his way to Iraq at 0330 the next morning. When I reached him on his cell phone later that evening, he was standing outside the Austin Music Hall waiting for the doors to open. Nothing, he informed me, not even Iraq, was going to keep him from a Willie Nelson concert.

We talked for a little while, to the familiar accompaniment of street sounds in the background. Joey is as unflappable as they come, and the only signs of apprehension were a few long pauses punctuated by humorous observations about the sergeant who had predicted with great confidence only a few days before that they wouldn't be leaving for at least another week. They still hadn't given Joey an APO address, but he promised to e-mail once he arrived. At Thanksgiving I got a message from Baghdad with an avian theme: "Well the goose is loose," he announced, but no platoons were available yet, and he was doing his best, as the lone second lieutenant at headquarters, to stay out of the way. Eager to latch on to a patrol as soon as possible, he had read Bernard Lewis's *The Crisis of Islam* in the meantime to find out what everyone's "feathers [are] all ruffled up about." I shipped him a box of books and some turkey jerky to help him pass the time until he got his platoon.

Joey is a country boy who believes in Willie, beer, and pickups. He considers my newfound enthusiasm for Johnny Cash's *At Folsom Prison* a very positive development. But Joey is an odd country boy, and his musical library and literary tastes are eclectic and cosmopolitan. Whenever we talk, he shares a new discovery: one day it is the poetry of Pablo Neruda, the next a novel by Michael Ondaatje, and, most recently, Nicole Krauss's *The History of Love*. He thought Virginia Woolf's *A Room of One's Own* "wonderful" and once proposed that her book *Orlando* should be required reading for all cadets. Joey also writes poetry and fiction awash with sensuous description and a love of words. At West Point, in addition to writing a senior thesis on the poetry of Anne Sexton, he played rugby and lifted weights. Indeed, his looks and charisma would make him a natural for an Army recruiting poster; his smiling charm, forthrightness, and good nature made him hugely popular with his fellow cadets.

While in Ranger School, he called from Georgia to ask me how to translate "Fear no man" into Latin so that he and his buddies could inscribe it on their Kevlar helmets. I don't know whether that's the helmet he brought to Iraq. Toward the end of his time in the desert, Joey sent a melancholy e-mail with the subject line "Green Thoughts and Green Shades." He was paraphrasing a line from Andrew Marvell's "The Garden," a poem in which the speaker finds himself in a fecund garden ensnared by flowers and tripped up by vegetation. Overloaded with the stimuli of war, Joey perhaps found a parallel to his own fatigue in the description of what happens to the speaker's mind once his body has fallen onto the grass:

> What a wondrous life is this I lead!
> Ripe apples drop about my head;
> The luscious clusters of the vine
> Upon my mouth do crush their wine;
> The nectarine and curious peach,
> Into my hands themselves do reach;
> Stumbling on melons, as I pass,
> Insnared with flowers, I fall on grass.
>
> Meanwhile the mind, from pleasure less,
> Withdraws into its happiness;
> The mind, that ocean where each kind
> Does straight its own resemblance find;
> Yet it creates, transcending these,
> Far other worlds and other seas,
> Annihilating all that's made
> To a green thought in a green shade.

What a remarkable counterpoint to the sights and sounds of a Baghdad street patrol Marvell's "happy garden-state" must have been.

Joey wrote to me soon after he returned from Iraq to Fort Hood to report one friend dead and another blinded. From Hood he moved to the Old Guard, a ceremonial unit in Washington, D.C., where one of his duties was the Arlington funeral detail. Joey confessed that he felt a little "guilty" that he was not sharing the risk of those still deployed. This guilt, I told him, is the soldier's inevitable lot. Working as he did near Walter Reed, Joey met up with more friends and classmates who had been wounded. One of them works for the Army's Wounded Warrior Program, established a few years ago to help the wounded return to the Army or reintegrate into civilian life.

That reintegration will be one of the important domestic challenges of the coming decades. As Freud noted in *Reflections on War and Death*, published in 1918, war transforms our attitude toward death by destroying our strategies of denial. Examining the psychological impact of war deaths on "those who remain at home," Freud concludes that we are thrown by them into a state of "confusion and paralysis." We try to heal our own psychic wounds by turning each death into a story, by giving each life lost a shape and a purpose. All deaths gain the luster of patriotic sacrifice, but the presence of the wounded, like the rupture of war itself, is far more difficult to assimilate.

Improvements in body armor and in the procedures for treating and evacuating casualties from the battlefield have markedly reduced mortality rates. The lethality of war wounds in Vietnam, for example was 24 percent. It was the same for the First Gulf War, but in the current conflicts in Iraq and Afghanistan, the rate is only 10 percent. Today soldiers are living with wounds that they would not have survived in earlier wars. "The cost, however, can be high," as Atul Gawande reminds us. In *The New England Journal of Medicine*, Gawande details by way of example the "devastating injuries" of one survivor of a mortar attack: "The airman lost one leg above the knee, the other in a hip disarticulation, his right hand, and part of his face. How he and others like him will be able to live and func-

tion remains an open question." Today soldiers are given unprece-
dented levels of surgical care at Walter Reed, but, once released,
they return to local VA clinics and hospitals that do not boast the
same state-of-the-art facilities.

Flown into Andrews Air Force Base at night without fanfare,
thousands of soldiers wounded in Iraq have passed through the
wards at Walter Reed, which has, despite "its contemporary architecture, high-tech wards, and superb physicians," Lawrence Kaplan
reported several years ago in *The New Republic*, "the feel of a Civil
War hospital." Furthermore, *The Washington Post*'s report on the
deplorable condition of out-patient facilities at Walter Reed in February 2007 suggests the degree to which the Army's commitment to
long-term rehabilitation programs lags behind its surgical prowess.

More than two centuries ago, George Washington, concerned
about the government's failure to adequately compensate noncom-
missioned veterans of the Revolutionary War, warned: "Nothing
could be a more melancholy and distressing sight, than to behold
those who have shed their blood or lost their limbs in the service of
their Country, without a shelter, without a friend, and without the
means of obtaining any of the necessaries or comforts of Life; compelled to beg their daily bread from door to door!" The increase in
the Veterans Administration's discretionary spending budget in fis-
cal year 2007 was prompted by last year's embarrassments. According to a December 2006 story in *The Washington Post*, the VA will
receive $80.6 billion. "Officials hope to avoid a repeat of last year,"
wrote Christopher Lee, "when the VA received $1.2 billion in emer-
gency funding after it had underestimated the number of personnel
returning from Iraq and Afghanistan who would seek VA medical
treatment." The VA "expects to treat 5.3 million veterans" in 2007.
We are still a long way from fulfilling our debt. More recently, questions about the willingnesss of some officers to refer soldiers to
mental-health services at Fort Carson have surfaced.

Stories of the wounded have always been difficult to tell, while
those of the dead are the stuff of national newspapers, CNN, and

epic cinema. We much prefer the dead to the wounded in part because they can be more easily honored and lionized. Documentary filmmakers, however, are now beginning to break the silence. The 2005 film *Purple Heart*, for example, chronicles the lives of several wounded veterans returned from Iraq. Caring for them is a responsibility that will last for decades, and what makes it even more difficult is the fact that not all injuries are readily visible.

If the physical wound is difficult for us to contemplate, psychological wounds are even less comprehensible. The Vietnam experience raised civilian awareness about war's psychological wounds and the Army's own sensitivity to the reality of PTSD, but in a culture that so valorizes the physical, the realm of the mind remains largely invisible. Sergeant Steve Cobb, who suffered a traumatic brain injury in Iraq and was diagnosed with depression and PTSD, explained in a story reported by Joseph Shapiro on NPR in November 2005 that during his three months at Walter Reed he felt the amputees received the lion's share of attention. They had become, Shapiro suggested, "the symbol of what an injured soldier is supposed to look like." Sergeant Cobb put it this way: "There's just as much or more wrong with me than there is him. They can put prosthetics on him—he's fixed. What can they do for me? You can't put prosthetics on our brain. I'm not fixed." Cobb's theory about a hierarchy of the wounded makes sense to me: it echoes our lingering suspicion that psychological wounds are unmanly, something not to be discussed by real warriors.

West Point's alumni association maintains an online memorial page that honors "those members of the Long Gray Line who lost their lives as a result of the attack against our country on September 11, 2001, or have given their lives in the defense of freedom while fighting the war on terrorism." The list includes a graduate who had left the Army and who had the misfortune to be working at the World Trade Center on September 11, another graduate killed while working for a private contractor in Baghdad, and many younger graduates killed in Afghanistan and Iraq. Yet Ted Westhusing's name does not appear. His suicide, deemed in military parlance "a non-combat-related injury" yet indissolubly linked to the fact of war, does not fit neatly into the page's heroic story of defending freedom, and so it is passed over in silence. It is a gap in communal remembrance that reproduces the individual soldier's own repression of the traumatic memory of war. It also suggests the uneasy place this war, like Vietnam before it, will one day occupy in national memory.

In *The World According to Garp*, a book in which the author John Irving makes so much of the ball turret's symbolism, the nurse Jenny Fields distinguishes in her mind the injuries that befall most of the patients in intensive care from what happens to soldiers: "What happened to them was no accident," she concludes, calling the wounded soldiers who appear in the ward "non-accidents." But in fact accident and chance are always part of war's narrative: one person is hit while another is not; one vehicle rolls safely away even as the next one explodes. Remember how Margaret recounted that her brother "narrowly missed" riding in the HMMWV that was blown up. The story of Bill Hecker's death by IED has already acquired a communal significance beyond its devastating personal import for his family and friends, but soon after it happened, one officer told me, "I'm angry. It's like convoy roulette out there."

Often imbued with survivor's guilt, war stories are filled with accidents, missed encounters, hairbreadth escapes, and the distortions and gaps characteristic of traumatic memory. Mistakes and near misses are also the stuff of war literature—of Odysseus's postwar wanderings as well as of Tim O'Brien's "true" war stories. Whenever I read the *Odyssey*, I am struck anew by the tale of Elpenor, the youngest soldier in Odysseus's band of drifters. In the underworld, Odysseus is startled to see the shade of this callow soldier, whose body the commander had neglected to bury on Circe's isle. Homer takes pains to tell us that poor Elpenor is "none too brave in battle, none too sound in mind." He has died not in a battle—not even in a training accident—but by a fall from a roof after a night of drinking. Elpenor pleads with Odysseus to return to Circe's island to bury his body, and his impatient commander honors his request for a warrior's funeral, burned on a pyre "in full armor." Odysseus also erects a tomb on a promontory by the sea so that future generations will learn of Elpenor's luckless story.

It has always seemed to me that Odysseus is just going through the motions. Homer's description of the ceremony is hurried and unsentimental; to the funeral he devotes less than ten lines. Epic journeys to the underworld seal heroic status, allow the living to make peace with the dead, and reveal news of the future. Heroes generally emerge with newfound resolve to face the challenges that remain. In the figure of Elpenor, however, Homer confronts us with a soldier's death that cannot easily be made to fit heroic models. The story told at home, however—the story Odysseus might have told to Elpenor's grieving family were he a modern officer charged with writing the dead soldier's next of kin—works against error, blunder, and chance with a rhetoric of heroism and sacrifice that consoles and that also nourishes an easy patriotism. Witness, for example, the long delay in releasing the information that the former professional football player Pat Tillman's death in Afghanistan had been caused by friendly fire. Death provides an occasion for revision, redemption, and transformation. The revised narrative that results replaces accident with heroic determination.

The wonder of our own age is that we can preserve so many of the living, yet our national subordination of the wounded body to the sacrificial ideal of the corpse camouflaged by a flag in a funeral ceremony risks further dehumanizing the U.S. soldiers who continue to risk their lives. To complicate matters even further, our national preoccupation with the dead coexists with an inability to look at them until they are ready to be buried. The return of bodies to Dover Air Force Base has been closed to the press for thirteen years; even the photograph of flag-draped coffins on a cargo plane published by *The Seattle Times* in April 2004 was greeted with outrage in certain quarters. We send Joey and an honor guard to pick the bodies up, but the camera can't follow him there the way it does on the battlefield.

In large part perhaps because of the ways in which it is packaged for us, the war has given to many American spectators a chance to atone for Vietnam. Never again, we have determined, will we forget that soldiers don't choose their wars. Instead, supporters and opponents alike lay claim to patriotic feeling and to fuller understanding of the soldier's sacrifice. In his World War II poem "P.O.E." (short for point of embarkation), Lincoln Kirstein articulates one soldier's resentment of what he perceives to be a kind of sunshine patriotism. He writes of the women who have volunteered to serve cocoa and cake to soldiers about to ship out:

> They've parked their limousines the while;
> Their natty uniform is spick
> And span, their hairdo and their smile
> Pronounces patriotic chic;
> And THIS IS IT for these dames too.

Today's patriotic chic provokes outbursts such as that of Representative Jean Schmidt, who, soon after being elected to Congress, decided it would be a good idea to suggest that John Murtha, the representative from Pennsylvania who is also a Marine Corps veteran, was a coward. On November 23, 2005, *The Washington Post* reported Schmidt's response to Murtha's call to bring the troops home: "A few minutes ago I received a call from [Retired Marine] Colonel Danny Bubp," Schmidt announced to her colleagues. "He asked me to send Congress a message: Stay the course. He also asked me to send Congressman Murtha a message: that cowards cut and run, Marines never do." Perhaps more disturbing was Schmidt's apology: "Asked if she would change anything if she could do it over again," the *Post* reported, Schmidt said, "I wouldn't have used Congressman Murtha's name." "I am quite willing," she maintained, "to suffer those attacks if in the end that policy [recalling the troops] I so strongly oppose is exposed as unsound. First and foremost I support the troops. They dodge bullets and bombs while I duck only hateful words."

Our national discourse today is remarkable for ecstatic embraces of others' sacrifices. The idolatry of sacrifice animates the argument that the only way to honor the soldiers who have died in Iraq is to send more soldiers to do the same. Followed to its absurd end, of course, such logic leads to the extinction of nations and species. Even in less extreme and provocative formulations, however, the rhetoric of sacrifice continues in 2007, to submerge any real moral and practical arguments that might be made for troop surge or phased redeployment in a morass of sentimentality. It recalls the self-destructive honor displayed by the ancients: "While I'm happy for him," the Spartan woman said when her brother brought news of the death of her son, "I'm equally sorry for you, since you've missed making the journey with such a valiant companion."

The days are gone when the iconic Spartan mother exposed her stomach to her son when he fled from battle and demanded: "Do you plan to creep back in here where you emerged from?" We are kinder and gentler than the Spartans: we expect mothers of the war dead to grieve, but we also expect mothers of yet-living soldiers to sign on to the notion that only the possible deaths of their own children will somehow honor and validate the sacrifices that have already been made. More must die to prove that the first to die have not done so "in vain." That's why no one—neither supporters nor opponents—really knew what to do with Cindy Sheehan, and why she didn't really know how to use her own anger effectively. General Grant noted in a passage that resonates today: "Experience proves that the man who obstructs a war in which his nation is engaged, no matter whether right or wrong, occupies no enviable place in life or history."

One day in the fall of 2006, the nine seniors in my seminar came
into the room comparing notes on an exercise they had just completed in their military science class. The conceit of the exercise
was that, as a result of a plane crash, they would be stranded in the
desert, but only for a few days, after which time they would be rescued. They were then given a list of items they could salvage from
the plane and told to rank them in order of their utility for survival.
Among the available items were a raincoat, a flashlight, a parachute,
a mirror, a knife, a pistol, food, and a bottle of vodka. Fresh from my
reading of Saint-Exupéry's *Wind, Sand and Stars*, I was fairly confident that I knew what to choose, but when Saint-Exupéry crashed,
he didn't know that he would be rescued, and so I was planning for
the long haul. "Remember, ma'am," the cadets warned me as I was
taking the test, "you're going to be rescued in a few days." Those
were the conditions of the exercise. "But how," I asked them, "could
anyone be so sure?" I brought all the wrong things, of course—
loaded myself down with food and weapons—when I should have
brought the raincoat to protect me against the cold desert night, the
parachute to collect any rain that happened to fall, and the mirror
to signal a rescue plane. Some of the cadets had fared well, while
others seemed as ill-prepared for the crash as I was. "You could just
take the vodka, ma'am," teased one. "That's what I did."

Designed as a capstone experience for those majoring in our
program, this course on life writing demanded a great deal of introspection from the cadets: we talked about their educations, about
their professional identities, about the ways in which technology
had reshaped concepts of the self. Sometimes, when class was over,
we found that we had more to say, and those who had nothing
scheduled for the next hour stayed on to continue the conversation.
Even the most heavily armored among them proved willing to ex-
pose a great deal both in discussion and in their semester-long projects, which ranged from a journal of a solitary Thoreauvian sojourn
in the woods to a volume of poetry illustrated by hand.

All of our ruminations on education, training, custom, and tradition had a different valence than they might have done when we were at peace and everything seemed hypothetical, just like the exercise of being stranded in a desert. Then, one day toward the end of class, the cadets turned the tables on me. "Ma'am," one of them said, "it's time you told us why you teach here." As often as I have heard it by now, this always strikes me as a bizarre question. It isn't one I thought to ask my professors, but the idea that someone not in uniform would want to teach those who are evidently still seems odd to cadets. Usually the question comes from the plebes, who don't entirely know themselves what they are doing or why. These seniors, however, knew themselves and me quite well, and I had never found it so difficult to answer this question, which was in effect just another version of the groundskeeper's long ago query, "Miss, what's your function?" "I bet it's because of your dad, right?" offered one. I agreed that my father surely had something to do with my coming to West Point, but that didn't explain why I stayed. "Is it because of patriotism?" asked Kevin. Suspicious of patriotic chic, mindful of Samuel Johnson's observation that it is the "scoundrel" who seeks "refuge" in self-aggrandizing boasts of patriotism, I was leery of this explanation as well.

"I like to think I'm arming you with something you may need," I ventured, "something of value." I hoped that we were becoming travelers of the sort Montaigne describes, wayfarers who visit "foreign lands" not "the way others do so (knowing how much longer and fatter Nero's face is on some old ruin over there compared with his face on some comparable medallion) but mainly learning of the humours of those peoples and of their manners, and knocking off our corners by rubbing our brains against other people's." Whatever we were discovering in that room wasn't tangible. It lacked the particular satisfaction of a well-built bridge or the marvelous utility of a well-aimed M-16, but one day whatever it was might help them in war, and one day it might help them come home.

I can't be sure, of course. "Only fools," Montaigne warned, "have made up their minds and are certain." Make the student understand, Montaigne insisted, advocating the study of Plutarch and others, "that confessing an error which he discovers in his own argument even when he alone has noticed it is an act of justice and integrity, which are the main qualities he pursues; stubbornness and rancour are vulgar qualities, visible in common souls whereas to think again, to change one's mind and to give up a bad case in the heat of the argument are rare qualities showing strength and wisdom." I think I see this capacity in cadets such as the Three Musketeers. Kevin, Renée, and Grant strike me as the sorts of adventurers who, wherever they may find themselves, will be trying to discern people's "humours" and "manners" rather than comparing notes on Nero's nose. As I envision them in those "foreign lands" that Montaigne conjures, I find them not only courageous in confronting the physical dangers they will likely encounter but also unafraid to change their minds. There they'll be knocking their metaphorical corners off and peering into the brains of others, just as we used to do in the corridors of Thayer Hall.

Lately I've been carrying around a copy of Cormac McCarthy's *Blood Meridian* that Joey passed along to me. On the first page, McCarthy describes how his protagonist, the kid, gets to be the way he is: "He can neither read nor write and in him broods already a taste for mindless violence." The kid is the antithesis of Joey, of the Three Musketeers, and of the majority of soldiers I have met; their tastes don't run to mindless violence. Over the last several years, cadets have had to think a lot about their function, too. They know their lives may contain a share of necessary violence, even the possibility of death, but they have the courage to meet brutality with imagination as well as ammunition, with questions as well as convictions, with books or without. They have the wherewithal to resist the abstractions of sacrifice with the realities of leading soldiers in combat and in a peace that one day will come. And that kind of patriotism isn't chic at all.

Ave atque Vale

◆

Ave atque vale—hail and farewell. If there is one thing I have learned from a decade's association with the military, it is how to say goodbye. It is something at which I have had a great deal of practice. Soldiers are creatures of arrival and departure. They rarely stay in one place for very long. One of the oddities of West Point is the relative stability of its population. Senior military faculty, at least, might remain for ten years or more. There is, nonetheless, a significant annual turnover as officers arrive from graduate school or return to the field army. Each academic year is punctuated by two department gatherings: a "Hail" in late summer and a "Farewell" in the spring. In most units, where the cycle is less predictable, such functions are more frequent, their purposes united as a "Hail-and-Farewell."

In 1997, in a large cohort of new faculty in the English Department, there were only a few civilians. One day in the late spring of 2000, one of the officers, a major whose deadpan wit had kept me laughing for three years and with whom I often talked about Grant, Washington, and other research interests, came into my office. "I want to talk to you about something," he said. Because his gloomy expression never changed, I eyed him suspiciously and readied myself for the usual barbs. "No," he said, "I'm serious. When we all leave this summer"—he was referring to the officers, who would be moving on to their next assignments while I stayed on—"it's going to be hard for you. You don't think so now, but it will be." He was right. The weeks of orientation and the various first-year rituals we shared forged an unmistakable bond that today survives infrequent contact. While I don't imagine our cohesion approximated that of a unit, I had a firm sense of kinship with this group and a feeling of belonging that extended to the entire department in those early years. I have valued friends among those I have met in the years since, but I have never identified so closely with a particular group.

In part because they must do it so often, soldiers have strange ways of saying goodbye. The active-duty Army feels small enough to them that there is an expectation that paths will cross again: "I'll see you downrange," one might say to another, and today that means Afghanistan or Iraq, the "sandbox." And, remarkably, soldiers do meet up in unexpected places. There is, however, a competing sense of the future's fragility and what seems to me a superstitious dread that actually saying goodbye stamps the encounter with too much finality. Cards and letters are a preferred method: things that can never be said out loud can at least be written around. Personal send-offs are important: drinking a beer on someone's back porch, sitting in a living room full of moving boxes, meeting for a last dinner at a local restaurant. But you can't act as if they mean anything. This atmosphere of unreality dominated my visit to Dan's quarters the night before he was to leave for Afghanistan several years ago. A few of us stood around on the lawn "giving him shit" as if he were about to embark on a pleasure cruise.

When officers resign or retire, of course, they must say goodbye to the Army itself. Al's transition has been an easy one, but not because his current life bears any resemblance to the Army. He was just ready to go. Before reporting for his last out-processing appointment, he left me a message: "I am outside . . . waiting to watch the fat lady sing, and she is beautiful." If it is true that Al was saved by the Army, it is also true that he was born again by leaving it. Now he has retired to a plot of land in Nebraska about the same size as New York's Central Park: he calls it "Central Park Way Out West." One of the things he wants to do is work that land, for he has the same faith in green things that he does in young people: "I tell you the army in the rearview mirror is one helluva pretty sight, and how. Really. Double really. People getting out of prison can't feel any better." Now he's building a house and working the land. (After all, this is a man who has long subscribed to a newspaper for muleteers.) Liberated, he has time to listen and to look ahead: "The cattle are lowing this morning as calves are separated from mamas, lots of unhappiness. All is well here, whiskers a growin', boys coming and going. Plans afoot . . . I'm headed out for a walk with the dog and then to the potting shed to repot some . . . West Point acorn sprouts. I'm hopin' they shade the drive and the yard before I die."

Ironically, after resigning his commission and entering what he thought would be the entirely alien universe of film school, Max reported, "It amazes me how much a film set runs and operates like a military unit. Commands, phonetic alphabet, chain of command, etc." The former Army captain is right at home; he certainly understands teamwork and knows how to take charge of a group. I think of how many directors from his favorite Hollywood era behaved as if they were generals in the field: Raoul Walsh, with his eye patch and bravado, C. B. De Mille, with his jodhpurs and riding crop. All most of us really ever want is to play at being soldiers. We prefer attenuated crises to the real thing, and we envy those who know how to face them. "I have no idea what I'm doing here," I once confessed to Colonel X when I was in the middle of some project. "Don't worry," he said, "we're all just making it up as we go along." Maybe that's true, but soldiers certainly seem calmer and look better than the rest of us while they're improvising.

One Friday afternoon in October 2005, I find myself headed downtown on the 6 train with four cadets after a tour of Central Park and a visit to the Frick. They all want to escape for the three-day weekend: cadets will go anywhere, even if they have to spend more time on trains, buses, and planes than at their destination. We have arrived here by chance. After saying goodbye to the group outside the museum, I cut over on Seventieth, while they have walked down Fifth Avenue. We meet up again on the corner of Madison and Sixty-ninth, en route to the subway. For some reason I turn around, and there they are behind me, four cadets in billowing gray raincoats. "We're following you, ma'am, making sure you don't get into any trouble. Where are you headed?" "I'm going downtown," I reply. "To party?" they ask. (It's 2:30 in the afternoon.) "Where do you live, ma'am?" "I live here, now," I say. "Really? That's so cool." They are excited by this discovery. New York means escape to them (as it does to me).

We are still soggy from our rainy day in the park, but I at least have a leaky umbrella, a luxury the regulations do not permit them. We have had a solid week of rain from the weather systems that have torn through the South. They've gone to Greek letters for the hurricanes now, where they ought to have been all along. Who names a hurricane Katrina or Andrew? It is no wonder we habitually underestimate them, thrown off the scent by their names, so innocuous, like those of members of the family. As with attack dogs, so with hurricanes: the more antique and imperious the names, the better.

The cadets reminisce about their miserable experience the week before at the football game during what is called a "white out," a tradition that involves responding to a challenge from the superintendent by taking off their raincoats and standing in their short-sleeved white dress shirts, a gesture that can be thought of as West Point's version of the inside-out rally cap. One of the cadets' mothers reported to him that the television announcer had celebrated the fact that the cadets stood for the whole game cheering in the rain. What the announcer didn't know was that their attendance is mandatory. He also got choked up when he heard the cadets sing the Alma Mater, an incurably melancholy tune. One of the cadets, Tom, says that the line "live, serve, and die" is always sung the loudest. He's okay with the first two—with the living and the serving, that is—but he's not so sure about the last part. Superstitiously he won't say, "with dying." Phil reports that when he sang the "Battle Hymn of the Republic" with the Catholic Choir a few weeks before at a church in New Jersey, the congregation started crying at the line about dying "so that others might be free."

Cadets grow used to being the reasons or excuses for the emotional exercises of others, be they announcers or congregants. On the subway, however, we are somehow relieved of our status as spectacle. The assembly of wet commuters is miserable and preoccupied, and no one seems to be paying any attention to us. At least I'm not conscious of it, and we continue to talk about the cadets' travel plans. Tom and Phil are headed to South Bend for the Notre Dame–USC game. Lucas is going home to Arkansas. James, a quiet young man with a healing stress fracture who has tromped through the park along with the rest of us, asks me if I know the way to the soldiers' and sailors' club, where he can stay for the weekend on the cheap. At Grand Central we wave goodbye, and they seem to me very young and very courageous indeed. *Ave atque vale.*

Recommended Books and Films

———◆———

Prince Andrey lying wounded on the field, unable to move after the battle of Austerlitz, and staring up at the sky's "blue infinity," is one of the most enduring images of *War and Peace*. In a less celebrated but equally revealing scene that takes place before the battle, Andrey visits a Vienna bookshop, where he goes "to lay in a stock of books for the campaign." I like to speculate about what titles he chose to take with him: Were they novels or histories? Old books or new? Were they French, German, or Russian? Was their subject peace or war?

Joey took a copy of Anthony Briggs's new translation of Tolstoy's epic novel (Penguin Classics) with him on his most recent deployment. Many readers still enjoy older translations of *War and Peace* by Constance Garnett (Modern Library) and by Louise and Aylmer Maude (Everyman's Library Classics). My former student Nick sends a copy of Joseph Heller's *Catch-22* to every friend who returns from Iraq or Afghanistan. I like to see graduating seniors off with a copy of Evelyn Waugh's Sword of Honour trilogy (Everyman's Library); paperbacks of Waugh's three novels *Men at Arms*, *Officers and Gentlemen*, *The End of the Battle* are also available individually (Back Bay Books).

Books I know to have sustained Joey and other former students and colleagues both at home and abroad include Fyodor Dostoyevsky's *Crime and Punishment*; Charles Dickens's *Bleak House*; Edith Wharton's *House of Mirth*; Ernest Hemingway's *A Farewell to Arms*; James M. Cain's *Double Indemnity*; Dashiell Hammett's *The Maltese Falcon*; Virginia Woolf's *Orlando* and *A Room of One's Own*; J. M. Coetzee's *Waiting for the Barbarians*; Zadie Smith's *White Teeth*; Jonathan Franzen's *The Corrections*; David Hinton's translation of Li Po's *Selected Poems* (New Directions); the poetry of Andrew Marvell (a complete edition of which is available in Penguin Classics); Wallace Stevens's *The Collected Poems* (Vintage); Horace's *Odes*, translated by David Ferry (Farrar, Straus and Giroux); the plays of Shakespeare, especially *Macbeth*, *Othello*, *Troilus and Cressida*, *Measure for Measure*, *Henry IV Parts 1* and *2*, and *Henry V*; Sophocles' *Antigone*; Henry David Thoreau's *Civil Disobedience*; the essays of Michel de Montaigne (which are available in complete and selected editions in Penguin Classics). Francis Palgrave's *Golden Treasury*, introduced into the West Point curriculum by Lucius Holt, has been reissued and edited by John Press (Oxford).

Among the books my father remembers reading in Armed Services Editions during World War II are Joseph Conrad's *Lord Jim*; James M. Cain's *The Postman Always Rings Twice*; A. J. Cronin's *The Citadel*; Ben Ames Williams's *Leave Her to Heaven*; Somerset Maugham's *The Moon and Sixpence*, *Of Human Bondage*, and *The Razor's Edge*; and C. S. Forester's *The African Queen* and *Commodore Hornblower*. Armed Services Editions have become collectors' items, but all or most of these titles are easy to find in modern editions. A full list of ASEs is available online from the Library of Congress Center for the Book: www.loc.gov/catdir/toc/becites/cfb/84600198.html#appendix.

Anyone interested in what literature can tell us about war and war about literature would do well to start with Homer's *Iliad* and *Odyssey*, in translations by Robert Fagles or Richmond Lattimore;

and Virgil's *Aeneid*, in the Fagles translation or that of Robert Fitz-gerald. The Civil War stories of Ambrose Bierce are available in multiple editions, while the work of World War I's soldier-poets can be found individually and in collections. Recommended editions include *The Poems of Wilfred Owen*, edited by Jon Stallworthy (Norton); *Collected Poems, 1908–1956*, by Siegfried Sassoon (Faber and Faber); *The Poems of Edward Thomas*, edited by Peter Sacks (Handsel Books); and *Isaac Rosenberg: Selected Poems and Letters*, edited by Jean Liddiard (Enitharmon Press). Useful anthologies of poetry from World War I and other conflicts include *The Penguin Book of First World War Poetry*, edited by Jon Silkin; *The Oxford Book of War Poetry*, edited by Jon Stallworthy; and the Everyman's Library Pocket Poets volume *War Poems*, edited by John Hollander. The poetry of World War II has been largely neglected. *Poets of World War II*, edited by Harvey Shapiro, collects the work of several soldier-poets of that war (Library of America). "The Death of the Ball Turret Gunner" and other war poetry by Randall Jarrell can be found in *The Complete Poems* (Farrar, Straus and Giroux).

These works of imaginative literature can be read in relief against works of nonfiction such as Thucydides' *The History of the Peloponnesian War* and the writings of Plutarch (available in Penguin and Oxford Classics editions and in a two-volume Modern Library edition). Ulysses S. Grant's *Personal Memoirs*, a book that changed the way I think about soldiers and war, is available in several versions; I recommend Penguin Classics or Library of America. The latter also publishes the very different *Memoirs of General W. T. Sherman*. Theodore Roosevelt's *The Rough Riders* is an energetic account of war as grand adventure (Modern Library War). I am not alone in thinking Edmund Blunden's *Undertones of War* (Penguin Modern Classics) the subtlest memoir to emerge out of World War I. Barbara Harshav's translation of *Memoirs of a Warsaw Ghetto Fighter*, by Simha Rotem [Kazik] (Yale), made a powerful impact on the plebes with whom I read it. The rich meditations of Antoine de Saint-Exupéry on war and many other themes can be found in *Wartime Writings, 1939–1944* (Harcourt) and in a collection of his books, *Airman's Odyssey* (Harcourt). War memoirs are illuminating in sometimes surprising ways, especially perhaps when they blur the line between fact and fiction, as is the case with Robert Graves's *Good-bye to All That* (Anchor); T. E. Lawrence's *Seven Pillars of Wisdom* (Penguin Modern Classics); and Siegfried Sassoon's *Memoirs of an Infantry Officer* (Faber and Faber).

Alfred Hitchcock once declared that the "chase" was "the final expression of the motion picture medium," but sometimes it seems as if there is no subject more cinematic than war. The war film is our modern epic. My students refer frequently to *Braveheart* (1995, dir. Mel Gibson), *Saving Private Ryan* (1998, dir. Steven Spielberg), *Black Hawk Down* (2001, dir. Ridley Scott), *Jarhead* (2005, dir. Sam Mendes), and the older but still powerful *Apocalypse Now* (1979, dir. Francis Ford Coppola).

The films that shaped the way I thought about soldiers and war growing up included *Sergeant York* (1941, dir. Howard Hawks), *Desperate Journey* (1942, dir. Raoul Walsh), *Wake Island* (1942, dir. John Farrow), *Guadalcanal Diary* (1943, dir. Lewis Seiler), *Five Graves to Cairo* (1943, dir. Billy Wilder), *They Were Expendable* (1945, dir. John Ford), *To Hell and Back* (1955, dir. Jesse Hibbs), *Run Silent, Run Deep* (1958, dir. Robert Wise), and *Patton* (1970, dir. Franklin J. Schaffner). A trio of films from 1964, which I didn't encounter until much later, combine Cold War hysteria with a still-pertinent commentary on the civil-military relation: *Dr. Strangelove* (dir. Stanley Kubrick), *Fail-Safe* (dir. Sidney Lumet), and *Seven Days in May* (dir. John Frankenheimer). *Grand Illusion* (1937, dir. Jean Renoir) remains for me the most powerful cinematic study of war.

Max, the former Army captain who is now in film school, insists that the horror film *Jacob's Ladder* (1990, dir. Adrian Lyne) is "the most realistic war movie ever made." His other favorites—the films he grew up on—include *Little Caesar* (1931, dir. Mervyn LeRoy), *The Public Enemy* (1931, dir. William A. Wellman), *The Roaring Twenties* (1939, dir. Raoul Walsh), *Casablanca* (1942, dir. Michael Curtiz), and *Cool Hand Luke* (1967, dir. Stuart Rosenberg).

Among the films old and new that seem to have had an especially powerful impact on Max and other students are *Metropolis* (1927, dir. Fritz Lang), *His Girl Friday* (1940, dir. Howard Hawks), *The Lady Eve* (1941, dir. Preston Sturges), *The Maltese Falcon* (1941, dir. John Huston), *Citizen Kane* (1941, dir. Orson Welles), *Double Indemnity* (1944, dir. Billy Wilder), *Notorious* (1946, dir. Alfred Hitchcock), *The Treasure of the Sierra Madre* (1948, dir. John Huston), *Sunset Boulevard* (1950, dir. Billy Wilder), *Night and Fog* (1955, dir. Alain Resnais), *North by Northwest* (1959, dir. Alfred Hitchcock), *À bout de souffle* [*Breathless*] (1960, dir. Jean-Luc Godard), *Yojimbo* (1961, dir. Akira Kurosawa), *Hud* (1963, dir. Martin Ritt), *The Battle of Algiers* (1966, dir. Gillo Pontecorvo), *The Conversation* (1974, dir. Francis Ford Coppola), *The Player* (1992, dir. Robert Altman), and *Prisoner of Paradise* (2002, dir. Malcolm Clarke and Stuart Sender).